PARENTS UNKNOWN

PARENTS UNKNOWN

A Ukrainian Childhood

MORRIS STOCK

ANDRE DEUTSCH

First published in Great Britain in 1971 by
André Deutsch Limited
105 Great Russell Street London WC1

Set in 'Monotype' Ehrhardt
Printed in Great Britain
by Ebenezer Baylis and Son Limited
The Trinity Press, Worcester, and London

ISBN 0 233 96277 8

To Sonia

CONTENTS

I. THE BABY
AT THE SYNAGOGUE

The things I am going to tell you happened in Russia, in the small town of Verchneprovsk, by the River Dnieper in the Ukraine, and my story begins in January, 1892. There are some sad things in the story though it is not all sad, and the end of it, at least, is encouraging.

There were 50,000 people in Verchneprovsk, 15,000 Jewish and 35,000 Russians. For the Russians there were three smaller churches and one very big, very old church in the centre of the town; for the Jews there were three synagogues. Each of the synagogues would have a Christian couple, a man and wife, living in a cottage near by, who would clean and scrub the building, polish the candlesticks and do the other caretaking work. Because they were Christians they could work on Saturdays when the Jews could not, and they had their Sundays free. These caretakers were poorly paid, but they could add to their wages by getting work outside, and they would also have a big piece of ground behind the synagogue on which to grow vegetables and fruit.

On a morning in the third week of January, 1892, one such care-taker went to the synagogue to open up ready for the early morning service. It was not yet six o'clock when he heard a knock on the door, and opened it to find a young woman carrying a basket, who pushed past him, saying she must see the Rabbi. The caretaker explained that the Rabbi would not arrive before half past six. The young woman put her basket down, saying she would wait but would go out first to pay her cabman, and out she went. When after a few minutes she had not returned the caretaker went out to look for her. There was no sign of the young woman or of any cab, only her basket left behind. The puzzled caretaker closed the door, took the basket into the Rabbi's office, and went on with his work.

After the Rabbi had arrived and had said his prayers at the altar, the caretaker told him about the young woman who had left her basket behind, and together they went into the office to examine the basket and see if there was anything in it to say who she was. They took off the light cloth which covered it, and saw two big eyes looking up at them. In the basket was a baby a few days old with a mop of black hair and a little red face. From the way he was wriggling the caretaker, a family man, guessed he was very wet. By the baby's side was a small bottle of milk.

The caretaker wanted to fetch the police, but the Rabbi said the man had better first fetch his wife to look after the baby until they could find out why the child had been left there. The caretaker's wife was hurriedly called; she picked up the baby and cooed over it. The Rabbi dug further into the basket and found a letter. He would not open it then, but waited until the service ended at eight o'clock and the congregation was about to leave. Then he stopped half a dozen men, leaders of the Jewish community in the town and, first reassuring them that he wasn't going to ask for money, invited them into his office while the caretaker went to fetch the baby. When they had all seen the child, they asked the caretaker's wife if she would continue to look after it for a while, and she agreed. Then the caretaker and his wife left, and the Rabbi brought out the letter, opened it in front of them all, and began to read it aloud.

'I am a Jewish girl, twenty-three years old,' the letter said. 'Six months ago I was expelled from my college. My father does not know why . . .'

Her father was very rich, she said, and she had never been short of money. She attended a mixed college and the year before she had gone abroad for the vacation with a crowd of students. They had enjoyed themselves walking, talking, sunbathing, dancing in the evenings. One evening she had danced late with the boy who was her favourite partner, danced until it was past midnight and the rest of their party had gone. Unable to find a cab to take them back to the hotel where their friends were staying they had walked; walked and talked and lost themselves. Eventually they had found another hotel for the night, together.

When she returned from the holiday she realized that she was pregnant. The college sent her home, with discreet excuses. Her

father was away, travelling on business, and her mother had agreed
to help hide the daughter's disgrace.

The letter ended, 'Although my heart is breaking, I have to put
the baby into your care — I cannot face the consequences, ever.'

When the Rabbi had finished reading there was silence. This was
the first time anything of the kind had happened at the synagogue.
The elders discussed what should be done. The caretaker's wife
had said she was willing to care for the child as long as they liked;
Jewish or Christian made no difference to her. It was a baby, and
she did not care what religion it was. But after the elders had talked,
they decided that a wet-nurse must be found for the baby, and the
police notified.

Word spread among the Jewish community of Verchneprovsk. A
midwife remembered that she had not long left a Jewish mother
whose child had been still-born; Zelda Marcovsky, wife of Shloma
the bootmaker. The Jewish authorities and the police made inquiries about her. The Marcovskys already had three girls aged
eighteen, fourteen and twelve and a son of sixteen; they were poor
and Shloma was inclined to drink too much, but there was nothing
known against them and Zelda was kind and very clean and a good
mother. So the baby was put into her care, and eight days later he
was circumcised and named Moysey, which would be Morris in
English, or Mosh for short.

The Rabbi appointed two Jewish women to call on Zelda to see
that the baby was well cared for, and the police paid visits too. The
women were impressed by the way Zelda looked after Moysey, but
they reported with surprise to the Rabbi that she would not accept
any help with clothes or money. Zelda insisted that God had sent
her this child after her youngest had died, and Moysey had saved
her life as perhaps she had saved his, so she would not take any
charity for looking after him. The baby's arrival had seemed to
make all the Marcovskys happy; the two elder girls Vera and Esther
were out at work and helped buy things for him; the youngest girl
Monica liked to play with him and watch over him. And Papa Marcovsky, Shloma the bootmaker — well, that was most surprising of
all. He had given up the bottle, and people who had once tired of

waiting for the new shoes which Shloma could never get round to making were now finding him sober and hard at work, so his business was improving.

It was Shloma who felt it hardest when the two Jewish women visitors pressed Zelda to take their charity to pay for Moysey's keep; he argued with them, telling them that it was the baby who had stopped him from being a drunkard, so that now his other children no longer turned away from him in the street: 'I'll fight for this child with my life,' said Shloma, and taking his cap he went out. He went straight to the Monopol, the state liquor store, to buy a bottle of vodka to quench his great aggravations; but when he got there and saw the line of people waiting to be served, and a few drunks already lying around, he thought differently and went back to his house again.

So it was in the Marcovskys' house that Moysey lived, until he was three years old. It was a poor house, like many in that little town; a single-storey house of timber and mud and plaster, with three small rooms, the walls whitewashed, the floors of mud — they had to scrape and flatten them every now and again to keep them level. The furniture was as simple as the house; half a dozen wooden chairs, three iron bedsteads picked up somewhere second-hand, a table with a little oil lamp on it, curtains stretched across corners to make cupboards. In the living room there was a brick stove; a big, high square stove with the round-arched fire-opening running into the front of it like a little railway tunnel. It was a wood-burning stove, and Mama Marcovsky would push the ashes aside to bake her bread on the hearth. At that time in Verchneprovsk many people richer than the Marcovskys baked their own bread. And that wasn't the end to the use of the stove; the big square mass of bricks would hold the heat for a long while, and in winter people would spread their bedding on top of the stove and sleep there in the warmth.

Time passed; the happiest time Moysey would know for a long while. But the Rabbi and the elders of the synagogue were worried. They felt he should be adopted formally by someone, for he still had no proper surname and it was very important for a child to have that, and a real settled home. The Marcovskys wanted to adopt him legally; so did fourteen other Jewish couples. The two women visitors were given the job of investigating all these people, and they eventually brought the number down to four from which a choice should be made. A committee examined the four, and finally chose not the Marcovskys, who were poor and already had four children, but the Sverdlovs, a couple who had been married for six years but were childless though they very much wanted a child.

Mr Sverdlov was thirty-five, a tall, stooping, thin-faced man who worked in one of Verchneprovsk's flour mills; his wife was twenty-nine, a dark-haired girl with a nice figure. She was a dressmaker, and between them they made good money. They were both smartly dressed and had a very comfortable home — it had carpets on the floor, which not many people in the town possessed. They lived not far from Zelda Marcovsky, and Mrs Sverdlov had often seen the little boy as she passed on her way to market.

The Sverdlovs were told they might look after Moysey for six months and at the end of that time, if everything was satisfactory, they could apply to adopt him and give him their own name. So that the little boy should not be too upset by the change, they agreed that he should at first come to visit them, and that afterwards, when he came to stay, Mama Marcovsky's youngest daughter Monica, should visit him at the Sverdlovs' house regularly.

Moysey seemed to settle down in his new home, and Monica brought home good reports; every time she went there she would find new toys that had been bought for Moysey, and his bedroom was fitted out like the room of a little prince, she told her mother.

But Zelda never got over the loss of the boy. There were times when she thought about him so much, especially in the evenings when she would have been giving him his supper and talking to him, that she would make up her mind to go herself and visit him; but always she would decide that it would not be fair to disturb him in his new home, and instead she would cry herself to sleep.

The Sverdlovs had long wanted to emigrate to America and had been saving for this. After the boy had been with them for a year they made out adoption papers and bought three tickets to America, and began selling up their furniture. There were delays in getting the adoption completed, and this worried them, for they had been warned they could not take Moysey with them until he was formally their son. Eventually Mr Sverdlov went to the synagogue to consult the Rabbi and to tell him of their plans.

The Rabbi shook his head: 'This is the first we've heard about it,' he said. 'If you had let us know your intentions when you first took the boy, we would have told you that you can't take him out of the country until he is of age. And you can't just smuggle him out — some people have tried that sort of thing and landed themselves in jail.'

Mr Sverdlov protested that he had a good job waiting for him in America and that he and his wife loved the boy; but sooner than stay behind in Verchneprovsk working in the flour mills all his life he would have to drop the idea of adoption and leave the boy behind. They argued it and considered it from every direction, but there was no way out, and at last Mr Sverdlov went home to tell his wife, who broke down and cried. He comforted her, telling her that in Verchneprovsk there was only one parentless child and many people who wanted to adopt him, 'but in America there are heaps of children with no parents, and girls there get in trouble every day,' he said. 'America is a great city.' At that, Mrs Sverdlov stopped crying and gave in. She agreed that she would go to America and try to forget Moysey.

Another meeting of the synagogue elders was held, to consult the list of other people who had wanted to adopt Moysey. The next people on the list were Herscho and Hannah Levine, another childless couple, and to the Levines the elders now wrote — this time warning them in advance that if they wanted to go to America it would be no good asking to have the little boy.

Herscho Levine was fifty-one, a tall man with a touch of grey at the temples, grey eyes with long eyebrows, a small ginger beard, a birthmark on his right cheek, long arms with meaty fingers. He was a water-seller; a hard-working man who had his own horse and a cart with a barrel on it, with which he brought water to people's houses to sell. He wore long boots always, never shoes, and a long overcoat like a government official, and people in Verchneprovsk thought him a good-hearted man, always happy and never drunk. His wife Hannah was forty-five, and as they told the synagogue committee, it was time they had an heir. Hannah was a short, plump woman with a small face, beady eyes and blue lips; she looked severe and she was thought by the neighbours to be strict, though clean and kind-hearted; she was known to give sweets and coppers to children in the street.

The Rabbi urged the Levines to think it over very carefully before deciding to take Moysey; the boy could go to neighbours after the Sverdlovs left while the Levines were making up their mind, he said, for it would be a cruel thing to change his parents any more now that he was growing up. But Hannah and Herscho refused to go away and think it over; they were sure now, they said. So when inquiries by the police and the Jewish authorities found nothing against them, the Levines were told they could take the boy as soon as the Sverdlovs left, and if all went well they could adopt him after six months.

The Sverdlovs were sure Moysey could be happy with Hannah and Herscho, and they invited them round while they explained it all to the boy, who was now nearly five.

'You come to live with us,' said Herscho to Moysey. 'You will be happy because we have a horse you can play with.' And Hannah gave Moysey a coin, a five kopek piece. When Mrs Sverdlov began dressing the boy for Hannah to take him away, Moysey began to cry. Both women comforted him, but Moysey noticed that while Mama Sverdlov kept kissing him, his new mama, though she held him, did not kiss him once.

But Hannah took Moysey home. They walked and walked until they came to a big house. He asked her if this was where they lived, and Hannah explained they lived behind the big house, which belonged to the landlord, in a smaller one. They climbed over a stile, taking a short cut across the grounds of the big house, until they came to the Levines' house, a house of three rooms and a kitchen, a little better than that of his first mama Zelda Marcovsky. Inside she took him up to the little room she had prepared for him: 'And all these toys are yours,' she said. He played with them until supper time, and after supper returned to his room to play again until he fell asleep.

And that is how Moysey came to live with Hannah and Herscho, and eventually came to bear their name. Some of these things I pieced together from what people told me, in that little town of Verchneprovsk beside the River Dnieper, years later; some I remembered and remember still. People manage to forget many things that are no longer of interest to them: the tender outlines of our childhood are little by little worn away, wither and fade. But I could not forget, and these memories are not erased from my mind. They are my memories, from so many, many years ago.

II.   MY TOWN

I would like to tell you something about Verchneprovsk as it was then, two wars and a revolution ago, and some stories about the people in it, so you may know the town where I grew up and the sort of people who lived in it; so far away and yet not so very different, perhaps, from your town and the people you know.

Verchneprovsk lay between two larger towns, Kremenchug and Ekaterinoslav, about one hundred and sixty miles apart; and all around it were peasant villages, about one hundred and twenty of them including those on the other side of the River Dnieper. The peasants from all these villages would bring their grain into Verchneprovsk to sell to the forty-five grain dealers of the town. From the dealers' shops it would go to Verchneprovsk railway station twelve miles away, eventually to be sold abroad. The peasants would also sell the other things they had grown, in the town's market which was set up on the large pavement outside the railings of the big old church in the centre of the town; cheese, butter, eggs, potatoes, nuts, fruit.

Monday was the big market day, when the peasants would come into the town in their carts drawn by oxen, to sell their grain and their other wares, and to buy what they needed from the four hundred or so shops and beer-houses. The peasants worked very hard in the summer, even bringing tents into the fields and living there with their children; this open-air life was probably the reason why they were so strong. In winter they would take life a bit easy; they would have saved enough grain for themselves, selling the rest to get some cash. They would have their cattle to look after, and all the poultry they wanted; if they were short of meat they could kill a pig. The peasants even wove their own cloth; though in my time I noticed that the younger peasants didn't like the homespun clothes their parents made and preferred to buy cloth in the town from which to make their clothes—the plain long dresses of the women, with beautifully embroidered blouses for special occasions, and the thick blue blouses and baggy trousers of the men.

You could buy almost anything from the shops and beer-houses of Verchneprovsk, but not spirits. Those could only be bought in special shops called 'Monopol', operated by the town council. The Monopol opened at ten-thirty in the morning. A little window would be pushed up and a queue would form and money be handed in, and everyone served with bottles of vodka of different sizes. The Monopol did not close for lunch, but went on selling until six o'clock in the evening. Soon there would be drunks around, who would be picked up by the police and fined. A fine thing: first they sell them the drink, then they take more money off them for being drunk.

In the town there was always a certain amount of unemployment, some of it genuine, some because people were lazy and didn't want to work—but somehow they would always be able to find money to buy drink, though when their wives would ask for money to buy food the answer would be a good hiding. It seemed that among the peasants if a man did not beat his wife he did not love her.

The nearest railway station was twelve miles away from the town. Everything was brought from there, and the grain taken out from the town to the station, by horse-drawn carts. About fifty or sixty carters worked taking goods to and from the station, and there was a section of street where they would wait and talk between journeys.

In the main boulevard there would be a fine line of horse-drawn cabs also waiting, ready for anyone who wanted to travel about the town or out to the station; and there were also many hotels, with stables attached where people who came in their own carriages could put up their horses while they were in the town.

There were three theatres, which were always packed. Well-known Russian actresses and actors, and many from abroad, would come and go. The town hall was a very big building, where once a week the twenty-eight councillors would meet to look after the town's affairs. There was also a large building, the police head-quarters, where in the morning if you went out early enough you would see the police night patrol march in and the day patrol march

out, like a regiment of soldiers. So early in the morning everything
in the town would be very quiet, except for the noise of the town's
two big flour mills which never stopped day or night. These mills
stood along the great lake fed by the River Dnieper, and used its
water.

Sometimes on a summer weekend boys and girls would come
and row on the lake. In the winter the lake would freeze hard, and
then there would be more fun to be had by the boys and girls skating on it. Parents would bring their little children, too, to teach them
to skate, and it would look as if the whole town had gathered there
on the ice.

On the other side of the town was a big park, where courting
couples would stroll and children would play, and little teashops
would be busy. Every amusement was there in the park — it had
its own boating lake, too — but there were very strict rules, and
everyone had to be out by ten o'clock. Once a week an open-air play
would take place in the park, and then anyone wishing to see it
would have to pay at the gate, though boys would climb one on top
of the other to wriggle over the high railings and get in.

Schooling was not compulsory in Verchneprovsk. Any child
who was needed at home could stay there, so that many of the
poorer people, and even some of the richer ones, could not read or
write. There were a few free schools kept up by the Jewish community, where children were taught to read and write in Hebrew
and in Russian. These schools were open to Russian children as well
as Jewish, but few Russians took advantage of this free education.
Very seldom were girls sent to school; the parents would say: 'The
mother teaches them to cook, to sew and do the housework. What
more should a girl know?' When Russian children did go to the
schools, they and the Jewish children would not mix, and animosity
was great between them. There were other problems; one of the
teachers' duties was to see that the children were properly clothed.
If a child was found to have torn clothes and bad shoes the Jewish
authorities would be notified and new ones provided. But this
clothing might be too big or too small for the child, and then the
other children would laugh, and often the child would leave school

and go away and get work of any sort, to get away from the school.

In spite of the animosity shown by the children, the Jews and the Russians of Verchneprovsk could usually get on together after a fashion. Most of the people in the town were very religious. As the sun set on Friday the Jewish people would close their shops and leave their work, though the Russians kept their shops open sometimes until far into the night — there were no laws restricting shop hours. All Jewish shops would be shut on Saturday, and the Russian shops open; on Sundays the Jewish shops would be open, except for an hour and a half when they had to shut during the church services, while the Russian shops would be shut.

The Jewish people would get up at six-thirty on Saturday mornings, but because it was the Sabbath they could not, if they were strictly religious, light the samovar for making tea. They were allowed a cup of tea and a biscuit before going to the synagogue. So on a Saturday morning they would find someone not of their religion to light the samovar for them, and there would be many Russians waiting to be called on to do the job. The Russians would also light a small oil lamp and put the Jews' dinner over it to warm so that it would be ready when the Jews came back from the synagogue. Their religion did not allow the Jewish people to ride around on carts or horses that day, either. If a Jew employed people he must not allow them to work that day. Even if the postman delivered a letter for him on the Sabbath he would tell the postman to put it down on the side, for he could not open it until the Sabbath was out.

The synagogues were crowded on the Sabbath, though they were by no means so full on other days. But every synagogue had to have a service every morning and evening to keep it a holy place, and for the service there must be ten people; under that number a service could not be held. It happened sometimes that only nine people would arrive, and then a passing Jew would be brought in from the street to make up the number. On one such occasion in one of the synagogues of Verchneprovsk a man was brought in from the street to make up the number, and given a prayer book and the service held as usual. It was not until everyone was going out afterwards that one of the nine recognized the tenth man and said: 'What are you doing here? You're not a Jew, you're a Christian.' They all went off to tell the Rabbi, very disturbed; but the Rabbi said: 'We didn't know—as long as we had ten people everything is all right.'

The Jews and the Russians of Verchneprovsk could work together on big and important occasions too, like the time of the cholera outbreak.

There were few real doctors in the town, and not enough hospital care for those who needed it. The patients in the hospitals were looked after by unqualified doctors and nurses, and seen only once a week by a fully trained doctor, but even so there were a great many people waiting to get into these hospitals and so no patient could stay until he was fully recovered; as soon as he was seen to be on the mend he would have to leave to make room for someone else.

Outside the hospitals few of the poorer people could pay for a real doctor; if a child fell ill the mother might send for the unqualified man, but the proper doctors would rarely come unless they were offered pay in advance. They knew that otherwise they would never get paid at all. At times there would be a lot of sickness, especially on the outskirts of the town where a great many poor people lived; rents were low there but conditions were appalling. In such places you would often find twenty children ill at the same time in the same street.

Now it happened once that there was such an outbreak and there was great unrest among the poor people, who were afraid that their children were going to die because they could not afford to pay for doctors. The police noticed the unrest, and told the town authorities about it, and the town council sent two men to investigate.

At the first house they went to, a boy of ten opened the door, going out to play. The men thought he did not look well, but the mother said there was nothing wrong with him. They pushed their way into the house past the woman, who smelled strongly of vodka; it was a house of only two rooms, a kitchen and one bedroom where the whole family slept, and there they found a little girl lying in bed, very hot and feverish. As they went out again they found the small boy lying in the street where he had fallen while playing; they picked him up and carried him into his house, and while one of the investigators went to bring a doctor the other stayed to carry on the inquiries. It didn't take the authorities long to get doctors to the street; nothing like the time it would take ordinary people to persuade one to come. In all, they found thirty-three children very ill, and returned to report to the town clerk. A meeting of the town council was called there and then, and it was decided that the matter was serious, too serious to worry about payment for the doctors.

The police chief was instructed to get the children into hospital, but the hospital authorities told him they did not have room for one more person, let alone thirty-three; 'We're full, we can't help,' they said. The police chief wouldn't take this for an answer; 'If you won't help soon there will be more and more children ill,' he said. 'Think of your own children. They might become ill. You would find room in hospital for them. You love your children; so do the poor people love theirs,' said the police chief. 'This system is all wrong; because they have no money they have to die.'

They invited him to look round the wards to see for himself, and as they had said there wasn't one empty bed. But there was room for more beds, and he told them: 'I will get the beds for you,' and hurried back to the town meeting. The council acted quickly; they called together the leading Russian citizens, and they sent four policemen to the Jewish community with a list of people who must also attend the meeting — the rabbi, leading members of the synagogues, and eight leading Jewish tradesmen. The Jews were worried and did not understand why they were being called, but the police told them the matter was very important and if necessary they should take a cab and the authorities would pay; they must be at the town hall in twenty minutes.

When they arrived they joined the others sitting round a big table, and soon the Chief Justice came in; they all stood as he entered but he told them to sit down, thanked them for coming, and began at once to read the report of the two investigators. The Chief Justice explained that something must be done to help the children, if only for the sake of their own children who might become infected by the disease, whatever it might be, if it were not arrested right away. Jews and Russians alike agreed to help, and then the police chief read out a list of the things he needed — beds, mattresses, sheets and pillows.

In two hours all the items were ready, and two cart-loads were being delivered to the hospital. Next day the police called on the town's carters and cab-drivers, and the sick children were picked up from their homes and taken to the hospital. A Jew and a Russian also asked the police for permission to go round to all the shops of the town and collect donations of money to help pay for the hospital treatment and to provide little luxuries for the sick children, and this, too, was done.

When the children were examined in hospital it was found that some were suffering from cholera, and could not stay without endangering the other patients. So again the police acted, and had big tents set up in the fields a mile outside the town. In a week there were fifty children and adults in the tent hospital with cholera.

The expert in treating this disease was a doctor named Torganov who lived in Ekaterinoslav. He was telegraphed to come to Verchneprovsk, and when it was known he was coming cab-drivers rushed to the station, competing for the privilege of driving him to the hospital free of charge to show their appreciation. Accompanied by the chief of police Torganov drove to the field where the tent hospital had been set up. A crowd of parents of the sick children were waiting when he arrived, and they watched him go from tent to tent, escorted by the nurses. He examined each patient, and confirmed that every one was suffering from cholera. To each he gave an inoculation of the serum he had brought. When every patient had been seen, he came to where the crowd was waiting. 'It is a bad disease,' he told them. 'I cannot guarantee a cure. We must wait until tomorrow.'

Six of the children did not recover, and some of the adults, the very aged, died too. But the rest recovered, and the cholera in Verchneprovsk was stopped; there were no more cases.

When the crisis was over the Jewish and Russian leaders met again. A Jewish merchant presented the town with a big house to be used for the welfare of the poor and sick; the town council fitted it out as a new hospital and arranged that doctors and nurses should always be on duty there. Placards were posted through the town advising parents that if their children needed medical treatment they could have it at the new hospital without charge.

The whole town got together, too, when it was decided that there was a danger of the cholera lingering in the homes of the people who had had the disease. The town council put up tents for the people from the infected area, and then all their furniture and bedding was taken from their houses and burned, and the houses fumigated and painted fresh to get rid of any traces of the disease. Then a collection was made all round the town to supply everything new for these people. Some even found when the cleaning-up was over that they had things such as they had never owned before, like little carpets. Perhaps they would never have such things new again; but nor would Verchneprovsk, everyone hoped, have the cholera again either.

No, having different religions did not stop the Russians and the Jews of Verchneprovsk from being people of the same town, people who could work together. It didn't stop them from sharing the excitement over the town church, either.

This was the big church right in the town centre, the very old one around whose railings the peasants and townspeople had held their market as far back as anyone could remember, sitting on the wide pavement with their home-made cheeses and their eggs, their vegetables and fruit, their tomatoes and cucumbers and potatoes.

Then, one day, when I was a boy in Verchneprovsk, there appeared large notices on the railings of the church, telling the townspeople that because the church was so old it was to be pulled down and replaced by a new one. Four weeks' notice was now given for everyone to move, because the market could not be held there any longer. To compensate them for the loss of their old market, a place had been assigned to them outside the town. It was difficult to get people to understand, for many of the peasants and some of the townspeople could not read or write; in fact it took many policemen to explain the notices to them, and even to escort them to their new place until the new church could be built, when they could return once more.

In a few weeks' time you could walk through the new market and see that people were getting used to it and happy again; though there was a complication. The peasants, on their way into the town to sell their grain, would now drop their wives off at the edge of the new market outside the town, and go on into the town alone. With the wives not coming into the town, and the men not being willing to stop and look in the shops when their wives were not with them, the shopkeepers were losing business. This made the shopkeepers complain to the town council, but the council only told them to take their wares out to the market and set up stalls there. Most of the shopkeepers did this, but they found their expenses higher, and a lot of them could not carry on business and had to shut up their shops and go out to work. This did not seem to worry the council, who pursued their original plan regardless.

Weeks and weeks went by, and brick after brick was pulled from the church. People stopped and watched as slowly the old church was demolished. In twelve months nothing was left but a flat surface and sad memories; nobody would have known that a great church had once stood there. Now the site was ready, but more complications arose. The authorities wanted to dig up the graves in the churchyard, but the relations of those buried there did not take kindly to the idea. Higher authorities were approached and asked if it was right to disturb people from their last resting place. The authorities gave permission for the remains to be moved. So one morning there passed along the Volkov Street a burial procession such as the people of Verchneprovsk had never seen in their lives, with all the relations following to a new graveyard which had been made ready; and now everyone was happy and satisfied.

From the day the church began to be pulled down until all the graves had been removed took about eighteen months; now the time had come to begin building the new church. Bricks, cement and timber started pouring into the site. In addition to the iron railing, the builders surrounded the place with fencing nine feet high, leaving only two large entrances. Weeks went by and nothing could be seen of any building, and people were wondering and talking about why nothing had been done. Then came the day when one of the gates was flung open and a dozen men were seen going in, some with long rulers and measuring tapes and papers; but the thing that people noticed was that these men were strangers. It now became known that the reason for the delay was that there were not enough educated men in Verchneprovsk to undertake the building, so men had to be brought in from other towns.

The measuring went on for three weeks, and then gradually more and more men were seen entering the site — rougher men with picks and shovels, and oxen were seen drawing carts with loads of bricks and cement and long iron girders. After a long while, when people were getting used to seeing all this building material going in, they were relieved one day to see, just above the fencing, the new building gradually rising, brick by brick.

Now notices appeared telling people that the new church would hold two thousand people, instead of the mere eight hundred and fifty which the old church held. Many people stood looking at these notices, some reading them, others who couldn't read just standing and wondering, and waiting for someone to explain to them. During the winter months, which are very hard in Verchneprovsk, nobody could work, so it took about four and a half years for the new church to be completed. In the winter the men who came from outside the town to work on the church went back to their own towns to live until the weather was better and they could resume work once more.

But in the end the church was built. More notices appeared to tell the public that the archbishop and four assistant priests were coming from Kiev to bless the church and open it; and now the town really got busy. Everyone talked about this great thing, and the newspapers spread the news to other towns. The trains began to disembark many people and the hotels began to fill up. The rich people in the town offered their houses to accommodate strangers coming to see the new church opened, and poorer people let rooms and even shared their beds with the visitors. As more and more people crowded into the town it looked to us as if all Russia was coming to gaze through the iron railing at the new church. Three hundred extra policemen were drafted in from other towns, and people out for their evening stroll saw them on duty, guarding the church all the way round.

Day after day the excitement grew. On market day every corner was blocked by peasants crowded around their oxen-drawn carts; but nobody could get into the new church except for the workmen putting the finishing touches to the building; the big front gate leading into the church was guarded by four soldiers with rifles, to see that nobody climbed over the fences and to check the passes of those who were allowed in to work. One man I knew bribed the foreman of the painters with ten rubles to let him take the place of one of his men and go in with the man's pass, wearing his white overalls. The foreman told him that in all his forty years of painting and decorating he had never seen a building as beautiful as this one, and warned him that if he was discovered he would probably be shot, but the man went all the same, and afterwards he told me that the great wall paintings and the magnificent altar were so beautiful they filled him with wonderment, until he could hardly bring himself to get on with the decorating he was supposed to be doing.

Now fresh placards appeared in the town telling people that the consecrating of the church and the opening ceremony would be in ten days' time, and that people must close their shops, and that everyone who didn't have to go out that day must stay in his house and not block the streets. The peasants who were already collecting outside the town, hoping for a glimpse of important people, were warned by the police to clear out and told that if they were not away within six hours they would be fined five rubles. Many of the peasants who couldn't afford such a fine did go away, but the better-off ones took a chance and stayed. Little did they know that they would be fined and still made to get out of town.

On the Friday before the Sunday when the church was to be opened the bishops and assistants from Kiev arrived in the town, and the greeting they received was so tremendous that it might have been the Czar of Russia who had arrived. As they passed, the shops were closed and torches were burning on both sides of the streets, all the way until they reached the hotel where they were going to stay.

Sunday dawned, and the shops opened just until nine o'clock; then everything closed up. The great procession came along, with the archbishop from Kiev, and many bishops and priests from neighbouring towns. To the people of Russia the opening of a new church was a rare and very precious event at that time. The church was soon filled to capacity, and those who couldn't get in surrounded it. The noise was very loud, and then suddenly everything was quiet and still. The service had begun, and in the silence you could hear the swelling of people's voices from within the church. But after half an hour there was trouble; the church gate was becoming blocked and the police came to clear the crowd away, and it seemed that people were saying that every time the bishop said a sentence there was an echo, as if someone were answering him. An echo was expected, as the church was so big, but what puzzled people was that even when the bishop stopped speaking the echo was still heard, and it seemed to come from below. But the service went on, and eventually it was over and the church was consecrated and open.

Once the church was empty the police became suspicious about that echo, and began a search. They looked everywhere in the building, but they could find nothing wrong, and the head policeman was for calling off the search; perhaps, he said, the sound they thought was an echo was angels answering the bishop, for the church is a holy place. One young policeman, however, said that only children believe in such things, and asked to be allowed to make another search. He was given sixteen men and allowed to search again. After placing a man on each exit, he went round the building and then he asked if anyone had examined the altar. They said they were not supposed to touch that because it was too holy, but he said that as they were looking for something that didn't seem to be right they must look everywhere.

On his instructions the heavy velvet cloth was removed from the great altar; they then tried to remove the top but found that it was fixed. But the panel on one side of the altar, they noticed, was pierced with a lot of little holes. This panel they levered open, and to their surprise they saw steps leading down beneath the altar, and when they climbed down they found a man in priest's clothes and twelve nuns, all standing round a table with hymn books, lit by candles. The man was frightened, but when the young policeman questioned him he refused to talk except to someone of high rank. The police chief was called, and dismissed the nuns; he told the priest that he had committed a great crime and must answer for it in due course. But why the choir of nuns was hidden there under the altar, and what really happened to the priest who organized the angelic echo, nobody in the town ever knew.

This, then, was the town where I grew up; Verchneprovsk with its poor people and its rich, its Jews and its Russians, its excitements and its quiet, its carts rattling to and from the station, its cabs and carriages jingling about the town, its lakes and its river and the great wheatfields stretching away to the horizon. This was my town.

III. HANNAH AND HERSCHO

Herscho and Hannah Levine puzzled me. I was not yet six years old when I went to them, and ever since I could remember I had always had a lot of fuss made of me; with Mama Marcovsky and with Mrs Sverdlov there were always kisses, but with my new parents kisses did not come very often, and it was a long time before I could remember to call them Mama and Papa and not Aunt and Uncle. In spite of her severe looks Hannah cared for me well enough at that time, and there were plenty of toys for me, but I remember crying that I wanted to go home to my real mama, Mama Marcovsky, and Hannah telling me that I couldn't because theirs was now my only home. That day, when Herscho came home he took me on his knee and comforted me, and calmed my fears that one day someone would come and take me away from this home as I had been taken away from my other two homes. 'There in the kitchen is your mother and I am your father, and you will stay here until you are a big boy and can go to work and please yourself,' he said; and I remember running into the kitchen and putting my arms round Hannah's waist, trying to hug her. She gave me some milk and put me to bed; but still she did not kiss me.

Members of the Jewish committee came to visit the house when I was first there, and were satisfied with what they saw, and finally decided that the Levines could adopt me legally. I remember Herscho bringing all his friends to the house to drink wine to celebrate, and everyone having a jolly time; the day was my sixth birthday, and I remember Hannah going out of the room and coming back with a big cardboard box which held a train set. I was so pleased and excited, and hugged her; but I remember still feeling a bit disappointed because she made no attempt to kiss me.

Herscho decided at this time to give up his watercart business and to earn more by becoming a carrier with a pair of horses and a cart, delivering goods between the town and the station. This meant moving to another house where there would be more stabling. While he was waiting for this move, he went to see the solicitor who was dealing with the adoption. The solicitor told him that these things took time, but promised that in ten days' time my name would be Moysey Levine. Herscho hurried home that day and told Hannah, and she and I danced for joy at the news. A fortnight later the postman knocked at the door and delivered a large envelope. Hannah could not read, so she had to wait for Herscho to come home; she waited at the window, and when she saw him coming with his horse and cart she ran out and gave him the envelope. He left the horse and opened it and read it, and said: 'It's here, now everything's settled,' and so I became a boy with a name, Moysey Levine.

Next day we all went to see the new house; it had a big kitchen and three rooms beside, and outside was a big yard that Herscho would need for his new business, and stabling for eight horses; Herscho said he would start with one pair but he intended to have more.

Eight days later we moved into the new house, and Herscho sold his watercart business and went off to the market to buy two horses and a big cart suitable for the journey to the station. I jumped for joy when I saw those horses.

Everything went right with the new business; Herscho would go off in the mornings and Hannah would ride with him. While Herscho was loading up the cart with wheat in the town she would buy something for him to eat during the day, and then return to the house where I would be waiting.

When I was getting on for seven she showed me how to mix the horses' food and clean out the stable, and after a while I was able to do it without her help. Herscho bought two more horses and another cart and hired a man to drive them, and they were glad I could help. But now a member of the Jewish committee reminded Herscho that he had promised to send me to school, and must not delay this any longer, so Hannah had to get on with the work of looking after four horses herself. The hired men would never stay to feed and bed down their horses; they would just leave the cart and hurry home at the end of the day and expect it to be ready to drive out again next morning. And I had to go to school.

I did not enjoy that school. It was bad enough when I began, for the rest of the class could read and write a little while I still had to learn my ABC; but it was worse after a while when I had begun to learn and was doing better than the others. Then the laughter stopped and they began ganging up on me, and calling me 'the little bastard', and after that there were fights and I seemed to find myself being punished whether I started the fights or not and whether I won them or lost.

But the words hurt as much as the fights; it wasn't anything new for me to see women looking at me when I went out with Hannah and to hear them talking about me, the boy with no real parents; but this was worse.

In the end, after one fight, the teacher called his maid to clean me up, and while she was doing so the teacher's wife came in and questioned me. I remember talking to her with my head down, and she saying: 'Lift up your head and look into my eyes,' and lifting my head and the tears rolling down my cheeks. She sent the maid for a glass of tea and a piece of cake for me, and then she took me home herself, and told Herscho and Hannah that it would be best if I stayed at home for a while, and perhaps started at another school later on.

I wasn't sorry; I loved horses, and liked to feed them and rub them down and clean the stables, and every day now I begged Herscho to let me go to the station with him on the cart, to help. Herscho at last agreed to take me to work with him next day, and I was so happy that I went to hug him; but he said: 'Men do not hug and kiss,' and pushed me away. I was not so upset by this now, for I told myself that these people were not my real parents.

When I was a little older, Herscho bought a third cart and another pair of horses, and I was very proud and happy, thinking that I would soon be able to drive into the town with him and the hired man, and out to the station, sitting high up on the cart and holding the big carter's whip. I painted the cart and got everything ready, and one Monday morning we all set out, Herscho, then me, and the hired man Anestrat following behind.

First we went to the grain shops in the town to load up with wheat to take to the station. All the other carriers were there, and one said: 'Herscho, is that the boy you took and made your son?' I felt terribly embarrassed by this, and I think Herscho felt the same. Others, seeing the three pairs of horses and the three carts being loaded said to Herscho: 'You'll soon be a rich man with someone working with you for nothing.' Herscho didn't like this kind of talk, and there would have been a few fights if Anestrat had not stepped in. But I didn't care what they said, when we set off for the station, Herscho first, then me, then Anestrat; I had the whip and the reins in my hand and I felt proud and happy — even though the whip was bigger than I was, and very heavy.

From then on, that was my life; the journey into the town centre to the grain shops, waiting to load up — I wasn't big enough to lift the sacks of grain; Herscho and Anestrat did that — and then setting off out of the town, along the streets and out on to the open road; slowly up some little hills at first, and then the wide road with its telephone poles stretching away down a gentle slope all the way to the station, with the great open fields on either side. Our loads would be twelve sacks to a cart, and each sack held five poods; a pood was forty pounds, so a cartload was about a ton. All the same, with two horses to each cart, we made good time out to the station; and good time back again too, when the carts were empty.

The only drawback for me was that when we all returned home in the evening, Anestrat would jump down from his cart and make off for his home, and Herscho would go into the house to eat because he was hungry, and I would be left with the big yard gates to shut, and six horses to unharness and stable and feed and water; only after all that was done could I go in for my own supper. It did cross my mind that if I had been their own son Herscho and Hannah would not have worked me so hard, but each day I would console myself with the thought that next day I would go out again with the horses and hold that big whip.

Anestrat the hired man was very good to me. Every dinner time

I would eat with him, and he always gave me some of his food, because he thought I did not have enough. Herscho never ate with us: he would go off somewhere to eat, perhaps popping into a beer shop. It was true that I always felt hungry now, and Hannah had started feeding me in a grudging way; she said I ate like a pig. For Hannah was getting worse as I grew older. I can't say when it began for she was always a cold, severe woman; but she began to grow more and more mean. Hers was a house where everything was kept under lock and key.

One Sunday morning — I was nine years old then — Hannah and Herscho went off early to a funeral. They left me orders to feed the horses and clean the stables; afterwards I could have the breakfast left on the table for me, Hannah said. But I was hungry, and when I had got up and dressed I went to have my breakfast first. When I went into the kitchen all I found on the table was a full saucer of sour milk and two pieces of dry bread, too stale and hard to eat. I went into the other room and looked at the food cupboard, which had glass-fronted doors, fastened with two rings and a padlock. I was very hungry; I pulled out one of the rings carefully, opened one of the doors, cut myself a piece of fresh black bread and put the rest back. I refastened the doors, fixing the ring back with a piece of wood to keep it in position, and then went to eat my breakfast. After I had eaten I went out to my work, taking the horses from the stables, clearing the night's dirt away, mixing their feed and fetching them water from the well. It was my hard luck that Hannah and Herscho came back before I had finished. Herscho walked into the stables and said everything looked all right, but Hannah, who had gone into the house to begin preparing dinner, came running out again with a whip in her hand and before I could dodge she had given me two strokes with it, and then pulled me into the house, sending me sprawling across the floor and kicking me with her sharp-toed shoes.

Herscho heard me screaming and ran in to see what was going on, and when Hannah told him I had eaten my breakfast before attending to the horses he backed her up, telling me I must always obey my father and mother whatever they told me. I thought: 'They are not my father and mother; real parents wouldn't behave like this,' but I was too afraid to say anything, and afraid, too of what would happen if Hannah discovered the piece of bread missing.

Later on Herscho came up and asked me, 'Where does it hurt?' and took off my jacket and shirt. He looked at my back and shouted to Hannah to look at the marks she had made on me. She replied, 'It will heal like a dog — don't be so soft on the little animal.' Herscho washed the sore place and put a plaster over it.

I got no dinner that day, as punishment; and for tea Hannah gave me a piece of stale cake. When she wasn't looking Herscho took from his pocket a big new piece and gave that to me, before he went out to the horses. When Hannah saw it she snatched it from me and threw it on the floor, and I ran out before anything worse happened.

I helped Herscho pull pails of water from the well for the horses; they seemed very heavy that day, perhaps because I hadn't had very much to eat, but I was enjoying myself watching the water disappear from the pails as the horses drank. Then I remembered the cupboard I had broken into and the bread I had taken, and felt afraid again.

At supper time I went into the kitchen and sat down at the table; I put myself with my back to the window, and I unhooked the window fastener, thinking to myself that if Hannah discovered what had happened to her food cupboard and came at me I could make an escape out of the window. I was expecting a very bad end to the day; and so it was. Herscho came in and sat opposite me with his big boots and his meaty fingers. Hannah placed a big dish of food on the table and put smaller dishes in front of us; and then she asked Herscho to go and get the bread. He went into the next room with the key she had given him, and came back with the loaf of black bread and began to cut it. Suddenly Hannah said: 'Give me that bread. I left exactly half a loaf.' She gave one look at me and said to Herscho: 'You are bringing up a thief, a little bastard, and if you don't teach him a lesson he will put you in a lot of trouble.' She told him to come with her to look at the cupboard, and when Herscho pulled one of the rings hard it came out together with the pieces of wood I had used as wedges. Herscho took off his big belt, which had an iron buckle, and asked: 'Did you cut a lump of bread?' I told him that I was very hungry. He swung the belt, and I closed my eyes and felt the blow on top of my head. I opened them to see him raising the belt again, and I pushed open the window I had unfastened and threw myself out and began to shout.

The landlord of the house happened to be in his garden, and hurried up to help me as Herscho ran out. Before I could speak Herscho began making excuses; I'd just leaned on the window and fallen out, he said. I didn't contradict him; I still had to live with him. He sent me back indoors, and once inside he said: 'This time I forgive you, but if it ever happens again I will punish you for this as well.'

Next morning I gave the horses water and hay; soon Anestrat would arrive and Herscho and Anestrat would start harnessing them to the carts. I'd had no breakfast yet, and I told Herscho I'd eaten nothing since tea time the day before; he said he had food in the basket for me but there wasn't time to stop, so I got on to the cart and picked up the reins. With the reins in my hand, sitting up there on the cart, I felt so happy I forgot my hunger.

When we all got to the loading place, Herscho and Anestrat hoisted the sacks on to the end of the cart and I had to pull them into place; it seemed hard work with my stomach empty. The loading complete, we set off on our journey to the station, and after a while Herscho stopped and gave me some food to eat as we went along.

I sat munching my bread and cheese, but it was soon finished and then I started looking around. The trees were beginning to look a bit bare, and the sun didn't seem so hot now and there were times when it didn't show itself at all. Winter was coming, and that was something to be afraid of.

At the railway station Herscho and Anestrat unloaded the sacks of grain, but I had to pull the sacks to the edge of the cart for them, with Herscho shouting: 'Come on, we haven't got all day.' Presently all the sacks were unloaded, and I put nosebags on the horses and Anestrat and I sat down to eat while Herscho went off somewhere on his own. When we had eaten and the horses had rested, we began

loading up again with goods to bring back to the town, fruit, hard-
ware and fish. Anestrat caught me on the quiet and slipped a parcel
of food into my hand before we set off again: 'Eat that on the way
back,' he said. 'You didn't have enough for a mouse.' He was a
good friend, Anestrat.

We went on like this for a few weeks. It was not a nice life really,
but when I mounted the cart and held the reins in my hand, then
I felt happy. I loved the horses; but sometimes I wondered, who
was there to love me? Sometimes as I sat on the cart my mind would
be far away; and once when that happened Herscho must have
spoken to me but I didn't hear him, and I felt a blow from his horse-
whip: 'Perhaps you'll hear next time,' he said. I screamed so loud
that Anestrat thought one of the horses had kicked me, and he came
running up and saw Herscho with the whip in his hand. 'Why do
you keep beating that poor orphan!' he said, and Herscho replied,
'He's not an orphan—I buy him boots and clothes and feed him and
give him shelter.' Anestrat said: 'Yes, I can see how you and your
wife are bringing up that unhappy boy,' but all the same when we
reached home Anestrat jumped off his cart and rushed off home as
usual, leaving me to unharness the horses and feed and water them.

After a while Herscho came out into the stable yard to tell me he
had visitors: 'Your mother's mother and my mother,' he said. I'd
known they were coming to stay for the winter, for I had been
turned out of my room for them, and had to sleep now on the
kitchen floor. When I went indoors I saw a wrinkled old woman,
Herscho's mother, who shouted at me; and another old woman,
Hannah's mother, who gave me a piece of chocolate . . . a kind
thing to do, except that she had kept it in her pocket along with
her snuff and I couldn't eat it for the smell of snuff on it and that
annoyed her, and annoying her brought me a slap from Hannah.

When it came to supper time, with Herscho and the three women
seated round the table, there wasn't room for me; I had to wait until
they were finished before Hannah gave me my meal. Later I had to
wait for everyone to go to bed before I could stretch out my bedding
on the kitchen floor beside the oven.

I was almost asleep when I heard a voice shouting 'Moysey!

Moysey!' I pretended to be asleep but when I heard Hannah's voice telling me that one of the grandmothers was calling, I thought it best to get up or I would be for it. Up I got, to see what the old cow wanted. 'Bring me a pot!' the old lady shouted; and when I'd found one and brought it to her the other one wanted a glass of water. Then I could go back to curl up again on the kitchen floor like a dog. I didn't seem able to sleep, for my head was full of trouble. I began to think about what had happened to me in my short life; first Zelda Marcovsky's home, then the Sverdlovs, and now Herscho and Hannah, and I didn't know what might be going to happen tomorrow except it couldn't be much worse.

I woke about six-thirty, and that was late. I jumped up quickly, gathered up my bedding and hurried outside to the stables to give the horses their water. When I returned to get my breakfast, Hannah sent me to see what the old women wanted; and they told me to empty the pot and bring them water in which to wash. I did this and got snapped at for not bringing a towel. Then they told me to fetch them two glasses of tea with sugar and something to eat. I did this and then rushed back to see if there was anything for me to eat, for it was getting late. Hannah gave me a saucer of sour milk and a piece of bread; I was about to eat it when Herscho came in, saying it was late and I must come out to the horses, so I picked up my bread and followed him. Out in the yard Anestrat was already on his cart so I jumped on mine and we all left for the town centre.

All the summer I wore no socks or boots, and my clothes were pretty ragged by this time. But now you could smell the air getting colder every morning, and see the days getting shorter, and in winter I would have to be supplied with warmer clothes. One evening Hannah saw to that, by cutting down a pair of Herscho's trousers and a shirt and jacket for me. It was lucky for her that I was a tall boy for my age and the clothes didn't need so much cutting down, but it wasn't so nice for Herscho next morning when all the other carriers noticed my clothes, as the carts assembled in the town centre.

'What's the matter?' they asked him. 'Trade so low you couldn't buy the boy new clothes?' Herscho would turn such remarks aside by saying: 'I'm thirsty; anyone want to come for a drink?' and vodka would make them all the best of pals again.

Then winter set in. Being left to do the horses alone wasn't so bad in summer, but imagine trying to unharness three pairs of horses on a freezing winter evening, hanging the harness up, hoisting six pails of water from the well and carrying it into the stables through the snow . . . my hands would be blue and cracked with cold. When I finished and went inside complaining of the cold and of the pain in my hands, Hannah would say 'You'll survive,' and promise to find some fat for me to rub on my hands, but she never did. In the morning again I would have to go out in the freezing cold and get the horses ready while Herscho would look through the window and only come out when they were waiting to go — he was terrified of the cold. When he came out I would go in and Hannah would bandage my cracked fingers with pieces of rag where they bled, and then give me something wrapped in paper to eat at dinner time.

When we got to the town centre a lot of carriers would already be there. They did not bother Herscho about me any more; it was too cold now to worry about anybody, though I noticed that the wife of one of the carriers would bring her husband something hot to warm him up before he set off on his twelve-mile journey. When our three carts were loaded Anestrat would get up on his cart and I would get up on mine and we would wait while Herscho disappeared for a drink.

We were waiting like this one morning when the wife of one of the other carriers came up to me and offered me a glass of something hot to drink, saying she could see I was shivering. I didn't take it; my hands were so bad I couldn't hold it, and I told her so. She stepped up on the cart with one foot and pulled my hand from out of my jacket where I was holding it to keep it warm, and saw the black rags wound round it and the blood which had seeped through from the cracks. This woman was a Christian, not a Jew, but she knew all about my past life; Verchneprovsk was a small town. She asked, 'Where is Herscho?' and I nodded my head in the direction of the beer-house. She got down from the cart and hurried away.

It wasn't until much later that I discovered what happened after

2*

she got down from my cart. It seems she went straight to the synagogue, pushing past the protests of the caretaker who told her the
Rabbi must not be disturbed, and confronted the Rabbi and some
of his assistants. There must have been quite a hullaballoo with the
caretaker trying to hold her back and the woman demanding to see
the Rabbi; until the Rabbi shouted to the caretaker to be quiet, and
nodded to them to take her into a small room while he took his
taleth off.

When he returned she asked if he knew that a Jewish boy named
Moysey was driving horses to the station in the bitter weather, a boy
badly clothed and looking ill and with his hands all cracked with cold.

The Rabbi said there was no reason why a big boy shouldn't be
driving horses. With no hood over his head, and torn clothes and no
gloves? said the woman. On a twelve-mile journey? Fur gloves and
hats and coats, she said; that was the way to dress children if you
wanted them to work out of doors in the winter.

The Rabbi said they had a member who went to see Herscho
Levine every three months, and he had reported nothing wrong.
Why yes, said the woman, and the boy himself probably never happened to be around, and Herscho probably gave the gentleman a
good drink; everything would appear to be well.

One of the men asked her what her religion was, and she said, 'It's
not a case of religion. Good people, I'm telling you, take notice because this is your duty.' And she told them to send two men to the
carrier station where the grain was loaded next morning and look out
for the boy. 'If you don't send anyone I shall go to the police,' she
said. The Rabbi and the elders thanked her, but she only replied that
she would see their men the next morning at nine o'clock and went
out.

I, Moysey, did not know all this, and how I got through that cold
day I don't know either. It seemed so long, and at the end of it I still
had the horses to feed when I got home. Anestrat's cry was always
the same: 'I've got to get home,' and Herscho and Hannah would be
warm indoors. It took me about an hour to attend to the horses before
I could go in, shivering from the cold and my fingers hurting. I had
my supper of fish and bread, and the others got up from the table

leaving their dirty dishes and cutlery on the table — washing up was my job. I did not move, for my hands were just coming-to from the frost, and I didn't want to put them in water again if I could help it. When Hannah asked me why I was sitting there I started to beg her to get someone else to wash up because my hands were hurting me, but she said it hadn't hurt me to eat bread and fish. 'Besides, I'm doing you a favour,' she said. 'By the time you've washed up the rags that are stuck to your fingers will become loose and I'll be able to put more on.'

There was nothing I could do but obey. When I had finished washing up I started to wipe. Hannah saw a few rags still hanging on to my fingers, and with no feeling in her heart she tore them off. I screamed as the blood began to run, but she only said, 'Keep quiet; you won't die from this,' and put some fat on my fingers and tied them up with cloth.

I remember that evening. I can see, even now, Herscho sitting reading a letter. It must be an important letter, for he reads it again. The two old women are sitting holding their prayer books, which I'm sure they can't read. Hannah is mending socks for Herscho. Now, thank God, everyone is moving and leaving the room to go to bed, and Hannah tells me to go and get my bedding. I go to the cupboard and bring out my bedding, and as I am putting it on the floor one of the old grannies comes back and says, 'Look what I've got for you; I made it for you to put your head on.' It is a pillow stuffed with straw. It is difficult for me to sleep at first, with the unfamiliar pillow under my head, and my hands hurting. But eventually I fall asleep.

The woman who had complained to the Rabbi about me was up very early the next morning and accompanied her carter husband into the town. By the look of the sky there was going to be a heavy snowfall. When her husband had loaded up his cart and left, she waited until she saw the Rabbi himself with two other men. The Rabbi did not know one man's cart from another, but she pointed out Herscho's carts, and the Rabbi sent one of the men over to me. I heard a friendly shout: 'What are you shivering for, boy? What's your name?' I told him I was Moysey Levine, and when he asked how old I was I said I was very nearly ten. And where was my father? Over there, drinking with Mr Anestrat, I said.

'Where?' said the man, and I forgot and pulled one hand out from inside my jacket and pointed.

'Why are your hands all bandaged up?' said the man. I told him they had frostbite and it hurt.

'Let's have a look at your boots,' said the man. I didn't dare do that; I knew Herscho would whip me if I did. He knew what state the boots were in.

'Cheer up, son,' said the man. 'Everything will be all right,' and he left me and crossed back to the Rabbi to tell him what he'd seen. Then he went on into the beer-shop and shouted at the top of his voice: 'Which one is Herscho Levine? Come outside.'

Herscho went outside, followed by Anestrat. The man told Herscho that he came from the Jewish authorities, and had seen the boy whom Herscho had promised to look after. 'You can't take this boy on a twelve-mile journey; there will be no boy left when you come back,' the man said.

This wasn't the only shock for Herscho; as they got nearer the cart he saw a policeman standing beside it. 'That boy is very ill and you can't take him on a twelve-mile journey,' said the policeman.

'Ill?' said Herscho. 'You should see the breakfast he ate, you wouldn't say he was ill.' The policeman disregarded him, telling some of the men who had gathered round to get a cab before I froze to death. They got me down off the cart and bundled me into the cab quickly enough, and I was driven off to hospital.

A doctor saw me sitting on a seat in the emergency department of the hospital, almost bent in two, and told a nurse to undress me and put me to bed, but not in a hot room. This was done, and with another doctor he examined me, and then went out to the crowd waiting outside. I was told afterwards that he told them I was underfed and had frostbitten fingers; a few more days without treatment and I would have lost my fingers. 'God must be good, you have brought him in time,' said the doctor.

The policeman took out his book to prepare a report for his superiors, but the Rabbi drew him aside and said this was a matter

for the Jewish organization. He pushed a few rubles into the policeman's hand saying: 'Forget it,' and the policeman, people saw,
closed his book and walked away.

While I lay in hospital, there was more trouble for Herscho at
home. The two mothers blamed both Herscho and Hannah for
what had happened, and Herscho and Hannah blamed one another,
and there were quarrels. Hannah discovered what it was like to fetch
food and water for six horses, and how cold it was to mix a mash for
them, which you had to do without gloves on. And Herscho discovered it too, because Hannah wouldn't let him go running into
the warm house as soon as he returned, leaving all the work of looking after the horses to her.

Urged on by the old ladies, Hannah brought me cakes and sweets
to the hospital; but she was just as strict and cold inside as ever,
asking why I hadn't told her I had lost my gloves though she knew
she had refused to get me gloves many times.

I was in a little room by myself, because I had to be in a cool
place until my hands were better from the frostbite; and when she
came in and talked softly I thought what a funny thing it was that
this woman with blue lips and icy-looking eyes could be bringing
me sweets and talking kindly to me, and I knowing all the time that
she didn't mean what she said. And when she got up to go she still
did not kiss me.

But the woman who had seen me that day waiting on the cart in
the cold; she came to see me, and brought me cakes and sweets too,
and she kissed me when she left. She wouldn't tell me her name;
she refused to give it to the Rabbi or the hospital authorities because she did not want to become involved with anything; and
Hannah tried to find out who she was but failed, which made
her furious.

Herscho had trouble with his cartage business too while I was in
hospital. Anestrat had found him a boy aged eleven to drive the third
cart for him. But this boy, Vasil, had a mother, and she saw to it
that he was paid twenty-five kopecks a day just for driving the
horses, with no unloading or loading. She forbade him to touch the
sacks, not even to drag them from one end of the cart to the other,

to load or unload. And she would wait every evening at the gate of Herscho's yard to see that he didn't keep the boy late or get him working in the stables. She had heard a bit about Herscho and what had happened to me. He did have his three pairs of horses all working, though, until one day a piece of paper blew in front of one of the horses the boy was driving and they bolted, throwing the boy off the cart. Before he let go of the reins the boy was pulled about twenty yards along the ground; and when the horses did stop a wheel of the cart was broken. Luckily the boy wasn't badly hurt, only frightened, and Herscho was able to make it up with his parents by buying drinks for them. Not long after another of the horses died.

The Jewish leaders had told Herscho that he must appear before them, and were very severe with him, telling him that he was lucky the woman had reported the way he was treating me; if she hadn't done that he might have been charged with killing me, they said. Herscho's only defence was that his mother and mother-in-law had descended on him for the winter and with that and the worry of his business and repaying the loans with which he had bought the horses he had been too busy to look after everything and had left me to his wife's care. He promised that he would see now that I was fed and clothed properly, and in the end they gave him another chance.

When the day came for me to go home from hospital, Hannah brought a parcel with her, and I took from it a brand new suit and hat, long woollen socks and warm gloves and strong boots. I was very happy about that. Hannah helped me to dress, and we both went to thank the nurses for their kindness and I kissed the Sister's hand, and then we left for home. Hannah even offered to get a cab to take us home, but I knew she couldn't mean that, and I didn't mind walking when I had the new clothes to keep me warm. I remember as we walked along I looked back and saw our footprints in the snow; my small boots and Hannah's larger ones. It's funny how a thing like that sticks in your mind.

When we got indoors the two old ladies hugged and kissed me, but even now Hannah wasn't pleased and told them they were making too much fuss of me, like a big baby. When Herscho and

Anestrat returned in the evening I went out to help with the horses; Anestrat set off home, and Herscho still couldn't get indoors quickly enough. I heard Hannah say: 'You've left him on his own to un-harness the horses again,' and Herscho replied: 'If you're such a good mother you go and help him.' But nobody came out to help.

For me, it was like a new life to be going out with the cart wearing my new warm clothes; even though I still had to change into old ragged ones to clean out the stables. Every four weeks a man from the Jewish authorities would stop at my cart and chat with me, asking if I was happy and if Herscho ever whipped me. I told him I was happy and that Herscho didn't hit me now, though Hannah still did every now and again. I didn't tell him that I was still sleeping on the floor, with an old fur coat as covering to keep me warm.

Six months went by, and it was summer again and life would have been easier if Herscho's bad feelings towards me had not sud-denly revived. Every now and again he would let loose his hands or his whip on me; and now I was no longer seeing anyone from the Jewish community. I suppose they thought everyone would be happy in the summer. Herscho never liked the heat; perhaps that's why he let fly at me. If anything went wrong with the business or at home he could not blame Anestrat, for Anestrat would have left him, but I couldn't leave. All the same, those whippings were registered in my head now, and I began to live with the hope that one day I would pluck up courage and instead of waiting for the Jewish authorities to come and take care of me, I would find a way out for myself. I dwelt on this hope more and more as the summer passed and the five terrible months of winter came round again. Food became short for me again, too. Hannah would say: 'That's enough for you — you are fed enough.' I couldn't say anything, not while I still lived there with them. But deep in my heart I made plans to free myself from my bondage.

IV.   IVAN AND THE RABBI

For Herscho things were not going too well. After the unlucky incidents of the runaway horse and the horse that died he had more trouble. His mother became ill and had to be visited by the doctor and then sent to hospital, a big expense. After two weeks she died. It was very expensive to have her buried under the Jewish law, so he had to borrow money from the same man who had lent him money to buy the horse that died.

One evening Anestrat and his wife and their children, a boy of about eight and a little girl, arrived at our house. Herscho told me to go outside and give the horses a drink; what he and Anestrat had to talk about would be of no interest to me, he said; but when I got back Anestrat called me over to explain they had been discussing ways of helping Herscho pay his debts.

'If we got up earlier and did not waste time we could make two journeys and double the profit,' he said.

I said: 'Will the horses stand it? You know we have already lost one.'

Anestrat said we would have to take extra care of them and feed them better and they would be all right. He explained that he would not be taking any more money for the extra work, but would keep accounts, and when Herscho was out of debt he would get five rubles more a month.

Making more journeys was heavy work for Herscho and Anestrat, who had to load and unload the carts, but it was even worse for me, because we came home much later and I was still left to look after the horses alone. I managed to struggle through the winter and hoped that God would send the summer a little bit earlier this year. When I complained to Anestrat he only said that one day he would be able to help me and that very soon the sun would shine on me. I said to him: 'Until the sun shines, the dew will drown me.' He would urge me to be patient, and patient I was, but every day I would plan how to make the break away from Herscho.

Although we now did two journeys every day Herscho was still complaining about the price of hay and of repairs to the carts. The carters all had the same complaints, and in the end they all got together and hired a hall and had a meeting — about fifty-four of them — and decided to ask for more money for carting the grain. They demanded seven and a half kopecks a sack, instead of five — a kopeck and a half a pood instead of a kopeck a pood. They gave the grain buyers twenty-one days to agree with their demand or else, they said, they would stop work.

Most of the carriers took the idea of a strike as a chance for a bit of a holiday, but Herscho, who had three pairs of horses to feed, didn't like the idea. He wouldn't do anything about it, however, for he knew that if he went against them the rest of the carters would do a lot of damage to his property. So for the next twenty-one days Herscho, Anestrat and I worked very hard to get enough money put by in case we had to stop work.

After the twenty-one days had gone by another meeting was held. I sat outside with Anestrat while Herscho went inside to the meeting. Anestrat said to me: 'I know how Hannah and Herscho are looking after you but don't worry; the time will come when I will be able to do something for you. I can't do anything now because I have a wife and two children and another on the way and I can't give up my job yet.' I asked him if he really meant he would help me, and he crossed his heart and swore by Jesus Christ he meant every word he said. I knew that if a Russian man did that he really meant it.

As we finished talking Herscho came out from the meeting and told us the grain buyers had refused to pay any extra money. So we didn't go to work for some days. Then one day we noticed a whole line of peasants with their ox carts travelling along the road from Verchneprovsk to the station. We stopped them and asked them what was going on and they said they were taking grain to the station.

We told these peasants our plight — how expenses were rising while our pay remained the same — and they told us theirs; the buyers were refusing to take any more of their grain, they said, because there was nowhere to store it in the town; offering to deliver the grain to the station granary was the only way in which the peasants could sell it.

Luckily the grain buyers soon found that the peasants' ox carts were too slow — the oxen took twice as long for the journey as horses — and that they were losing trade, so they had to give in and employ the carriers again at the higher price.

When work started again Herscho became very greedy. He started hurrying us up and he himself worked harder than before. When we had begun making two trips a day to the station instead of one we had always returned from the station to the town empty, for hauling goods back to the town up the long hill into Verchne-provsk would have made us very late. But now, though we still re-turned empty on our first trip, we carried a return load on our second trip. This made us so late getting back that we had to knock up the shops after they were shut to deliver their goods.

It was fun at first to hurry everywhere, the horses going at a fine pace, but it was telling on me and on Anestrat. We got very tired, and even on a Saturday and Sunday that wicked woman who called herself my mother would not let me rest; she would always find work for me to do while she sat talking with Herscho.

One Monday morning we were in our usual hurry. I went out first to the horses and Herscho was not long after, quickly harness-ing the horses and jumping up on to the first cart while Anestrat arrived to climb on to the second cart and I took the third. Herscho set off very fast; the horses had got so used to following each other that even if I hung my reins up on the side of the cart they would still gallop on. The day was very warm and I had not had much sleep. I must have dozed off while the horses were still going. Sud-denly I woke up to the sound of a whip. I looked up and saw Herscho standing over me. He began to whip me all over, angrily and without mercy. I realized I must have fallen a long way behind for Herscho to have noticed and to have been willing to stop. When we moved off again I took care not to fall asleep again.

I rode along, trying to stay awake and listening to the wind singing in the telegraph wires beside the road; it sounded like sweet music. And I watched the peasants ploughing in the huge fields which spread away from either side of the road.

A few days later, however, I was so exhausted that I did fall asleep again. It was a Sunday; I remember that because Herscho had taken on a new contract with a big furniture company to deliver goods on Sundays — and because on that day there were no peasants ploughing in the fields. I was woken from my sleep this time by a cabman calling to tell me that my horses were straying off the road, and I woke to see that Anestrat and Herscho were very far away, but I also noticed that Herscho had turned his cart and was coming back towards me, and had brought out his whip.

I jumped down from the other side of the cart and started running back towards the town. Herscho was shouting to Anestrat to catch me, and Anestrat began running towards me, but Herscho must have realized they would not catch me on foot and he stopped and began to unharness one of the horses from the cart so that he could ride after me. Anestrat came pounding on after me, but Herscho was having trouble with the horse, who was not used to being mounted. Anestrat came close to me and then pointed: 'Get on to the ploughed fields — Herscho won't be able to gallop after you there. I'll pretend to fall. Find a peasant — they'll help you, they're good people.' Then he pretended to fall, and I ran on, scrambling across the big ditch beside the road until I could hide in the line of bushes which made up the hedge just beyond it.

Peering through the bushes I saw Herscho ride up and get off his horse and begin stumbling across the rough ploughland, and I heard Anestrat shout that it was useless because I was probably back in the town by now. They both went back to the carts while I lay there getting my breath back and wondering what to do. It had been late when I fell asleep, and now it was getting dark.

When I heard the carts moving off, I waited a little longer and then decided to take Anestrat's advice and make for a peasant village. I could see a light just beginning to show a long way off in the dusk, and I got up and began walking across the ploughed field towards it.

As I got nearer I could see a peasant cottage, whitewashed mud walls and a low-eaved thatched roof which seemed to go down almost to the ground. Suddenly there was a voice shouting 'After him!' and a big dog appeared out of nowhere and leaped at me, knocking me down and tearing at my clothes . . . and at me. Then the voice shouted 'Stop it, Bobca!' and I twisted from where I was lying face down and looked up. There was the dog, a big ginger-haired rough-coated dog with a long sharp muzzle; and there was a young man in the baggy trousers and rough wool blouse of a peasant.

'You Jewish bastard, you're thieving!' he said. 'I'll take you to my father.' And he caught me by my collar and hauled me to my feet. My legs and hands were bleeding and my clothes hung in tatters where his dog had pulled me about, but I didn't think about that. I thought, if the son does this to me, what will the father do? But I could not do anything but follow him, and as I plodded over the field towards the cottage I wondered if Anestrat had expected something like this to happen. Was this a way for him and for Herscho to get rid of me?

When we got to the cottage the boy shouted, 'Father! Look what I've found — a Jew boy in the field thieving!' A tall man came out from the cottage, a big straight man. He looked at me and said: 'How old are you?' I told him eleven years and seven months. The father turned to the son and said, 'Vassil, why let the dog pull him about like this? Could the boy steal a lump of earth?' Angrily he told his son to go away, and then more gently he asked me my name, and when I told him he said: 'Come inside, Moysey.'

I followed him into the cottage and looked about. I'd never seen a place like this before. There was one big room, a very big room, tall, open right up to the roof, with rough poles supporting the ridge — not sawn timber but just tree trunks. In this room there was a long table of planks, and two rough benches, one on each side, and on the table an oil lamp.

The peasant shouted: 'Marie, look what your big son has done to this poor boy. Take him and clean him up,' and his wife came in. The man was tall, but she was even bigger, tall and very stout. She washed the blood off me and dressed my wounds while a tall girl, her daughter, tried to clean and sew up my jacket. I must have fainted or fallen asleep then, but I heard the woman shouting, 'Ivan, come quick,' and then the farmer was back and asking when I had last eaten.

I told him seven o'clock that morning, when Hannah had given me a dry piece of bread and a plate of sour milk. He shouted: 'Marie, he was fainting because he had had nothing to eat. Make him a big meal.'

The woman went out and brought back a big glass of milk and a small piece of cake. 'I could give you a larger piece but we are going to have a big supper soon,' she said. I took the milk and put it on the table, and took her fat hand and kissed it and thanked her. The daughter looked on amazed and the mother said, 'Tatania, what's wrong with you? Come along,' and they both left the room.

Ivan sat down opposite me and began questioning me. Looking at the bandages on my legs he said: 'It looks as if you've been in the wars,' and I said: 'Yes, and your dog won.'

He said I must forgive his son for being so stupid as to set the dog on me; but now he wanted to know where I lived and what I had been doing. 'I don't like lies,' he said. 'But nobody here will hurt you.'

I began to tell him about Hannah and Herscho and my life with them, and I could not stop tears coming out of my eyes. His wife came in and said, 'Leave him alone for now. We'll have supper and then let him go to bed to rest,' and she started bringing in the food.

I could not remember ever having seen so much food as the portion she gave me and she kept giving me more, telling me to eat as much as I liked. Vassil the son came in and sat at the table with his dog, who came up to me. I was frightened, but Ivan said: 'The dog won't hurt you now you are with us, so don't worry,' and I stroked the dog's head and he licked my hand, and I felt better then.

Afterwards Marie brought in a big water melon and we all had some, and then they sent me to bed. Ivan showed me into a little room with a wooden bench for a bed, with some straw, coarse sheets, and for a pillow a sack filled with straw. In the corner hung an icon with a little oil lamp alight beneath it. Although I was a Jew I went down on my knees and prayed to that icon before I got into bed.

I had hardly shut my eyes when Vassil knocked at the door and came in with some sweets in his hand for me, asking me to forgive him for setting his dog on me. Before I fell asleep I thought: Anestrat was right about the peasants. They are kind people.

In the morning I got up and washed outside in the rain barrel. There was no soap but the water was soft and Tatania the daughter gave me a clean towel to dry myself. Indoors Marie and Tatania brought in the breakfast and Ivan bowed his head and said the daily prayers. Then we started to eat. It was a wonderful good breakfast.

Ivan gave Vassil his instructions for the day, saying he would be out to help him after he had talked to me. When the others had gone he turned to me, 'Now,' he said, 'tell me what it's all about.'

So I told him about Herscho and Hannah, about the three pairs of horses and the three carts, and about how I loved horses and was very happy driving them in the summer but how bad things were for me in the winter. I told him of the long hours I had to work and of the scraps that were left for me to eat and of my bed on the floor.

Ivan listened to it all and then he said: 'How old were you when you went to live with these people?' I told him I was five years and four months old and that Herscho had adopted me legally for his own son and promised to look after me. Ivan asked if I remembered where I was before that, and I told him all about my other mothers, and of the woman who had seen me one day sitting shivering on my cart, and had saved my life by getting me taken to hospital, and of the frostbite that nearly made me lose my fingers.

I told Ivan it would probably have been better if I'd died then, and he said: 'Don't talk so soft. You'll have plenty more trouble before you reach ninety! Now just tell me how you came to be on my land, in my fields.'

So I told him how I had been so tired that I fell asleep on the cart, and how I was frightened of Herscho whipping me again and ran away from my horse and cart.

After I had finished Ivan called his wife and told her to look after me and see I didn't run away. He would go out in the fields with Vassil, and that night they would see what was to be done with me.

When Ivan returned that night he was worried. He had been to the village during the day, and it seemed that Herscho had told the police I had run away and the police thought I might be being kept by some peasant family against my will. 'I'm not keeping you against your will,' said Ivan. 'I'll take you wherever you want to go.' I told him that the chief person over Jewish boys would be the Rabbi, and Ivan offered to take me to him, and went out to harness his horse for the journey to the town. I bade Marie and Tatania good-bye; I clung to Marie and kissed her, and she told me that when I was a big boy I must come back to see them. I promised that I would, and then hurried out to get on to the cart with Ivan and Vassil. They were good people.

In Verchneprovsk I directed Ivan to where the Rabbi lived, and when we got to the house Vassil stayed on the cart while we went to the door. The Rabbi came out, and Ivan said: 'I've brought you a boy who has run away from that wicked man Herscho Levine.'

The Rabbi told us to come in and sit down; Ivan at first refused, saying his clothes were too dirty, but the Rabbi told him not to worry about the dirt and to sit down. Then Ivan asked him to promise that he would not send me back to Herscho: 'Otherwise I will take him back with me.' The Rabbi promised, and Ivan said, 'You are a holy man, and I will take your word.' Next the Rabbi asked if he could pay Ivan for looking after me, and Ivan looked at him and said: 'Do you think I looked after the boy for money? You, a man of God, insult me . . . but how much did you have in mind to give me?'

'Five rubles,' said the Rabbi.

'I'll take it,' said Ivan, and when the Rabbi handed it to him Ivan turned and gave it to me straightaway, saying: 'You might need this, son.' Then he said: 'Goodbye, and God be with you,' and went out.

V. RABBI BRODSKAY

The Rabbi took me into his study and asked me the trouble, and again I told the story of how Herscho and Hannah treated me. While I was talking the Rabbi's daughter came into the room and listened for a while, and as she walked out I saw tears in her eyes. Then the son came in, and the Rabbi told him my story. The son said he couldn't believe it, and asked me if I'd read a story like it or had been told such a story by other boys. I was terribly upset that he didn't believe me, and before they could say any more I got up from my chair and took off my shirt to show them the whip marks on my back.

They looked at each other and then the Rabbi asked if it wasn't the farmer who had given me such a beating for being in his fields? I said, 'No; the farmer was kind and I wish I could have stayed with him for ever.' The Rabbi and his son went out of the room, and I heard them saying that they must send for Herscho Levine. I rushed after them, begging them not to send me back to Herscho. The Rabbi assured me that he would not send me back, and made me sit down, giving me a prayer book and telling me to try to read some of it.

After a time a maid came in, bringing an armful of clothes for me; they were not new and they looked old-fashioned but they were not torn, and the clothes I had were only fit for the dustbin, as she said. I changed into them and then the maid came back and took me to a room which she told me was to be my bedroom, and left me.

I looked round. There was a wooden bed, a chest of drawers, a wardrobe, two chairs and a big book case. A lamp was hanging from the ceiling . . . only rich people, I thought, had lamps like that; it seemed to me that only a millionaire could live here. I lifted the covers of the bed and everything looked so clean and new I was afraid to touch it.

In a few minutes the Rabbi's daughter came and asked me if

I'd ever had a bath. I told her I'd heard people talking about baths but I'd never been in one. She took me to a room which looked so fresh and clean, and in it was a bath with the water already run. When she had gone I took off my clothes and got in. It felt beautiful to lie in a bath of water.

When I'd finished and dressed again it was time for supper, and I found everyone seated round the table — the Rabbi, his wife, and his son and daughter. The Rabbi cut a long loaf of bread into pieces and as he gave each person a portion he said a prayer over it. Then we all started to eat.

After supper we thanked God for our food, and they told me to go to my room and go to bed. I went into my room and sat looking at the bed, half afraid to get into it as I might spoil it. After a while the Rabbi entered, saying he had seen my light on, and asking why I hadn't gone to bed. I told him I couldn't get into the bed as I was frightened of making the sheets dirty. He said: 'Sheets can always be washed — have a good night's sleep.' And I did.

I was used to waking early, and it was still dark when I woke next morning. I tried to go back to sleep again in that wonderful bed, but my memories kept going back, and I wondered how anyone could have a baby and abandon it so that it was left to the mercy of people like Herscho and Hannah. My mind wouldn't stop running on this, and I was feeling very sorry for myself; so much so that when the Rabbi came in and spoke to me I could not reply but burst into tears.

The Rabbi said: 'Don't worry, boy. God will look after you. He told you to run away and He sent you to good people. Get dressed and we will go and pray.'

I did what he told me, and went downstairs to where the Rabbi was waiting. He handed me a prayer book and asked me to read a passage to him. I couldn't read it properly.

'No good,' said the Rabbi. 'Of course you don't know how to pray if you can't read God's words.'

I explained that Herscho had never taken me to the synagogue and that I'd never been taught to read properly. 'We'll soon alter that,' said the Rabbi. He drank up his cup of tea and ate his biscuit before setting out for the synagogue, and I was left to have break-fast with the Rabbi's wife and daughter. That was a meal such as I had never had before. When I had finished I thanked the Rabbi's wife and kissed her hand; and to my astonishment she bent down and kissed my cheek.

Later that morning the Rabbi's daughter told me to get ready so that I could go shopping with her and carry her parcels. I was very shy of walking with a beautiful girl whom everyone would know and respect and bow to, especially in the rather old clothes the Rabbi had found for me the night before, but she insisted, and when I hung back behind her she scolded me, but smiling, saying: 'I don't want to think I have a dog with me,' and she made me stay beside her even when she stopped to talk with other important people.

One shop at which we stopped was a big store selling men's and boys' clothes; when we went in the assistant bowed to her and fetched chairs for us both, and called the head assistant who greeted her with, 'Good morning, Mademoiselle Brodskay; what can I do for you?' She told him to fit me out with everything new, even to a cap, and he took me away.

When I came out from the dressing room in all my new clothes I returned to her and said: 'Mademoiselle, meet the new Moysey.' She smiled and said: 'I am pleased to meet you, Sir,' and signed the bill and told the assistant to send my old clothes back to the house. So we walked out together, and when we got outside the Rabbi's daughter said: 'Now you can walk beside me like a person.'

I told her I would be grateful to her all my life; and so I was, but she only said: 'In five year's time you will be a fine young man and my father will find you a job and you'll be like anyone else, Moysey.' That sounded very nice, though I wondered what would happen in those next five years, and who I would be living with next.

Rabbi Brodskay had an answer to that question at lunch time. He told me he had spoken about me to Habinski, one of the biggest grain dealers in the town — I knew who he was because we always carried his grain to the station; all the small men sold their grain to Habinski. The Rabbi assured me that Habinski wasn't anyone to be frightened of; he was a family man with three sons, the eldest my age, and one daughter; he was rich, keeping a cook and a maid and a driver for his horses. Horses: I liked the sound of it. So next day we set off to see Habinski; if I liked what I saw I should take a job with him living in, but it was up to me, the Rabbi said.

Habinski lived in a big solid, well-built brick house on top of the hill opposite the town church; a house which stood back behind big iron gates. There was another big gate on the right for his carriage to go in, and on the left a big wooden building, the shop and ware-house and store where he bought grain from the peasants and from which he sold them all sorts of agricultural machinery. This wasn't a shop as you would know one now; there were no big windows, just the plain doors, but outside was a long veranda with an over-hanging roof where people could stand and wait or talk, and shelter from the sun or the rain when they had business at the store.

The Rabbi led the way to the front door of the house and knocked. A maid opened the door and showed us in, and went off to tell Mr Habinski we were there, and in a few minutes the man I came to call the Guvnor walked in. He was a very tall man with bright eyes and a long nose, and a big black beard and moustache in which his mouth seemed to disappear entirely.

Rabbi Brodskay got up and shook hands with him, saying: 'This is the boy I was telling you about,' and Mr Habinski replied: 'I've seen him many times with Herscho Levine . . . but it was not my business to interfere . . .'

Then he looked at me fiercely and said gruffly that he was willing to take me into his house and give me a job for three years — but he would have to let his wife see me first.

When he brought his wife in, I looked at her with amazement. I'd thought that Marie the peasant's wife was big, but this woman was bigger still. She was huge, and she looked, so far as I could judge, about forty, and she didn't look very pleasant — but that was something I would find out.

I stood there, and Mrs Habinski looked me over and asked how old I was, and when the Rabbi said I was nearly twelve she began to talk about some boys growing in spite of their struggles in life. But Mr Habinski told her: 'That's enough talk about that — are you willing for him to stay here and to feed and clothe him for three years?'

She replied that she had four children already and she didn't suppose another one would make much difference. And I thought that I'd better accept because I couldn't believe the Rabbi's family would want to put me up much longer; so I bowed to both the Habinskis and thanked them, and it was settled that on the coming Monday I should move into the Habinskis' house and start work.

That night when I'd gone to my room the Rabbi's son knocked on my door and came in, bringing some books with him. He was as fair as his sister was dark, a young man in his early twenties, with a big forehead and a ginger beard. He was a medical student, and I knew he went off every day to the hospital to study.

He put the books down and said: 'I want to hear you read in Russian and see you write, because unless you can do these things you cannot live a happy life.' Taking his watch from his pocket he said he had no time to give me a lesson that night, but he would leave the books with me so that I could try to read a little in them.

I told him I didn't know how I was ever going to be able to thank him and his family for all they were doing for me, but he said: 'My reward will be when you grow up and tell your children about the young doctor who taught you to read and write.'

I spent a lot of the next day at lessons; it was hard, but the Rabbi's daughter made it easier, bringing me a bag of sweets, and telling me: 'It's easier to learn if you've something to chew.' I found she was right; it was nice to chew and learn.

The son would not test me that evening, however, because it was Friday and the beginning of the Sabbath. As a Rabbi's son he was very strict in such things; years later I was told that he had once had to take an examination for his medical studies on a Saturday; the Russian authorities arranged such things in that way because they knew that many of the medical students would be Jewish and they did not like the Jewish students doing well in the examinations. Jews always did much better in proportion to their numbers than the Russians. When the Rabbi's son had to take this examination on a Saturday he was in great doubt about what to do, but he managed it by travelling to the distant town where the examinations were held, well before dusk on the Friday, and on the Saturday he got the authorities to agree to let him dictate his answers to a Christian who wrote them down for him. And in spite of this difficulty the Rabbi's son passed.

This evening in the Rabbi's house, however, I did not understand at first. I had seen the special candles lit at dusk, but I had seen that in Herscho's house and Herscho and Hannah had never told me it was a sin to work on a Friday evening.

'Well, here it is different,' the Rabbi's daughter told me. 'The Sabbath has started and my father said you should come along to the synagogue.' I didn't like that idea so much, but I went along and the attendant gave me a good seat and a new prayer book. I was surprised to see how packed the synagogue was, and after the service the Rabbi introduced me to the head choir singer and told me that later on he might put me in the choir.

When we arrived home there was a bottle of wine and glasses on the table, and a large Vienna loaf covered with a white embroidered napkin. The Rabbi filled a large glass for himself and four smaller ones for his wife and son and daughter and me; then he picked up his own glass and said a prayer over it. We all stood up, and as the Rabbi sipped from his glass we sipped from ours. Then he cut and blessed pieces of bread and handed us all a piece to eat. It was a rite I had never seen before, and I thought it was fun. Then we sat down to supper.

After supper prayers were said and then we all went to bed. In my little room I stood looking at my bed, and thought that six months like this, living like a lord, would just suit me — but I had only tonight and two more nights beside.

Next morning, Saturday, I was awake very early as we all had to go to the synagogue. We had tea and a biscuit together in the dining room and then set off. At the synagogue I saw how everyone welcomed the son with warm greetings; I suppose they were especially pleased to know him because he was going to be a doctor.

The service was a very long one on Saturday morning, and it did not end until half past one. Once it was over everyone tried to get out as quickly as possible, but on the way home they all greeted one another and talked. When we got back to the Rabbi's house the son kissed his mother and sister, and I bowed and kissed their hands; and then we all sat down to dinner because it was nearly two o'clock and we'd had nothing to eat since seven-thirty.

Later that day I was sitting in my room, trying to learn from a book, when I glanced out of the window. In the distance I saw a couple walking, and they looked to me like Herscho and Hannah. I ran into the dining room where the Rabbi's son was sitting reading; he looked up from his book and said: 'Why are you so pale and upset?' I told him I'd seen Herscho and Hannah coming. For a moment he couldn't remember who they were, and then he said: 'What are you frightened of?'

I said: 'They'll kill me if they get hold of me,' but the Rabbi's son got up and held me and comforted me, telling me to go back to my room and trust the Rabbi, who wouldn't let them even see me.

I went back to my room, but I left the door open a little bit so that I could hear what went on. I heard a knock at the front door and Herscho's voice saying: 'I am Herscho Levine, and I've come to take my son home,' and I trembled. But then I heard the Rabbi's voice saying he could not see anyone then because he had afternoon prayers to attend, and whoever wanted him must come back afterwards; and then the door shut and Herscho and Hannah's footsteps went away.

The Rabbi told me that Herscho and Hannah would be coming back at seven o'clock that evening; he promised that I would not see them and they would not see me and that I had nothing to worry about, but all the same, when the evening meal was over and I was sent to wait in my room, leaving the Rabbi awaiting his visitors downstairs, I trembled as I heard the knock at the front door.

I'd left my door a little way open again, and I heard Herscho and Hannah shown in by the maid, and then Herscho's voice complaining that his son Moysey was hiding in the Rabbi's house. He told the Rabbi that I had run away leaving the horses, and that he had had to hire another driver and had been late making his deliveries to the station; he would forgive all that, he said, but I must return home with him.

Then the Rabbi's voice asked Herscho if he had finished, and Herscho's said: 'Let my son come home and I will forget all about it. If not I will go to the police.'

I trembled more than ever then, and I imagined Herscho bluffing or persuading the Rabbi to hand me over; or perhaps even Herscho and Hannah overpowering the Rabbi and coming through the house room after room until they found me.

But then the Rabbi's voice came again saying: 'Are you finished now?' and I could tell from his voice that the Rabbi was angry, though I had never heard him angry before. Then he said: 'If you and your wife had not worked that boy to exhaustion and had let him have his proper food and proper sleep it would not have happened. If you had not whipped him when he fell asleep on the cart it would not have happened.'

As I stood there listening from behind the door of my room, I heard Hannah sobbing that she wanted to see me, and protesting that she had been so good to me, had looked after me. And scornfully the Rabbi's voice saying: 'With your fists and shoes you looked after him? You kept your bread under lock and key, you fed him on leavings, you kicked him and punched him and you still want to see him? The boy is here in this house but you are not going to see him.'

Hannah began protesting that she had legally adopted me, and began threatening to go to the police. The Rabbi's voice answered: 'You promised to feed and clothe and look after him and you have broken all those promises, so he is your son no longer. But go to the police, and I will tell them I am keeping Moysey, and he will tell them why, and you'll get twelve months for the way you've beaten him.'

There was a long silence, and then a scraping of chairs and Herscho's voice saying it was getting late and he had to be up early in the morning, and then footsteps and the front door shutting.

And that was the end of my fears of Hannah and Herscho.

*

Next day, Sunday, after breakfast I was busy doing lessons with the Rabbi's son when his sister butted in, demanding that he let me off because she wanted to take me out. The brother laughed and said I could go where I liked after I'd completed the lessons, and left me to it. I took good care to be finished by noon so that we could set off as soon as lunch was over.

She wanted to go to the town park; I'd told her that I had never been in the park before. She asked if I would like to walk or whether we should take a cab, but I said I didn't enjoy driving unless I could drive the horses myself, so we walked, talking all the way.

The park lay behind two huge iron gates. Just inside was a little wooden hutch where a girl sat to take the entrance money — it was two kopecks each, I think. Mademoiselle Brodskay paid, and we walked past. To me it was all wonderful; the broad paths with their wooden benches, the brilliant big beds of flowers, the great space round the open-air theatre, the bandstand, and the boating lake, a huge lake fed from the Dnieper, ornamented by trees and with small boats scattered about on it.

We sat to rest on a bench, looking about us and still talking, and then we walked on, and eventually came to where the boats were for hire. Mademoiselle Brodskay hired a boat for two — there were bigger ones that would take four people — paying thirty-five kopecks; that enabled us to have the boat out for as long as we liked . . . an hour or all day long, it made no difference. She rowed the boat, and I rather wanted to try, but when I asked her she said I could row another time.

'There is no other time; tomorrow I will be gone and be in service for a long while,' I said.

'You are not going abroad, Moysey,' she said. 'You can come to us in the evening — my brother wants to go on giving you lessons. And I've spoken to my fiancé and he is going to get tickets for the theatre and he will take you as well.'

I had not known she was going to be married, and asked her when it would be, but she told me I shouldn't ask that, and why did I want to know?

I said: 'If you get married I will never see you again, as you will move away from your father and mother.' She said that could cut both ways — after my three years with Habinski I might find a different job and move away from Verchneprovsk and forget them.

I told her: 'I could never forget you or your parents who have been so good to me, never as long as I live.'

The boat was going as we were talking; she wasn't rowing but it was just sliding along through the water, and that's how it came to an end. We left the boat and the park and returned home. But I never have forgotten the Rabbi, or the park and the boat sliding through the water, or Mademoiselle Brodskay.

When we arrived home it was already six o'clock. The Rabbi's wife and daughter said I might take my jacket off to sit down to supper. It was then that for the first time I heard Madame Brodskay call her daughter by her first name, Marie. But I could never bring myself to say it; to me she was always Mademoiselle Brodskay.

We all sat round the table together, as always. I say as always because to me it seemed I had been there for years, as if I was one of the family. I forgot all my troubles and fears, and we all enjoyed a pleasant evening. Then everyone set off for bed, the Rabbi reminding me that I must be up early in the morning for my first day with Habinski, to show that I was a good worker. 'And don't forget to come and see me in the evenings to continue your education with my son,' he said. Then he opened the prayer book and said: 'Read the evening prayer with me,' and we read it and both went off to bed.

I was up early next morning . . . I found it hard to sleep anyway. I went into the dining room and I couldn't hear a soul until the maid came in and lit the samovar. After a time I heard the others stirring, and eventually they came down and we had tea and biscuits together, and then it was time for me to leave.

I said goodbye to them all, shook hands with the son, kissed the hands of his mother and sister. The Rabbi's wife told me to remember that I could always come and tell her of anything that worried me about my new life at the Habinskis. Then I opened the door and walked out — backwards, as I thought it would be rude to turn my back on them. Now I was on my own.

VI. HABINSKI THE GUVNOR

I walked up the hill in the early morning, until I came to the two big iron gates of Mr Habinski's house, went through the gates and knocked at the door. A maid answered the door, dressed as maids were at that time in such wealthy houses — in peasant costume for they were peasant girls; a blouse with big puffed sleeves, tied at the neck with a red ribbon with a little bow in front; a long dark skirt, and over all a white apron, very long, even longer than the skirt, down to the ground. She didn't wear a cap such as maids wore in the West, but the mistress always insisted that her long hair must be kept clean and tidy.

Smiling, she asked what I wanted — she was always smiling and laughing, this girl. I told her I had come to live there for three years, and she turned her face away — I suppose to hide the laugh that was on it, for I was so serious. Then she said: 'Come in — everyone is asleep, no one gets up so early here.' She showed me into the big hall, and I sat on a chair. She gave me some magazines to look at, and said, 'Can you read?' and seemed very surprised when I said I could.

After she left me I sat turning over the leaves until a loud commanding voice shouted: 'What are you doing? This isn't a college. Everyone here works for their keep.' It was Mr Habinski, standing and looking down at me from his great height, bright eyes and long nose looking out from his thickly bearded face. I stood up and said: 'Good morning, Guvnor.'

He said: 'What?' and I realized he must want me to show some other mark of respect, so I bowed to him and he said: 'That's better!' Then he let out another shout: 'Sanca!' Another maid appeared, and he told her to take me and give me tea.

We went into a big kitchen with a large table with six chairs round it. All round the room there were shelves with plates — I'd never seen so much china in one house before. The maid poured me a glass of tea and gave me a piece of bread and butter, saying that I would get a proper breakfast when the cook arrived. I'd hardly begun drinking my tea when I heard another shout from Habinski: 'Moysey!' I hurried out to him, and he complained impatiently that everyone was in the shop by this time and the peasants waiting with their grain, so I should be there.

He took me round to the shop and introduced me to the head assistant, who gave me a broom and told me to sweep up. When I'd done that he took me on to the next part of the building where the grain sacks were stored and told me to sort out the bad sacks from the good ones and stack them neatly.

I looked at the hundreds of sacks and thought: 'Sacks for life here — I'll never be able to finish,' but I set to work. Now and again as I moved the sacks I saw a mouse run out, and I would jump a bit, but the assistant said: 'That's nothing — you'll see rats before long.'

But before I had got to the rats the assistant took me back to the first part of the granary, where the peasants were now bringing in their grain. He said: 'This is where you have to learn to buy grain from the uneducated peasants.' I didn't like the sneering way he spoke about the peasants, but it wasn't my place to argue, so I stood and watched the peasants carrying in their sacks of grain and heaving them on to the biggest scale I had ever seen.

As each sack was weighed an assistant made a note and gave the peasant a ticket to take to a little hole in the wall where a girl sat at a pay desk to pay him what was on the ticket. When he had finished dealing with one man the assistant turned to me and asked if I understood, and when I said I hadn't understood he told me I couldn't be very bright and had better watch him again.

I spent many days in the granary, and I learnt. I learnt a lot — even to know how the peasants were sometimes swindled. Some peasants were too poor to buy their own sacks to put their grain in, and had to carry the grain into town in their carts loose. When they got to Habinski's they would borrow sacks, fill them from the carts and carry them in to be weighed, one at a time. A man couldn't be filling and carrying sacks and keeping an eye on the total number of sacks weighed all at the same time, so he would usually bring along a son or daughter to wait in the shop and keep count of the sacks after they had been weighed, while the father was outside filling and carrying. As these people could neither read nor write, the weighers would help the children keep count by giving them a small coin, a twenty-kopeck piece, for each two sacks weighed. In that way the peasant would know, by counting the coins, how many sacks he had carried in and should be paid for. He would give up the coins at the paying-out desk and be paid for the grain accordingly. But, as Habinski's assistants well knew and as I soon found out, the peasant's sons or daughters would sometimes keep a couple of these twenty-kopeck coins for themselves; they didn't understand what they were doing but thought they were only taking it from old Habinski the Jewish merchant. Of course, each time they stole twenty kopecks from Habinski they were robbing their own father of the value of two sacks of grain — ten rubles.

Even if a peasant had his own sacks, Habinski's assistants would fiddle the weight to cheat the peasants. The man in whose charge I had been put told me that peasants knew no better, that this was the way the grain trade was carried on, and if I went on in the same way as the other assistants I would become a rich man too, like Mr Habinski, one day. For Mr Habinski was rich all right, very rich, even though he couldn't read or write and had to pay a book-keeper to do it for him.

For the time being, however, my main job was looking after the sacks. Every week half a dozen women would come to the store to mend the torn sacks. They would sit outside under the shelter of the overhanging roof, and I would give them the torn sacks, needles, thread and scissors. Each woman had a little notebook in which I would mark down the number of sacks they had mended day by day, and on Fridays they would be paid—it came to about a half-penny a sack.

In the afternoons there was no trading in the shop, but there was plenty for the dozen or so assistants to do, and plenty for me to do, especially since I was the youngest and the latest arrival. And in the evenings I would go into the office, which was in Habinski's house, and run errands for the book-keeper.

This book-keeper was Mr Goodman; a short man, thickset, with ginger hair and moustache, always badly dressed. He was very good to me; it was he who told me not to worry about Habinski because the Guvnor's bark was worse than his bite and I would soon get to know him. One of my duties was to wait in the evening for Mr Goodman to finish writing all the day's letters and then take them to the post. The Guvnor had told me I must never go into the kitchen for my evening meal before I had posted the letters, but Mr Goodman used to let me off early for my meal and take the letters to post himself on the way home.

The Habinski house was the richest I had ever seen, with its fine new furniture and its painted floors with carpet-runners right through. The two maids lived in, but the cook lived out, and the coachman who looked after the four horses and the smart carriage lived in the solidly-built summerhouse in the garden. Among this coachman's other duties were to fetch water in a cart with a big barrel attached; the house had a well, but this was not considered fit for people to drink, only for horses, and so fresh water was fetched in the barrel from the river. The coachman also saw to the cow which the Habinskis kept to provide fresh milk.

All the servants were good to me, especially the cook who turned out, to my surprise, to be Vera, the daughter of that Zelda Marcovsky who had first taken me in as a tiny baby and fed me on her breast and cared for me until I was taken away from her at three years old. When I first saw Vera she made signs to say nothing. It wasn't until later that she got a chance to explain that she thought it would be better for me if people did not know.

I used to have my meals in the kitchen with the maids and the driver, and when the door was open we could hear the Habinski family talking in the dining room. Sometimes Mrs Habinski would walk into the kitchen to give the cook her instructions, and I would get down from my chair and bow down to her. Her fat hands were covered in rings and her dress would almost sweep the floor. The

Guvnor barked a lot, as people had warned me, but underneath he was not so bad; but his wife was not so pleasant at all.

Mrs Habinski's parents also lived in the house; I saw them first as I was sitting waiting for supper. The grandmother came into the kitchen; she looked a very frail old lady, slim but upright, and white-haired, but there was nothing frail about the way she treated people; she was strict, an aristocratic old lady. The grandfather came in after her; like his daughter he was of terrific size — he would have made three of his wife. He wore a long coat like the coats that rabbis wore and a little black skull-cap — he never wore a hat but always this little skull-cap — and he was white-haired and had a long white beard. The two of them walked round and then went out again. The grandfather, I discovered, kept a horse and trap and would drive round the villages buying up grain for his son-in-law.

We all waited, the maids and the drivers and the cook and I, until the mistress came in and told the cook what we were to have for supper. The cook then served us, and while we were eating she went to wait on the family in the dining room. I was very happy to sit round the table with a few people, the maids always laughing and joking; and the food was much better than I had had at Herscho's house.

This was the evening, too, that I first met the Habinskis' eldest son. Boris was a little older than I was, though not so tall. He was very smartly dressed; you could tell he was the Guvnor's son as soon as you saw him. One evening he came into the kitchen, walked up to me and said: 'My name is Boris and I know yours is Moysey. You have no father or mother.' Tears started in my eyes and I could not utter a word. He said: 'Can't you talk? You're not deaf or dumb, are you?'

Vera the cook heard him and butted in, asking why he was insulting me, and Boris said: 'I know he has no father or mother and I want him to know who I am. I have parents, and when he talks to me he should know I'm the Guvnor's son.'

I got my tongue back then and said: 'You've got a father and mother but you haven't got enough sense for a cat,' and he rushed at me and there would have been a fight there and then if Vera hadn't stopped him. He ran out, crying with temper, and I realized I'd said a bit too much but I didn't care; I didn't care if the three years' service with Habinski ended right now.

There was soon a fine old disturbance with Boris and his mother and sister and grandmother all crowding into the kitchen to tell me I mustn't talk to the boss's son like that. I tried to speak up like a man, telling them he had started it and that I wouldn't stand for insults, but I started to cry. Mrs Habinski shouted: 'That won't work; every time you insult my son you cry, and I should forgive you, you vagabond?', and I cried that I would finish my service right away, and went to run out. By this time Habinski himself had heard the row and appeared in the kitchen. He caught me by the door and said: 'You're not going anywhere until I find out what is going on.'

He went off with his wife and son and I waited for a long time. Then he returned, saying: 'You don't have to be afraid any more. My son shall not talk to you for a whole year.'

After supper, one of the maids showed me where I was to sleep — on the floor in the office, where Mr Goodman worked all day. The office was really the end of the corridor in the house, and it was small. A large desk with drawers and a black leatherette top, a smaller desk, rows of big ledgers, a huge old-fashioned letter-copying press, two chairs — these just about filled it. There was no telephone, and at the time I first saw it no typewriter, although one of those appeared a few years later. Just behind where Mr Goodman sat at his desk two doors into other rooms of the house faced one another across the corridor, so when I lay down to sleep my feet stuck out where people would walk across.

The maid brought in a mattress made from new sacking, and a pillow of the same kind. Then she went out again and came back with a rough army blanket. I tried the mattress and told her it was pretty hard. She smiled and said: 'You'll get used to it in a few weeks, but there's something worse.' She explained I would have to get up very early, before anyone else, because this room was used by people walking across from one of the doorways to the other. And I would have to be the last to go to bed, for the same reason.

That didn't worry me, because at Herscho's house I had got used to getting up early and going to bed late. But I didn't like the idea of sleeping on the floor, and while the maid was showing me a cupboard where I could put my bedding away by day and store my clothes at night, I told her so.

She told me there were two empty rooms in the house kept completely furnished and ready in case a relation should come to visit the Habinskis; but she said, as if it explained everything, that I was the first boy they had had live in.

When the maid left I lay down on my mattress on the office floor, and I must have been very tired for I fell asleep like a log. The next thing I remember is someone shaking me and saying, 'Time to get up, Moysey,' and the same maid was kneeling beside me shaking me.

When she'd gone I jumped up, full of life in spite of the mattress on the floor, put my bedding away and went to wash and then found my way into the kitchen.

Soon the old grandmother came in. I bowed to her and said good morning, and she answered, 'Good.' And when the grandfather followed her I bowed and said good morning to him too, but he didn't answer and I thought he was taking no notice of me until he said: 'What's your name?'

I told him, and he said: 'Until you are sixteen we are not going to call you Moysey, but Mosh,' and then he asked, 'Did you pray this morning?'

When I told him I hadn't, he said, 'If you don't pray you get nothing to eat,' and he got out a prayer book and told me to read, and I read from it for ten minutes before he let me go and sit down for my breakfast.

It was the old grandfather who gave me my first regular money, too. On Friday afternoon I was sorting sacks in the granary when he came in and asked me if I had any money, and I explained I had a few kopecks left that the Rabbi's daughter had given me.

He took out his purse and gave me a twenty-kopeck coin — about fivepence — and told me that if I was an obedient boy there would be the same for me every Friday. I wondered why he was giving me this money, and I soon found out. As I've said, he kept a horse and trap, and now he asked that when Mr Habinski's driver went home each day, I should throw him over some hay and oats in a bag for his horse; he knew that I always went to look after the horses and talk to them after everyone else had gone from the stables.

'No need to ask the Guvnor,' said the grandfather. 'After all, I am living here, and in any case it's all for him really — I go out to buy grain for him.'

Now I understood the twenty kopecks. But I thought, he was one of the family and I wasn't really selling anything — so I made up my mind to get that twenty kopecks every Friday.

When I'd finished what I was doing in the granary I went into the kitchen for some tea. Vera Marcovsky gave me the tea with a piece of cake, and slipped a piece of paper into my hand. I read it when I got outside again; it was a letter inviting me to go home to the Marcovskys after dinner the next day, Saturday, and explaining that she hadn't spoken to me because she didn't want Madame Habinski asking questions.

I thought Saturday, the Sabbath, might be a day of rest, but I was woken early as usual, and I'd hardly finished packing my bedding away when the old grandfather came in telling me I could have one glass of tea and must then get ready to carry his books to the synagogue.

This I didn't like at all, but I had to obey the old man, and so we set off, with me carrying his books and his robe. This was the white robe, the *taleth*, that everyone was supposed to wear at the synagogue; the idea was that everyone should look alike, rich and poor, when they went to worship, but it didn't work out like that, of course, because the poor Jews had to have cheap *taleths* and the rich ones had expensive ones and everyone could tell the difference.

When we arrived at the synagogue I saw that the old grandfather was treated as a great personality and shown great respect. He took his books and robe from me, and showed me the day's prayer in the prayer book, and shouted to one of the ushers to give me a seat somewhere, and then joined the other important men and took his usual seat.

3*

In the intervals of the service I recognized that among the boys with whom I was sitting were several from the school where I'd had so little education and such a lot of fighting. When the service was over a lot of the boys crowded round me as I waited outside the synagogue — the old man was busy chatting to various people. The boys wanted to be friends now; I suppose they had grown up since the days when we fought so much. And I couldn't believe my ears when several of them invited me to go to their houses. I didn't know if their parents would be pleased if they brought me home, knowing who I was, but they all said it would be all right now.

Then the old grandfather finished his chatting and wanted to go home, so I picked up his robe and books and followed him. As we got to the house the Guvnor was already there with his younger son and daughter; they all went into the house and the grandfather took his books and robe from me and followed them, telling me: 'Shut the front door behind me; then you can go round to the back door.' I did as I was told, but my heart felt very heavy; the boys could forget I was an orphan, I thought, but the Habinskis were not going to let me forget that I was a servant.

From the kitchen, I could hear the family laughing and I could hear the chink of their wine glasses, and after a while the mistress came into the kitchen and dished out the family's dinner ready for the maid to carry into the dining room. As she finished serving the family, the maid reminded her that I had not had any dinner yet, and I heard her reply: 'Let him wait.' And she did, for more than half an hour; I watched the plates coming back to the kitchen, some only half eaten, while I got hungrier and hungrier — I'd had nothing that morning except a glass of tea and a biscuit when I first got up, and it was now past two o'clock. Finally when the family had all finished the mistress came out to the kitchen, put some food on a plate and gave it to the maid to give to me.

When the mistress had gone the maid told me there wouldn't be anything else for me to do that day. And she said: 'They're not very nice people here, but the mistress is worse than all of them.' The maid was kind; after telling me all about the family she began to wash up, and I picked up a cloth to dry the plates for her, but she refused to let me. 'Go out before someone comes in and finds you another job,' she said. So I brushed myself down a bit and decided to accept Vera's invitation and go to see the Marcovskys.

When I got near the house I could see a lot of faces looking out of the window, and the youngest daughter came running out and kissed me. I felt very shy, but as I entered the house Mama Marcovsky got hold of me and hugged and kissed me and cried at the same time, and Mr Marcovsky and the others made a fuss of me, and I felt, 'This is my real family. These are my real mother and father.'

Everybody kept asking me questions at once, but when the others wanted to know about Herscho, Mama said quickly: 'Don't ask him things like that. We don't want to know.' Monica sat beside me and every few moments kept asking if I wanted anything, until Esther and Vera told her off, saying they wanted to talk to me as well. The Marcovskys wanted to know if the Habinskis were good to me, and Vera the cook said, 'You don't have to ask him that — I know all about it.'

I took the opportunity of asking Vera why I had to sleep on the floor of the office and get up before anyone and go to bed last, when there were empty rooms in the house already furnished. She said it was the mistress; in that house no one could go against what she said, and if she had decided I couldn't have a proper room, that was that.

'But there's one thing you can be sure of,' said Vera. 'While I'm cook there you'll never be hungry,' and she advised me to stick it out at least for a year, so that I could learn the trade.

We sat and talked for hour after hour. They told me about their son David, who had gone to America. He had written telling them that if they ever decided to join him there they should bring me with them because we should all have a better life in America.

When I got up to go, they all insisted that I must stay to supper, and so I stayed. I will always remember that evening, for this family behaved as though they had rescued me from the dead; they were so good to me and I was so happy with them. At last after supper I started to say goodbye; every sister kissed me so lovingly. And Mama! I couldn't get away from her arms.

Back at the Habinskis' house I saw that the big gates were open, and walking round to the stables I discovered that a pair of horses and the carriage were out. I went into the kitchen and the maid offered me some supper, but I was able to tell her I was so full up I shouldn't be able to eat for a month. She was just going to ask where I had been — which would have been awkward, since Vera didn't want the house to know we were connected — when I heard the horses coming in. I ran to help the driver unharness the horses, which saved me answering the maid's questions, made the driver friendly towards me, and pleased the Guvnor.

When I had been with the Habinskis for four months the Guvnor told me he was going to take me for a run to one of the big farms from which he bought grain. I wasn't a man yet but I was old enough to learn how the big farmers lived and how many people they employed, he said. So one morning he put a horse in a light cart, told me to get up in the back, and we drove off. On the way I asked him questions about the wheat trade. He explained that the grain hadn't grown yet; he bought it long before harvest time, setting a price in advance and not seeing the grain until it was delivered.

I found the Guvnor a different man when we were out in the country away from other people. He shared his food with me when we stopped for a break; he let me have a go at driving the horses, he talked to me, and we would be friends. But as soon as other people appeared he would be the master again. I wondered at this then, but later I supposed he just didn't want to seem different from them. They wouldn't be friendly to a servant or a boy with no real father, and so Habinski couldn't be friendly either.

I used to enjoy visiting the farms. These big farmers were what the Russians called *permirschic* . . . really important men in the neighbourhood. A farmer of this kind would own a whole village, perhaps forty or fifty houses, and all the people in the village would work for the one man. He would own perhaps two thousand acres, growing mainly grain, though there would be fields of tomatoes and cucumbers; and he would dress like a gentleman, not like a peasant, and have a good house, and perhaps two or three other houses where his friends could live when they came to stay. If they had children they would be sent away to one of the big cities, or even abroad, to be educated. He would have big machinery on his farm, too, that the peasants couldn't afford; great threshing machines —I liked to watch those at work.

When the Guvnor and I drove up to one of these farms, I would have to drop back into my place as a servant, and while he talked business with the farmer I would be outside looking after the horse or else waiting in the kitchen with the maids. They always seemed to be happy girls, these maids, always laughing.

It was about one of these farmers, Belocriss, that I heard the story of the first automobile that came to our part of the world. I had heard of automobiles, but I'd never seen one, and older people didn't understand them at all. I remember talking to one of the older men about it, and having a hard struggle to explain; something that moved without horses. I did my best, saying it must be like a clock only instead of winding it up you put some sort of liquid into it; but the old man only said: 'The end of the world must be coming,' and walked away crossing himself several times.

Well, Belocriss's son was studying abroad, and when he was due to return home for his three months' holidays the farmer proudly went round telling people that the young man would be bringing an automobile with him. The educated ones knew this was a big occasion for the neighbourhood, but the ignorant ones and the peasants just didn't understand at all.

Soon after the young man arrived, word began to go round the villages that there was something evil and frightening about. One peasant looking out of his shack in the night had seen two burning eyes moving down the road and, convinced it was a devil, he had prayed and crossed himself until it had disappeared into the darkness. He told his neighbours, and soon everyone in his village was scared to be out after dark; they all took care to be home by dusk, and if they had to go out to attend to their cattle they would take someone with them and carry clubs. Gossip like this soon reached the police in the nearest town, and the police chief took four men with him to the village to look into all this talk of devils. For a start they got the peasants together, and learnt that the devil had been heading in the direction of Belocriss's house.

So the five policemen set off for the farmhouse. When they got to the gates, dogs began to bark and the gatekeeper came out to find what they wanted. They asked to speak to Belocriss and the gate-keeper left them waiting outside the locked gates while he fetched his master.

Belocriss, however, welcomed them in, took them into his house, introduced them to his wife and rang for the maid to bring vodka and biscuits. The police chief explained that the villagers were complaining of some evil thing which came from within his gates at night. Belocriss smiled and called for his son, explaining what the police were troubled about. Together they went out to a big shed, swung the doors open — and there was the automobile, very long, shining, and painted red. The farmer opened the car door and touched something inside, and the engine began working. At the sound, one of the policemen crossed himself in fright, until his superior scolded him for being afraid of a machine. Then Belocriss turned on the car's headlamps; there, he said, were the devil's burning eyes.

Back in the house, over more vodka and biscuits, the police inspector asked Belocriss and his son if they would come to the village by daylight with the automobile, to show the peasants that there was nothing to fear; and to this Belocriss agreed. Next day they drove proudly down to the village, and when the people gathered nervously about the shiny red automobile Belocriss stood up and made a speech, declaring that there was nothing in the machine to be afraid of. Soon, he said, doctors would be riding in them to visit the sick, and so the machines would help to save lives; and in years to come the peasants would be cultivating their land with machines like these instead of horses. Whether the peasants believed this I don't know; but at least they were not bothered any more when the farmer's son drove through their village at night.

It was farmers like Belocriss that we would visit, the Guvnor and I, trotting along in a light cart, and talking. But when we had finished our day and headed back into Verchneprovsk, as we came into the town we would go back into our old positions of master and servant. All the same, I enjoyed those days.

Time went on and summer passed. Winter was setting in, and I realized that I hadn't once seen Herscho Levine come in to load up with grain, though I knew when I was with him we used to fill up at Habinski's warehouse at least twice a week. I went to ask old Mr Kovalevsky about it. Kovalevsky was about sixty-five, a short man with a white beard, who worked in the third shop where Habinski sold farm machinery. I liked Mr Kovalevsky, and we always got on together and were great friends. He told me that Herscho was still coming to the warehouse twice a week, but that as soon as any of the assistants spotted him arriving, they would think of an excuse to send me away out of the warehouse so that I wouldn't meet him.

'All the other carriers quarrel with him about his treatment of you, and we don't want any trouble: if you aren't here when Herscho arrives they won't think about it,' said the old man.

The next time the head assistant suddenly made an excuse to send me out of the warehouse I remembered this, and went out but returned soon afterwards. The head assistant tried to get rid of me again, and when I asked him if it was because of Herscho he admitted it. I said: 'Herscho won't bite me,' and stayed; and so for the first time for months we came face to face.

I said: 'Good morning, Papa,' and he was very kind and said, 'Good morning, Moysey,' and asked if I was well; and then right away began assuring me I was better off with Habinski and that it had been a mistake to try to make me into a carrier: 'Now when you grow up you will be able to have your own shop to buy wheat,' said Herscho, and he asked me to forgive him for all that had happened. I said I ought to be asking *his* forgiveness for leaving his cart in the middle of the road without a driver, and we agreed to forgive. I thought it is one thing to forgive, but I did not believe I could forget; all the same, when Herscho asked if I would visit him one Saturday I agreed. For however badly Herscho had treated me, I could not forget that he had given me a name; without him I would have been like a lot of other children in Russia who had no fathers and who had never been adopted. Such children had, in their papers, instead of a father's name the word 'Nepomnishy'—which means 'Forgotten', and everyone would know what that meant. At least Herscho and Hannah Levine had saved me from that.

Mrs Habinski had seen me talking to Herscho, and she was very angry; she had given me a home away from them, she said, and she demanded to know what we had been talking about; she was entitled to know, she said. I refused to tell her at first; I thought it was my own business and though I was a servant I wasn't a slave, and told her so; but I did tell her I had promised to go and see the Levines again. This made her angry, too, but luckily someone called out to me from the warehouse: 'Kuzovsky's here and wants two hundred new sacks,' so I was able to run out.

From about this time I noticed that Mrs Habinski was not cross with me so often. Her son Boris was nearly thirteen; an important age for him because up to that time, by Jewish custom, his father had to bear his sins, but from thirteen onwards Boris would have to bear his own. Maybe Mrs Habinski had realized that without a father I had had to bear my own sins all along; anyway, she began to be more kindly towards me.

One day early in the new year I came face to face with Boris in the yard. He said that though his father had said we were not to speak for a year, it was now the end of a year, and he wanted to be friends. I wanted to know how we could be friends when he was rich and I hadn't a penny to my name, but he insisted, and said that though his mother hadn't wanted him to go around with me he had persuaded her. So I agreed, and went back to my work sorting out sacks.

I thought about Boris, and remembering that he would be thirteen in a couple of weeks' time I realized that he would have more money to spend; he would want to go about the town more and go out at nights to the theatre. He would be afraid to go about in the dark on his own, that was why he wanted someone to go with him.

Each afternoon the old man in the machinery shop, Mr Kovalevsky, used to call me in and make tea over a little oil stove and give me a cup, and share with me the cake which his wife made for him.

The other assistants used to laugh at the two of us together, Kovalevsky old and white-bearded and me the youngest of the people working for Habinski. They would say: 'Have you got another child, Kovalevsky?' and he would say: 'Yes, I've got nine and this one makes ten.' And he told them that it wasn't my fault I hadn't got proper parents. As the weeks went by this talk of the old man's seemed to have an effect on the other men, and most of them began to be friendlier.

One afternoon when Kovalevsky called me in for tea he showed me an invitation he had received to Boris's thirteenth birthday party. There would be a lot of guests and the celebrations would go on all night, he said.

I knew something about this, because I had seen cases of fruit and drinks being brought into the house, and the week before a tailor had come to measure me for a new suit; I was to go for a fitting in two days' time. The tailor had asked me about the celebrations, and I had told him he ought to know; didn't he make the Guvnor's suits, and suits for Boris? But he had said the Habinskis went to a rich man's tailor; he had only been called in to make a suit for me.

Then Vera the cook told me she had been asked to work late the following week to get ready for the special occasion, and she had had to wash all the china and even buy more china because so many people had been invited—not only the Habinskis' friends but the fourteen assistants as well. The driver had been told to be sure to polish up the carriage and make it smart because there would be some elderly people who would have to be driven to the synagogue and back. I noticed, too, that all the curtains were being changed and that the chairs had new covers on them. Even Boris was busy, learning the piece he would have to say before the Rabbi on the great day.

But before the party there were a lot of other interesting things happening for me. On the Saturday a week before, I got up early and breakfasted and smartened myself up and set off to see Herscho and Hannah as I had promised them. As I got near my old home I was stopped by a neighbour who began asking me questions about my running away.

For Herscho's sake I told him that this was all gossip and that it was Herscho who had found me a nice place to work, learning to buy and sell grain, and I often saw him when he came to collect wheat for himself.

When I got to the house Herscho and Hannah were waiting, and one of the old grandmothers, and a lady I did not know, a woman of about thirty-five, very smartly dressed. Hannah introduced her as her sister, but she didn't look a bit like Hannah; in fact she was nice looking. 'Your auntie,' said Hannah, and the lady came up to me and said, 'What a beautiful looking boy!' and kissed me on the cheek. Embarrassed, I mumbled that there was nothing special about me, but she said: 'You must be different because I've brought you a present,' and gave me a parcel and told me to untie it.

Inside was a new book by Maxim Gorky. She demanded that I read a little, and so I started reading. Glancing sideways I saw Herscho sitting there dumbfounded: 'Where did you learn to read like that, you read better than me,' he said, so I told him that every evening I had been going to the Rabbi's house where his son was teaching me to read and write.

We all sat down to have dinner, and for once it was a good meal. I think for the first time Hannah looked at me as a son; she couldn't give me enough. After dinner I thought I would do my old job and wash up, but Hannah wouldn't let me; she told me I was a guest, so she and her sister cleared the table and washed up while I sat talking with Herscho.

He wanted to know what I had been talking about with the neighbour when I arrived, and I told him not to worry because I'd said the stories about my running away were all gossip. Herscho called Hannah in and told her this, and she was very happy that I'd given them a good name. They both told me how sorry they were about the way they had treated me but circumstances had compelled them to act like that. 'You are still our son,' they said. I told them I'd forgotten everything, but in my own mind I was suspicious, wondering what they were after.

Later on, when Hannah and Herscho went out to see to the horses, the aunt came and sat down beside me, saying she could

speak freely now they were outside. She hadn't approved of the way
they treated me, she said: 'Hannah and Herscho don't deserve a
son like you; they are very wild people.' And she kept saying that I
looked much older than my real age, thirteen. I felt very uncomfort-
able, the way she was sitting nearly on top of me, so I moved to sit
opposite to her. 'I won't bite you,' she said. 'You won't be frightened of girls when you get older and find a rich girl to marry.'

Directly Hannah and Herscho returned they were fussing over
me, asking me if I wanted anything to eat or drink, and Herscho
was telling me that Anestrat, the man who helped me run away,
wanted to see me again; but I kept quiet, afraid that I might find
myself coming there every Saturday and helping Herscho with the
work. Herscho told me that he was now doing very well and earning
a lot of money: 'All that will be for you. We want to make up for
what we have done,' he said.

When it was time for me to go, the aunt kissed me again and
pushed a whole ruble into my hand, and Herscho saw me to the
gate and took out a handful of money and picked out another ruble
and gave it to me. As I was going to walk off he said: 'Aren't you
going to shake hands with me?' and for the first time I shook hands
with my papa.

Then I made my way home. I was still suspicious; the pain in my
heart was buried too deep for me to become friends straight away.

When I got home to the Habinskis, I heard a lot of noises from
the dining room, and above them all the sound of the Guvnor laughing. The maid told me she thought the Guvnor was drunk, and the
mistress was very cross. Habinski had given orders, the maid said,
that I was to be sent in to him when I returned.

So I, Moysey, got up from my chair in the kitchen, took courage
and walked into the dining room. The Guvnor shouted at me,
'Moysey, come here!' Moysey, my proper name, not Mosh. I
walked up to him, and he put his hand on my shoulder and said to
his guests: 'This is my youngest assistant in the shop where we buy
grain. He knows the business better than some who have worked
for me four or five years.'

I could see the women whispering to each other, and the mistress suddenly shouted, 'Moysey, go back in the kitchen.' Then the Guvnor said: 'No, go and join the boys. You are not worse than Boris.'

So I went into the next room to join in with the boys, the sons of Habinski's guests. Boris introduced me to them, and I stayed with them until the guests went.

Next morning, Sunday, the Guvnor had a hangover from last night's drinking. There was a thin layer of snow on the ground and everyone started wearing their goloshes and extra clothes. Business was the same as usual on a Sunday, except that there was no sending out wheat with the carters, but for me it was like every day.

This was the week before the big party, but it was also my week of the big order. One afternoon I went into my shop, the sack shop, and found four orders: five hundred new sacks, five hundred seconds, and six hundred third grade sacks and one thousand old sacks; all to be tied up in fifty packs. The Guvnor told me the orders must be ready for the river boat to pick them up in two weeks' time. 'When the man comes he may try to bribe you to give him all new ones, but don't forget you can't cheat me,' he said.

Over supper that night I sat thinking about these orders — never had there been such big ones since I had been there. After I went to bed I could not sleep. I could see all those hundreds of sacks; two thousand six hundred sacks. How could they expect me, a boy of thirteen, to get them all ready in time?

When the morning came I didn't wait for breakfast, but went out into the shop to start sorting the sacks into different piles. I was so busy that I didn't hear one of the other assistants come in. With him was the man who had ordered the sacks, Mr Vaskevitch.

When the other assistant left, Mr Vaskevitch took out a wallet from his inside pocket, and took out a paper ten-ruble note and gave it to me. He said: 'That's for you, and it's not a bribe, but the sacks must be ready in time or they will miss the boat.' He said goodbye to me, and as I walked to the door to see him off he jumped into a waiting cab and drove off. Ten rubles! I had never had so much money in all my life, and it was all mine! At dinner time Vera asked, 'You are so happy, what's happened to you?' I told her, and I told old Mr Kovalevsky, but I didn't tell anyone else. I bought some tea and sugar for the old man, too, because I didn't think it right to be drinking his tea every afternoon and giving him nothing back, not now I had ten rubles; but he was very upset and insisted on paying me for what I had bought.

A few days later the Guvnor looked in on me to see how I was getting on with the sacks. He was surprised to find the five hundred new sacks and the six hundred third grade ones already packed. I told him the others were not ready yet because some had to be repaired, but I assured him they would all be ready on time. Then he said: 'How much did Mr Vaskevitch give you? I know he was here.' I told him, ten rubles, and he joked: 'You've more money than me now.' I asked the Guvnor if he would look after the money for me because I might lose it.

'Oh, no,' he said. 'You must learn to look after money yourself . . . it won't be long before you have wages, and you must not give it to people or you might not get it back. What did you promise Vaskevitch for those ten rubles?'

I told him I'd promised nothing except to have the sacks ready on time, and the Guvnor walked out with a smile on his face, leaving me with my sacks.

VII. THE BIRTHDAY PARTY

Vera told me that the mistress was hiring two more waitresses and some butlers for Boris's birthday, and that the music teacher who taught Boris the violin had been hired with a couple more musicians, to play for dancing. The driver told me he had been ordered to clean up the large sledge, as there would be people arriving from a good way away and they would have to be met at the station. This was January, so carts were not much used because of the snow.

On Friday the Guvnor came and told me to help the maid get in a lot of wood so that all the fires in the house could be kept burning. That evening he and the mistress and Boris were all missing; the maid told me they had gone off to the public baths. Even big houses in Russia in those days did not often have bathrooms, and there was no bathroom at the Habinskis. I went now and then to the public baths myself, though I had to go into the third-class baths while the Habinskis would go into the first class.

Saturday dawned. When I'd finished helping get in the wood I found that everyone else had gone off to the synagogue. I had a wash and changed into my new suit, which had been delivered only the day before, and set off to follow them. All the boys who were my friends were there, and they all admired my new suit.

After the service, a few neighbours came home for a drink, though the real party would not start until Sunday. Boris asked me to test him with the speech he would have to make, and I listened to it several times, though I would sooner have been free to go skating on the river. At dinner time I took my position at the table in the kitchen, along with the other servants, as always, but the maid told me I was wanted in the dining room. I wondered what the Guvnor wanted me for, but I got up and went in, and saw one empty chair at the dining room table, and the Guvnor bade me sit in it. Everyone was dressed in their very best, and I thought how good it would be to be rich.

We all had a glass of wine in front of us, and according to custom the oldest member of the family, the old grandfather, stood up and blessed it, and we all followed him; as he drank we also drank a little from our glasses. Then the dinner was served, all very nice; and after it was over I left while the family stayed together drinking and talking.

It wasn't usual for people to go to the synagogue on Sunday, but the next day was an exception, Boris's thirteenth birthday, and all the family set off for the synagogue at about nine o'clock. A lot of people were waiting outside the synagogue, curious to see who it was coming on a Sunday to pray. The driver took the family in the big sledge, but so many people blocked the way that the police had to be called to clear it.

We were home from the service about noon, and from that time onwards it was kissing and kissing, guests arriving, a big banquet being laid, the maids rushing backwards and forwards, and the hired butlers waiting behind the guests' chairs. After a while I heard the Guvnor's voice; he was already singing, 'Fill it up, fill it up!' and it was early yet.

After supper, which was at about seven o'clock, they pushed all the chairs to the side of the wall, took down the huge table, and the band started playing and people began dancing, while the maids took round the sweets and wine, and it went on like that until twelve o'clock. I had a fine time with the sweets and chocolates.

At midnight the guests began dwindling away, and the driver kept coming in to take people home on the sledge. He told me that one of the guests had given him a ten ruble tip. The man could have hired a cab for less money than that, but as the driver said, he was one of the rich men who would like such things known to make his name big.

I didn't have much sleep that night. I had to help the maids clear up and put all the bottles away. A few people still lingered on talking to the Guvnor, while we were putting everything out into the yard to be taken away next day.

About half past three everyone was finally gone, and the driver and the maid and I fell asleep on chairs in the kitchen, exhausted.

Next morning everyone got up with headaches, and the place looked a shambles, but the staff came back as usual and work had to go on. When I went in for my dinner I was told Boris wanted to see me in his room. I found him not even properly dressed yet. He showed me his presents, and the money laid on the table — five hundred rubles altogether. I said: 'It's good to be lucky,' and he said, 'You'll be lucky one day,' and picked up a fountain pen and a piece of paper money and gave them to me. I was worried about what his father would say, but Boris said: 'Tell him I gave it to you — he is not very interested in how much money I have, only if I have enough.'

Boris also told me that his father was thinking of putting me in the place of one of his old employees, who was about to be pensioned off; the man who looked after his wheat stores at the railway station. I wondered why the Guvnor wasn't choosing one of the workers who had been with him longer than me and who knew all about the job, but Boris explained that they were all married and would not want to work outside the town.

Boris also asked me to go with him to the theatre the following Saturday, and that made two invitations I had, for the head assistant had invited me to go home for dinner with his family that day.

So the following Saturday, instead of carrying the old grandfather's books and robes home from the synagogue after the service, I left them there to be called for another day, and went straight on to the head assistant's house. He had given me the address, but when I got to the house I was surprised to see what a poor district he lived in. He took me in and introduced me to his wife and his little boy of seven and his daughter of eleven; and the way they all got out of their chairs to greet me made me feel I was somebody. The wife and the little girl went to get dinner ready, and the assistant filled up a glass of wine for me, but I waited until his wife had returned so I could drink their health together.

It was a lovely meal, and they both kept chattering and asking questions. From the conversations I learnt that he earned sixty rubles a month, and I thought it must be hard to live on that with two children. After we had run out of conversation the little girl came up and asked me if I could read and write. I said, 'Certainly I can,' and she said she would like to see it, but that this was the Sabbath and I mustn't write on that day. So she went away and brought back a book, and asked me to read from it, which I did, though I was a bit shy. I asked her father if I could write something down, and he said he would be going into the other room so I could do as I liked. So when he and his wife left, the little girl got out some paper and asked if I could write a poem, which I did. This is what I wrote:

> *One evening there was a very hard frost*
> *A little boy was walking and was blue*
> *and shivering from the frost*
> *You can hear him saying*
> *'Whoever will take me in*
> *and give me food and warmth?*
> *And I hope God will not forsake me*
>
> *But send someone along to save me.'*
> *A little old lady was walking along*
> *All wrapped up in her rags*
> *She heard him talking*
> *So took him to her house*
> *And gave him food and warmth;*
> *After a few minutes he fell asleep.*

I wrote this with the pen that Boris gave me. When the assistant and his wife came back into the room they told how the wife went out to work to help with the expenses of sending the children to school. Nobody got good pay from our Guvnor, the head assistant said, and to prove it he told me what wages the other men were getting. They made me stay on for tea, but when the clock on the wall showed ten past five I cut short my meal, because I had to meet Boris, and got up, thanking them and saying I was sorry I had to go, as I sincerely was.

I met Boris outside the theatre, and he handed me a ticket, telling me to wait for him at the same place when the play was finished. Then he left me to go to his own seat. In five minutes the doors were opened and everyone went in. It was all new to me; wonderfully bright and the atmosphere so happy. The play was called *Life After Revolution*, and it was the first time it had been allowed to be performed.

My ticket was for right up in the top gallery, where people have to stand because there are no seats, but I was so happy I never noticed that I was standing up for two and a half hours; it was so exciting, with the actors and actresses dressed up in national costumes, and everyone saying what a wonderful success the play was.

When it was over, I met Boris where he told me, and thanked him for the ticket, but he said, 'Don't thank me, I'm not the Guvnor.' I thought we would be going home, but Boris said we would have some tea first. We passed one or two teashops, but he said, 'Not there,' and then we reached a posh one, and he said, 'That's the one.'

We went in and found a table for two, and Boris gave the waitress an order for tea and pastries; she went away but came back asking if we had the money to pay. Boris was very upset, and took from his pocket a five ruble note, saying: 'Will this be enough?' and she went to get the order. I asked Boris if he had been there before, and he said no, he'd never been in any teashop before.

The waitress brought the order and with a smile gave Boris the change, and from it he gave her a twenty kopeck tip. We drank the tea and ate four pastries, and then Boris called her again and ordered two big ice creams; and when she brought them he acted big, giving her some money and telling her to keep the change.

We walked home, Boris talking a lot of nonsense and I answering him in the same way. It was a quarter to twelve when we reached the door, and we went straight to bed. And tonight I found that I didn't have to get my bedclothes out of the cupboard where they were kept during the day; the maid had put them out for me. Next morning I was a bit late in getting up, and the maid put the bedclothes away for me too, and never reproached me; and after that she always saw to it for me every night and morning. It seemed that once the Guvnor's son took notice of me, everyone else would take notice of me too.

VIII.   A PAID MAN

When I had been with Habinski nearly two years, we were sitting together in the grain shop one day when we had nothing much to do, the foreman assistant, two other assistants and me. They reminded me that I'd been there nearly two years, and I said I had another year to do, according to the arrangements that had been made. Then they asked me if I had signed any documents, and I said no. I hadn't because I had been too young. So they asked why I stayed, without any pay, when I could go away and get a job somewhere else with pay; and I said the arrangements had been made for three years and I was going to stick to three years.

A few minutes later I heard the maid come out into the shop and say, 'Where's that lazy devil?' and I peeped behind the door and said: 'I'm here!' and she laughed, and told me the Guvnor wanted to see me in the office.

Habinski was with Mr Goodman the book-keeper; the book-keeper wanted to give me a chair but the Guvnor said: 'He's young, he can stand,' and then *he* asked me how long I had been there. I told him another ten days would make it two years; I knew it because I had kept the dates in a little book. The Guvnor wanted to know why I had put down the dates so carefully, and I told him: 'Three years is thirty-six months, and I can tell you I won't work thirty-seven months without money.'

'That's what I get,' said the Guvnor. 'I take you in, give you food, somewhere to sleep and clothes, and you just think of the day when it is finished.'

I said I was glad he had mentioned a place to sleep in, and asked if he knew that I had to wait until everyone else had gone to bed before I could lie down, and be up and out of the way before anyone else got up? The Guvnor said he didn't know that — of course, he did — and promised he would investigate it. Then he asked how much I earned — he knew that too, he was just pretending.

The book-keeper interrupted: 'Well, it says here in my book that Moysey is here for three years without pay, and in return for his service he is clothed, fed and given a place to sleep.'

'Now,' said the Guvnor, 'the last twelve months I am going to pay you three rubles a month, and that's because the foreman told me you are obedient and do your work properly.'

I thanked him very much, and went back to my place in the shop. They all wanted to know what the Guvnor wanted, and I told them about it. Then I went to the third shop where old Mr Kovalevsky was working, and told him, and said that the others were all happy for me because I was a paid man now. Old Mr Kovalevsky said: 'You know why he is paying you? Because he would have to pay a man twenty rubles a month for the work you do.'

With these words I felt lifted up on to a pedestal. I was worth twenty rubles a month!

In ten days' time I became a paid assistant, and was treated the same as the others, and they accepted me as one, though they all said I was silly to have agreed on only three rubles a month. But for me, time flew. I was often very busy, and almost every week Boris would take me to the theatre. A few months later I moved up another notch; I was allowed to sleep on a little divan in the lean-to beside the house. And then I was told that every Saturday I could dine with the family instead of in the kitchen with the maids and the driver.

I had to sit on the end of the table in case anything was wanted, so that I would be able to get it without disturbing anyone. The old grandfather saw to it that I was kept busy; it was never long before he said something like, 'Would you go and get another jug of water, Mosh?' and a big jug would be pushed at me and I would go and get it. These Saturday dinners were uneasy, too, because I thought everyone was looking at me, the way I ate; though I never knew for sure because I was always too busy trying to hold my knife and fork properly to be able to look up.

The old grandfather would tease me. He would say, 'Do you want lemonade, Mosh? To refuse is not nice,' so I would say, 'Yes, I will have a drink of lemonade,' and then he would say: 'You can drink water.' But he did this once too often; when he said, 'You can drink water,' I replied: 'To take water I do not have permission, but you suggested lemonade and that's what I am going to have.' That time all the family laughed at him; and the Guvnor said to the old grandfather: 'Don't tease him; you asked him to have lemonade,' and he poured out a full glass for me.

Lunch would finish with a prayer, and then I would turn to the mistress and thank her, and try to get away because the afternoon would be my holiday.

After I began eating with the family, the Guvnor took to trusting me with the job of going to the bank on Fridays to change a one thousand ruble note, ready for Sunday's trade. He never told me to be careful with it, but I was. He didn't realize how careful until one Friday he gave me the thousand ruble note and a moment later put his hand into my pocket and said, 'It's not there! Where is it?' I lifted up the bottom of my trouser-leg and showed him the note tucked into my sock. That sort of carefulness pleased the Guvnor.

There were guards standing on either side of the front door of the bank in Verchneprovsk; guards with drawn swords. The first time I went to the bank one of them stopped me, wanting to know what a boy was doing in the bank, but I told him the man at the cash desk would know, and after a bit of hesitation he let me through. I would go up to the cash desk and hand over the note, and say I was from Habinski, and get the change, mostly in small notes. At first I didn't use to worry about carrying all that money, because nobody except the cashier and Habinski knew that I'd got it; but as the weeks went by I began to get a bit nervous in case anyone was watching me; and I told Habinski, who from then on sent another assistant with me.

So the weeks went on, getting nearer and nearer to the time when my three years' service would be over. I had managed to save up eighteen rubles, what with the three rubles a month I was being paid, and another ruble Boris gave me every week in addition to paying for my theatre ticket. When I had the eighteen rubles saved I deposited it in the post office, and felt very proud at being a boy with a savings book! I was getting on better with the assistants, too, maybe because they were thinking that the end of my service was coming and they would be getting rid of me soon. I think they liked me, but they were afraid at the same time; they thought I knew too much and was working too cheap.

Herscho hadn't come to the granary for a few weeks, so I decided to go round and see him and Hannah the next Saturday after dinner, and find out what was going on. When I tried to get away after dinner the Guvnor wanted to know where I was going, and I told him. He shouted: 'The way those two kept you, and you still want to go and see them?' But he didn't try to stop me going.

When I reached Herscho's house, the landlord, who lived near by, came to ask what I wanted. He didn't recognize me at first, but when he did he invited me into his house and called his wife, who gave me tea and cake. They both kept saying how tall I'd grown, and declaring that I looked older than my age — I was fourteen and a half then. I asked them about Herscho, and the landlord's wife told me that he had been ill for a couple of months and had had to hire new men, and the men had swindled him and left him in debt so that he couldn't show his face in the town. In the end he had sold up and left for the next town, Kremenchug, away across the river: 'He lost face and ran away,' she said. He had changed his name too. She said that Herscho had told her he would have been a rich man by now if I hadn't run away and left him, because he could have trusted me to handle things and not cheat him; but Herscho blamed my running away on Hannah, not me, the woman said.

About four weeks before Easter the book-keeper, Mr Goodman, called me in and gave me a letter from the town of Kremenchug; he said he hadn't shown the Guvnor in case he confiscated it, and he advised me to tell people in future to write to me care of the post office so that I could collect the letters without the Guvnor knowing. The letter was from Herscho and Hannah, asking me to come to stay with them for a week at Easter. I wrote back saying I would try my best to be there and giving them a post office address if they wanted to write again; and then I caught the Guvnor when he was on his own and told him I wanted to go away for a week at

Easter; everyone had a week's holiday then. The Guvnor didn't
try to stop me going.

I told old Mr Kovalevsky I was going, and he urged me not to
be extravagant over the trip, and to save my money, because when
I was older I would need to spend money on clothes so I could mix
with business people. I told him rather proudly I had a post office
book and had already saved thirty rubles, but he only replied that he
had double that when he was my age.

I went shopping and bought a little case, and two shirts that I
liked—not the rubbish the mistress used to buy for me — and new
boots. When the time came for me to set off I found that I had spent
fourteen rubles, but I decided I couldn't go to see Herscho and
Hannah without a present, so I bought Hannah a warm skirt. When
I went home to pack the skirt in my case I thought to myself that I
must be mad to buy a present for a woman who beat me and
treated me like a dog, but then I thought I couldn't take revenge on
her, and shut the case up. I couldn't manage to buy Herscho a
present, but I knew he would be pleased if I bought something for
his wife.

On Thursday afternoon I went to the cab rank to ask one of the
men to call for me next morning and at nine o'clock on Friday I set
off in the cab with my case, to catch the river boat.

I arrived at the quayside much earlier than I had expected and
this gave me ample time to look around. For a long time it had been
one of my dearest wishes to watch the river steamers come and go
and to see the busy bustle at the landing-stage. Until now I had
merely accompanied Herscho to the railway station when goods
had to be consigned, but here at last I was going to travel on the
great river steamer myself.

There was a vast wooden building standing on brick supports
which had been sunk into the water. Inside the building was a
corridor off which there were three waiting-rooms, one for each
class; a barber's shop with two assistants, another shop selling gifts
and trinkets. There was one door which I found to be locked and
which turned out to be the door of a dormitory for the use of passengers who had missed their boat.

Each waiting room had its own tea-bar and since there would be some time before my boat arrived I entered the third class and bought a glass of tea. The room was crowded with nearly a hundred peasants and their families and they were making such a din that I was soon glad to swallow my tea and go outside.

When I had left the tea-bar I heard a bell ringing loudly. I asked what this meant and was told that the boat was due in twenty minutes. I looked downstream and there in the distance I saw a faint speck moving slowly towards me — the boat. There were so many people at the ticket office I decided to stroll down to the river's edge to watch the boat arrive before I bought my ticket. The boat was called the *Stolipin*; it was very long and painted white apart from its single black funnel and red portholes. In a few minutes its paddles had stopped and, having bought my ticket, I was aboard.

I walked along the decks and examined the paddle machinery through the iron rails surrounding it as the paddles began to turn again and the boat moved out into the stream. For the first hour of the voyage I could see quite clearly both banks of the river, with houses dotted along them, but as the Dnieper widened these disappeared and all I could see were the sky and the water. My fellow-passengers in the third class were a friendly crowd who passed the time in dancing, singing and other music-making; some played cards, some visited the shop to buy refreshments, including vodka. The voyage took eight hours but for me it was all too short — a holiday, just for the distance from Verchneprovsk to Kremenchug.

When we arrived at Kremenchug the boat stopped and a big plank was put up and I walked off and along the quayside until I came to the ticket collector's little house. There I gave up my ticket, and made for the line of cabs waiting along the quay, shouting the address to one of the men and asking him to take me there.

For the first ten minutes, we drove across a wide expanse of sand which made it hard going for the poor cab-horse. Beyond the sand, to both left and right, there were great piles of newly-cut timber, and there was the sound of saw-mills in the distance. When we reached the highway to the town, I felt the smoothness of the road's surface under the wheels and the horse's difficulties were at an end. Another half hour brought us to the town. The road here was wide and the pavements broad and clean. There were rows of splendid-looking shops and I asked the cab-driver if we could stop for a moment so that I could look in the shop windows, but he refused, saying it was not allowed for a cab to park in the main road.

When we got to the address I gave him a ruble and asked him for change, and he said: 'You're lucky I'm not asking you for more,' and drove off. I took my case and looked at the house and wondered if I'd got it right, for it was a very strange old building and it looked as if a lot of poor people lived there. But it was the right address, so I climbed the stairs to the second floor and knocked on the door.

Hannah flung the door open and hugged me. I felt confused; I could not feel it was the kiss a mother would have given me, and though I wanted to forget what had happened in the past I found that I could not, that the pictures of life with her as it had been kept coming back. But I tried not to show it. I hope I showed nothing. Herscho also embraced me, and then we all sat down to supper.

Time and trouble seemed to have changed Hannah and Herscho. For a start, they had taken to using a new name, Stocklinsky, instead of Levine. This meant that because I was under age I too became Moysey Stocklinsky, though it took me a long time to get used to it, and I used the name Levine for a long time afterwards. But the change I noticed far more, as I sat down with these people, was in their way of treating me. Hannah kept pressing me to eat more and more, and Herscho told me she had been working much more than usual that day to get ready for my arrival. I wondered why she couldn't have treated me like this when I was small — I was taller than Hannah now, and she had to look up to me when she spoke to me — but then I thought, if she had been kinder I would still be driving horses, and I decided that things had worked out for the best.

Herscho behaved differently, too; we sat up late talking, and he talked to me as if I were a grown man. He explained that Anestrat had inherited a piece of land from his father-in-law, and so had given up his job. Herscho had been unable to get another man to work like Anestrat, and had got into terrible difficulties with the

4

cartage business. Now he had a stall in the market at Kremenchug, selling tobacco and cigarettes. 'It is much better for me,' said Herscho. 'We don't need a lot so long as we get our food, and we don't need many clothes, we are getting on in years.'

I could believe that, but when he went on to say, 'Money does accumulate, and you are our own son so it will be all for you,' I found that harder to believe. Living with Herscho and Hannah, and then with Habinski, had made me suspicious.

After supper I opened my case and took out the paper bag with the skirt in it, and gave it to Hannah. She held it up to her waist saying, 'What a lovely present,' and hugging me again. And on the boat I'd found a present for Herscho too, a cigarette holder. He was pleased with that.

It was past one o'clock when we went to bed, and I discovered that they had only one bedroom with one double bed in it; Hannah made up a bed for me on the couch in the living room and I slept there until late next morning. Herscho didn't open his stall on Saturday, and after breakfast Hannah suggested we all go for a walk round the town and visit her relations. We started off with Auntie Fay and Uncle Noiyah — he was a cabinet maker who worked at home in a little workshop he had fitted up for himself — and their two children, Usher, a tall nice-looking girl of about sixteen or seventeen, and her brother Yakov who was learning to be a choir-singer. Usher was quite a shock to me. She started by wanting to know if I went out with girls, and asking if I would take her to the theatre, and when I said I was too young at fourteen to be taking girls to theatres she declared that she would take me instead.

When the old people sat down to talk, she dragged me out for a walk to show me the town, and kept asking me questions about myself. I tried to change the subject and asked her what work she did. She told me she worked in a stationery shop for ten rubles a month — everyone in Russia was paid monthly in those days. I told her that I would be earning more than that soon, and right away she came back: 'Then you can come here often, and take me to the theatre.'

I said: 'When I come back here, in twelve months' time, you'll be married,' trying to joke; and: 'You'll be my husband,' said Usher, just like that, making me shyer than ever. I told her I wouldn't be able to marry anyone until I had done my military service, and that was years ahead, when I was twenty-one. She looked so miserable that I said: 'Let's go home for tea, and perhaps when I come next Easter I'll bring you a present *and* take you out to tea and to the theatre,' but that didn't do any good either — it would be such a long time, she said. And there and then she told me she had fallen in love with me. It sounded rubbish to me, and I was glad when we'd got back to my aunt's house again, and I could say goodbye and set off with Hannah and Herscho for home.

Not that Hannah was much better in her way. She wanted to show me off to everyone as the son she had brought up. Every day in that week I stayed with her, she and Herscho found somewhere different to take me, and too many of the people she knew seemed to have heard about me, the boy without parents, until I felt I was being exhibited like some animal in a zoo. Nor was it just Hannah. My aunt pointed me out to her landlord's wife, and I found myself stopped by the woman, and questioned, and invited to come to visit her and her husband. I didn't want this at all; what would rich people like that want with a poor devil like me, except to satisfy their curiosity? But I didn't think I ought to refuse her invitation, especially when she followed it up with a written one, brought round by a maid; and Hannah and Herscho agreed, although they were frightened that I might tell too much about the way they had treated me. So at about six-thirty that evening I brushed my clothes and combed my hair and set off.

This landlord was a Mr Komaniev; he owned four big old houses in the street where my aunt and uncle lived, with about forty tenants, and lived himself in a very nice bungalow at the end of the street. I marched up to his door, and didn't have to knock; there was a button to press to ring the bell. A maid opened the door and before she could announce me Mrs Komaniev arrived and took me into a room full of books, their library, and then into a room with wonderful curtains and furniture, and rang for the maid to bring tea. Her husband came in, a nice-looking man and very hospitable, and they began talking, veering round soon to asking

questions, though they did it all so awkwardly, saying with embarrassment that they didn't want to upset me, that I had to help them out.
I told them: 'I'm not upset; I wasn't able to stop a woman from
leaving a baby in the synagogue and running away, and I couldn't
stop people pushing me from pillar to post, and I'm happy I can
stand on my own feet now.'

They had heard stories about Herscho and Hannah, and wanted
to know if I was frightened of them, but I told them I wasn't frightened any more. When I thought I'd given them enough of a look
at this monster Moysey, I wanted to get up and go, but they made
me stay and meet their children when they returned from school,
and I found myself trying to help the boy with some of his home-
work. Later Mr Komaniev explained to me that as well as owning
the four houses he had a stationery business, and he suggested that
when I'd finished my apprenticeship with Habinski I could come
to him for a job. I thanked him for this, but said I must try the
wheat business for a while. Otherwise my years of learning it would
be wasted, and he agreed. 'But next time you come to Kremenchug,
come to see us,' they said, and saw me to the door. Mr Komaniev
shook hands, and his wife held out her hand and I kissed it, and set
off home.

Hannah and Herscho seemed relieved to hear that I hadn't given
them away, and Hannah seemed more than ever determined to
make up for earlier days; she even brought me breakfast in bed one
morning, and glasses of tea when I went to bed at night. One evening she demanded that I take her to the theatre, and I took her,
though it wasn't much of an entertainment for me — inside the
theatre she kept chattering, asking me about the placards announcing
things — like a lot of people then, she couldn't read — until I had to
apologize to people round about us for the noise. Another day
Herscho took me along the town's high street with its big shops, and
sat down at a little boulevard café, ordering chocolate for me and
grapes for himself; Herscho liked grapes better than anything. He
said, looking at the shops, 'When you start getting high wages and
saving money, you'll be able to open a shop, and I'll be here to
advise you and help.' I told him it would take a long time for me to

save up money like that, and I thought to myself it would take even longer before I let Herscho help me with it.

But it was Usher who was a puzzle and a worry to me. She would not leave me alone, and I found nothing interesting in her company. Maybe a man of twenty would have found it interesting, but not me. She would be waiting for me when I got back to Herscho's; she would be waiting when I got up in the morning; and however much I told her she was older than I was, she would go on telling me I looked older than my years, and wanting to show me off to her friends. On the Thursday night I walked back with her to her house, and when I said goodnight she embraced and kissed me. I couldn't return this sort of affection, which made her very angry; she complained that I didn't love her, and when I protested that I *liked* her, that made her angrier still and she ran indoors. I felt a lot more comfortable when she'd gone, and turned back for home thanking God that tomorrow was Friday and I would be leaving Kremenchug on Saturday.

Usher was there again on the Saturday when I was to set off back to Verchneprovsk. Hannah and Herscho were shocked when I called a cab, telling me that nobody of Jewish religion should ride on a Saturday, but I told them I could only hope God would forgive me because I couldn't carry my case all the way to the quayside in time to catch the boat. And the sin of riding on the Sabbath didn't worry Usher either. When the cab arrived, I told her that I'd only called it to take one, but she asked the driver if he would mind her coming with me and of course, seeing a good-looking girl, he said she might, and so she jumped in beside me and we rattled off to the landing place. When I got out she caught hold of me, and I thought she would suffocate me; I said: 'You're killing me,' but she only replied: 'I can't help it — I love you so much and you don't know what love is.' I thought, as I climbed up the gangplank, that if love did this to people, then I was thankful for my ignorance. I watched her handkerchief waving from the quayside until the boat pulled away, then settled down to eight hours of rest from all the turmoil. I wasn't sorry I would be away from the lot of them for the next twelvemonth.

It was about two-thirty in the morning when the boat reached the Verchneprovsk quay; there were no cabs about and I started to walk until one overtook me, and the driver, recognizing me, called out, 'Jump in.' He took me back to Habinski's, and refused any money for it. I didn't like to bang at the door and wake anyone up, so I put my straw case on the porch and stretched out on a chair there. I must have fallen asleep, for I opened my eyes to find a policeman looking at me. He struck a match to look right into my face, and then he recognized me. 'Oh, I know you,' he said. 'The whole town knows you.' His match went out, and he left me and plodded on. I don't suppose he meant any harm, but what he had said hurt me in my heart. I didn't mind him knowing me, but the whole town . . . it made me feel I was guilty of something. After that I heard a clock somewhere strike every hour until eight, while I sat thinking to myself how I might some day find the people who had left me to the world and to a pain like this, and what I would say to them when I found them.

Then I heard the big gates open up for the horses to go out and fetch the water; as the driver came out I went into the kitchen and fell asleep again.

When I saw the mistress at dinner time, she wanted to know about Hannah and Herscho. I told her they seemed different people now, but all she could say was: 'They would be — they think you're going to earn money now and will give it to them.' The Guvnor told her: 'That's his business, don't keep pestering about it,' and soon I made my excuses and went back to work in the shop. There were a great many sacks to be repaired, and the women were waiting for me to hand out the work.

IX. THE WHEAT FRAUD

A few days later the Guvnor took me to the station to meet Mr Pevin, the man who worked for him there, checking the wheat brought in by the peasants from all the villages round about. We drove there along the road I had driven so often for Herscho, and I thought about the difference between the Moysey who had been a carter's boy and the Moysey who was now going to learn to take charge of part of a big grain business.

At the station the Guvnor introduced me to Pevin. Never one to give anything away, he didn't tell the old man straight out that I was to replace him, but just said I was there to help him. He told me that I should have my meals there, at the station, and he would pay: 'Go into the third-class café, not the first-class one; it's too dear and anyway you are not properly dressed for it,' he said. And I was to return each evening with Pevin to Verchneprovsk town in a cab. With that as all his advice, the Guvnor went home and left me with Pevin.

The old man took me off to lunch, not at the station as their food was not much good he said, but at a nearby cottage where he had arranged for a peasant woman to give him his meals. The woman was glad to earn a few extra kopecks and was happy to serve us both and I enjoyed it because I rather liked peasant cooking.

Over lunch Mr Pevin told me he had been working for the Guvnor for twenty-two years, and reckoned that Habinski now wanted to pension him off. If I looked after myself and learned quickly I might come in for the job, he said. I said I didn't want him to think I'd come to take his job away, but he said if Habinski made up his mind to get rid of a man he would do it, and if it wasn't me taking over it would be someone else. He asked how old I was, and when I told him I was nearly fifteen he said that explained it; the Guvnor wanted cheap labour, though I looked older than fifteen, he said.

It was an interesting job to learn. By the side of the tracks there was an enormous barn belonging to the railway, divided into chutes, each chute holding 900 pood of grain, enough to fill a railway wagon. The Guvnor rented 180 of these chutes, and there were several other grain dealers who also hired chutes.

The grain we bought from the peasants was unloaded into these chutes and when a truckload was complete, the railway inspector would give us a receipt which Habinski would deposit with the bank and on which the bank would lend him money until the grain was sold. It might not be sold at once; the dealers would keep the grain there, paying the railway so much for storage, until the price rose, then they would sell it, sometimes sixty or eighty wagonloads at a time, abroad.

It was Mr Pevin's job and mine to know how much went into each chute each day, and to keep tally until a chute was filled and the Guvnor's name was attached and a receipt was given for us to take to the bank.

I had been working with Mr Pevin for about a month, and had only a week to go before I finished my three years apprenticeship with Habinski, when the Guvnor called me into his office and told me that I could start on my own soon. 'I'm going to offer you a wage no boy of fifteen ever got before,' he said. 'Ten rubles a month, and I pay expenses as well.'

I was happy when he said ten rubles, but I didn't want to agree right away, so I said: 'That's not enough.' The Guvnor told me to go away and think it over, and I went straight round to old Mr Kovalevsky's home to tell him of my good fortune.

When I said I'd been offered ten rubles a month he replied right away: 'Not enough — Pevin gets thirty rubles; Habinski should pay you at least half that.'

I said I was scared; I wasn't really sure that I could do the job, and I wondered if it wouldn't be better to wait until I knew more about it before arguing with Habinski over the wages, especially since ten rubles seemed a big sum to me. But Kovalevsky told me to be brave and remember that if Habinski hadn't believed I was good enough he wouldn't have offered me the job. When I still looked uncertain, he made me tell him all about the work I did and explain how the grain business at the station was run. I went over the whole job, and when I had done so he said: 'You know all there is to know; now go back and tell Habinski you want fifteen rubles a month.'

The next morning the Guvnor said: 'I see you went for a conference with someone; what advice did they give you?' As bravely as I could, I told him that since I'd worked three years for him for nothing I'd like fifteen rubles a month now. If he found after a time that I wasn't worth so much I would leave, but I wouldn't work for anything less, I said.

The Guvnor looked at me with his bright eyes — you couldn't see if he was smiling because his mouth was hidden in his big black beard. Then: 'That's fair,' he said. 'I'll see you keep to that. All right — fifteen rubles.'

For another two months I worked as Mr Pevin's assistant, asking questions all the time. Life was going to be wonderful, I decided, when he retired and I became almost my own boss, out there at the station alone, away from Verchneprovsk and the Habinskis. My free time would be my own, too, and I might be able to take a room near the station, which would be cheaper than hiring cabs to and from the town.

At the end of three months working together Mr Pevin told me that in future he would just look on while I took over all the work. He was as good as his word, never interfering or talking about business, even over our meals together. After a little while longer he said: 'Another four weeks,' and at last the day came for him to go into retirement and he handed over his books and I was a man in charge, on my own.

The Saturday of that first week, as soon as lunch with the Habinski family was over, I was off to tell Mama Marcovsky all about it. There were kisses and hugs until I felt my breath going, and Mama Marcovsky cried and said how big and strong I was growing, and they tried to make me take the first glass of tea that was served — but I insisted that was still for Papa Marcovsky as the man of the house. Then we sat down, Mama Marcovsky and Papa and the girls Vera and Monica, and we talked and talked and talked, and told each other all our news. This was my real family, no matter who bore me

4*

or who brought me up for the most years, and these were the people I could never forget or turn my back on.

They all wanted to know why I had been to see Herscho and Hannah during my holidays the previous Easter, after the terrible way the Levines had treated me. I gave them the answer I gave everybody; I was grateful to Hannah and Herscho for being so unkind to me, for if they had been kind, like a real father and mother, I should still be driving a pair of horses to and from the station and by now heaving big sacks of grain on and off the carts. Instead I was living a gentleman's life working for an important firm, all because they had been harsh enough to drive me into running away. There was something else, too, which I could not forget; it was Herscho, after all, who had given me a name, so that I was Moysey Levine and not 'Moysey-the-forgotten-to-be-named-one'.

Mama and Papa and the girls told me their news in return; how Esther the middle daughter was working now in a tobacco factory, and how their son David in America was doing well enough to be able to send them money to pay for Monica to be educated so that she could later on get a job in an office. And both Monica and Vera were going out with young men. It was a happy day, that day with Mama Marcovsky.

The first week I was on my own at the station the Guvnor came to pick up the receipts for chutes which had been filled with grain, and he was delighted when I had fourteen to give him. At the weekend I took all the account books home, and spent Sunday trying to get them in order. While I was struggling to make them all tally, I discovered that there seemed to be four chutes begun and partly filled with grain but of which there was no record in Habinski's books. My first idea was to ask the Guvnor about it, but then I thought it might make trouble for Mr Pevin, and I'd best go to see the old man before I said anything to anyone else. So on the Monday evening after supper I walked round to Mr Pevin's house, and when his wife showed me in I told him, as soon as she had left us alone, that I wanted to discuss business.

Straight away he began telling me his life story; how he had been married for fourteen years but had no children and no one to help

him in his old age; how he had given up one good job at a station
grain depot because it kept him from home a fortnight at a time and
his wife had complained of being lonely; how he had taken low-paid
jobs in the town before Habinski hired him; how Habinski had paid
him only twenty-five rubles a month — enough to live on but not
enough to save on for his old age. 'So you ask for a rise now and
again, Moysey,' he said, 'don't be like me.'

I asked him why he had been telling me all this, and he said:
'Because I know why you came to see me. You've found four chutes
started with wheat, with no name on them and no record of them in
Habinski's books.'

I nodded, and the old man went on: 'You can fill these bit by bit
from the wheat in Habinski's chutes. When the four are filled you
get a receipt for each one from the railway inspector, and the
receipts you can sell to another trader who exports grain.'

I was silent with surprise.

'I've done this once before,' said Pevin, 'but these four chutes I
only started to fill about twelve months ago. It takes a long time
to fill them because you can't take big amounts from the Guvnor's
other chutes, but when you've got a hundred and eighty chutes to
look after a couple of pood from each isn't missed, and it mounts up.'

I don't know if I looked shocked or upset, but I suppose I must
have done, for he stopped there. Then he said: 'Moysey, you are
very young and it looks bad to you. But if you think our Guvnor
came to be a rich man from being honest, you are making a big
mistake. I've taken four truckloads of wheat before, and there's this
four started now, but that's nothing to what the Guvnor does. He
robs the peasants of more than that every day. And if he'd paid me
good wages I wouldn't have had any need to do a thing like this.'

I didn't know what to say, and I was about to get up and go when
he said: 'Wait a minute,' and went out of the room and came back
with a tray of two glasses and lemonade and some cake. We ate and
drank together, and then he took me to the door and said: 'I'm an
old man. Don't spoil the few years I have left. You are the only one
who can smooth things over.'

I went through the next days and weeks not knowing what to do.

I left the four chutes alone, neither filling them up nor saying any-think about them. I just worried about them, every day, and I worried even more when after three months on my own the Guvnor increased my pay to twenty-five rubles a month. Could I cheat a man who did this for me, even though he was rich and did trick the peasants? But could I betray old Pevin, who had worked hard all his life and now had nothing; betray him for the sake of a rich man who would never even miss the money Pevin needed? I couldn't stop worrying about those four chutes. They couldn't stay as they were for ever while I forgot about them; sooner or later the railway would want its rent for them. I couldn't sell them part-full. I either had to fill them up and sell them, which meant cheating the Guvnor, or tell the Guvnor about them which would go hard with old Pevin who was having a hard enough time already. I thought: 'I'm too young to take such worries on my shoulders, but who can I trust for advice?'

There was only one possible person, and that was old Kovalevsky from the machinery warehouse. I decided in the end I must trust him, so I set out one evening to his house. His wife showed me in; I kissed her hand and said good evening, but Kovalevsky soon realized I wanted to talk to him and dropped a hint to her; she brought us in a tray of tea and cake and then left, saying she was going to bed.

I didn't know how to begin; I told him it was a very delicate matter which I wanted his advice on; I told him it wasn't an unimportant childish secret like those I'd told him in the past, but something he must not tell even his own wife and children. I didn't know how a young boy could say it to an old gentleman, but I asked him for his promise that he would say nothing, because it was not my secret. He was upset at first, but then he said, 'Well, I will do more than promise,' and he got up and fetched a Bible and put his hand on it and swore that whatever I told him would be kept secret.

Then I said I had to tell him this because he was my friend and I looked on him as a father; and I told him all about Pevin and the four chutes of grain.

He stood thinking for a moment, then he said: 'This smells of three years' imprisonment. You are too young to undertake responsibilities like this. I'll think about it and then advise you; you go home and forget about it.'

He asked me not to come back until the next Saturday because he didn't want his family asking questions — his daughter and son-in-law lived with him and the son-in-law was a grain buyer in a small way. If I returned on Saturday he could tell them that we had met in the synagogue and he had invited me.

So the next Saturday I returned and he started by telling me that the four chutes of grain, if I got them filled, would probably be worth 4,500 rubles: 'From this, after the expenses of hiring the chutes are paid, you must get half for taking the chance,' he advised me.

I said: 'Poor Pevin has got these chutes ready to help him out in his old age, and you are telling me I should rob him?' Kovalevsky replied: 'We are all robbing each other in this world, Moysey, and a chance like this happens once in a lifetime. If you want to act like a Good Samaritan, leave it to Pevin; he'll probably give you a few rubles for your good heart. You are doing all the dirty work.'

A day or two later I went to see Mr Pevin, and when we were alone I told him I would see to getting the four chutes filled and sold. I didn't say how much I wanted for doing it; he himself suggested I should have a thousand rubles from the proceeds, and I thought that was a fair offer, for he was old. As the weeks went by I tried my best to fill the four chutes with wheat, and eventually succeeded. Then I asked the railway inspector how much I owed him in rent for the chutes. He said he was busy and couldn't do anything about them for the time being: by this time I understood what this sort of talk really meant, so I said I would give him five rubles for his trouble. He accepted the bribe and told me that so far as he was concerned the chutes had been empty and had not been recorded anywhere; but now he would give me receipts back-dated five weeks, showing them to be full. When the grain was sold it would cost twenty-six rubles to load it into the railway trucks, he said; I agreed to pay that and promised him another five rubles when it was done. He was very pleased; railway inspectors didn't get much of a wage.

Meanwhile I had got to know the grain-buyers who passed through Verchneprovsk station; every day they would stop and get out and come into the waiting room for five minutes and ask if anyone had wheat to sell, before climbing back into the train. I'd talked to them before and told them I had plenty of grain but no authority to sell, but now when one of the travelling dealers, Chernukov, came up to the table where I was sitting drinking tea, and asked me if I had anything to sell yet, I told him I'd permission to sell four wagonloads. I said the owner wanted one ruble twenty kopecks a pood; Chernukov suggested one ruble ten kopecks, with a kopeck a pood for me for my trouble. I told him I would have to consult the owner first; then another buyer came up and offered me one ruble fifteen kopecks; a moment later Chernukov came back and said he would match that and give me my kopeck a pood commission as well. I still told him I had to notify the owner, but he sat down and ordered some more tea and something to eat and then brought out his wallet and took out a ten ruble note. 'That's for you,' he said. 'And don't be like your predecessor Mr Pevin; I could do nothing with him and now he is retired and has nothing. When you get married one day, you will want to lead a good life. Of course you have to be careful, but if you deal with me I'll look after everything.'

So I made the deal with him, and he gave me five hundred rubles as a deposit.

That evening I went to see Mr Pevin. His wife was grumbling; Habinski had promised him a pension of fifteen rubles a month but was only paying him ten, she said; and she told us that she was going round to the shop to tell the shopkeeper not to send her grocery order that week unless he was willing to let her have it on credit.

When she'd gone I told Mr Pevin of Chernukov's offer. 'Sell,' he said. 'Sell it quickly. I must have money or we will have to go in the streets to beg.'

Next morning, when I was getting ready to leave Habinski's house for the station, Kovalevsky stopped me and asked what was happening. I told him; he seemed very happy about it, more happy than I was, and I began to be a little suspicious. He warned me not to sign my name anywhere on the papers for the grain deal; I'd realized that already. At the station Chernukov was waiting; he'd stayed overnight at lodgings beside the station. We both went to the granary, and he took samples of the grain. It passed the test, so he finished by paying me the four thousand rubles balance, and the thirty rubles commission he had promised me. When I'd paid all the expenses, the rent of the chutes and the cost of loading, there was four thousand rubles and ninety kopecks left.

Suddenly Chernukov said he had just remembered he would need some cash for another deal, and asked me to let him have two thousand rubles back and take a cheque for the rest. I wouldn't do that; I made an excuse, saying the grain belonged to a peasant who insisted on being paid cash, and suggested that he should leave the deal until next day and then pay me in cash if he was short today. To this he agreed, but I was worried; why should he suddenly act like that?

I was even more worried next day as I drove to the station; the thought of those four thousand rubles frightened me. Where could I keep the money? Suppose I was robbed on the way back from the station to Pevin; would Pevin ever believe me? Suppose Chernukov had tipped someone off that I was going to have a lot of money on me — money I couldn't make a fuss about if I was robbed?

In the end I told the railway inspector that someone was coming to pay me a lot of money, and I asked if he would mind waiting with me for a while. He agreed, and went out to tell the crowd of peasants who were waiting to unload their grain that they would have to wait for a while, and closed the gates. Soon there was a knock, and Chernukov came in with the money; the inspector pulled down a flap of the counter and started to count it for me. There was ten rubles too much; Chernukov said: 'Keep it, or give it to the gentleman here,' pointing to the inspector. I passed the ten rubles to the inspector, who said: 'Now everything is settled, you can walk along with me to the station,' and they went out.

I left the door closed and sat puzzling. Why should Chernukov first give me ten rubles and the commission, and now another ten rubles? It did not make sense that anyone should give money away like that — unless he expected to get it back.

I took all the money and wrapped it in newspaper, and looked out between the bars of the windows to see how far Chernukov had gone. He was talking to two strangers. As I watched, the two strangers began hurrying towards the granary. They didn't look like what I imagined crooks to look like, but I was taking no chances; clutching my parcel of money I slipped out of the back door of the granary, and hid in an empty railway wagon until they had gone into the building. Then I climbed out of the wagon and ran for the station and the cab rank, jumped into a cab and told the driver I'd a very urgent message to deliver back in Verchneprovsk. He whipped up his horse, and away we went.

Back in the town I directed him to Pevin's house; when Pevin answered my knock I thrust the parcel at him and turned to run back to the cab. He said, 'Wait a minute,' and with that tore the parcel open, took out ten one hundred ruble notes and gave them to me. I pushed them into my pocket, ran back and jumped in the cab and said, 'To Habinski's granary.'

I got the driver to stop opposite the granary and asked him to go and fetch old Kovalevsky; 'Tell him someone in the cab wants to see him,' I said. Kovalevsky came across to the cab, and I gave him the thousand rubles to look after, saying I'd no time to explain. And with that I had the cab wheel round and clatter back to the station.

At the granary the impatient peasants started shouting at me to hurry; they also said that two men were already waiting for me inside. I walked in as bravely as I could and asked them what their business was. They were the same strangers I'd seen talking to Chernukov. One of them said: 'Come further in,' and as I did so he held up a big fist and said: '*This* is my business — hand over the money or we'll kill you.'

I said: 'The money's behind the door we came in by — look,' and as they turned I flung the door back on them, letting the crowd of peasants in and shouting, 'Quick! They're robbers — and they want to kill me!'

The peasants all poured in and grabbed at the men; one of the two got away but the other was seized by two big husky men and dragged out to the station to be handed over to the police.

The poor peasants who had been waiting so long had to wait still longer while the police asked me questions. I told everyone the men must have thought I had a lot of money to pay out for the grain. When I was finally able to return to the granary and get on with my job the peasants complained bitterly about their long wait, but I got on with the work as quickly as I could and they soon calmed down.

It seemed that the man who had got away must have been the boss of the two, because the one who was caught didn't really know why I should be expected to have a lot of money on me; and this was a relief because I didn't want people asking me questions about it. The police let me see the man they had captured; he looked at me and said: 'You're a lucky Jew boy; I'd got a lump of iron in my pocket to hit you with, and sometimes I hit too hard.' I was feeling very glad to be alive when I left him.

After all the excitement I went to see Kovalevsky in the evening to get my thousand rubles. He asked me what I was going to do with the money, and I said I would put it into the post office bank.

'How much have you got in the post office bank now?' he asked. Ten rubles, I told him.

'And you want to put in a thousand rubles? Do you know what the clerk will say? He'll ask you where you got so much money, and the police will be called, and then you'll be in trouble.'

Then what could I do with the money? He stroked his white beard wisely and said: 'Lend it to me — I'll give you an IOU, and I'll pay you five per cent.' I thought I would be a bit wiser still and agreed — on condition that he made out three different IOUs for different amounts, and marked them with different dates; and this he did.

I wondered about old Mr Kovalevsky all the way home. When it came to so much money, I thought, his interest was in my getting it so he could borrow it, and that was the purpose of his advice, nothing more. From now on I should never be able to go to him, trusting him to give the best advice for me; but soon, I thought, I would be sixteen and able to think for myself and not have to consult anyone.

X. THIRTY RUBLES A MONTH!

Easter was coming round again, and it was almost a year since I had begun work at the station granary. I was still living with the Habinskis, and one evening after supper the Guvnor took me aside and told me he would be sending a man to work with me and to learn from me: Mr Greenspond, the man who taught me the wheat trade when I first joined the firm four years before. 'Let him see how you carry on, give him any tips he might need, introduce him to the railway inspector and to the station master,' said Habinski.

I wondered what was the reason for this, and the Guvnor explained: 'I wanted to send him to Constantinograd, as I've started buying there from a new district. But now he tells me he has a wife and three children and can't leave them here. So I thought of you, because you are single and it wouldn't matter to you if you couldn't get home for six months at a time. It would be just right for you; you would meet different people and find your way round a bit,' said the Guvnor.

I asked him what my responsibilities would be, and he said I would be buying different kinds of grain for him.

I said: 'People would not take any notice of me or my words because they would think me too young.' He brushed this aside: 'You look a nice young chap — nobody would know your age, you'd pass easily for twenty. Besides,' said Habinski, 'when they get to know you are buying for Habinski — my name is known everywhere, they'll be round you like flies.'

So that's how it was that on Monday he sent me Mr Greenspond to train for my job. Greenspond was a nice fellow, but a little upset: 'Four years ago I taught you all there was to know, and now I come here as a pupil,' he said. I introduced him to everyone he needed to know, and showed him everything, and at the end of a fortnight we were back in the office, handing over all the station granary books and receipts in front of the book-keeper.

That evening when I went into the house, I saw the table all laid and candles lit, and everyone already in the dining room. When I said, 'Good evening,' they all answered together in one voice, 'Good evening, Moysey,' and they all seemed rather happy. The Guvnor handed me a glass of wine; that seemed even stranger to me, so I plucked up courage to say, 'Everyone seems happy here. Could I know the reason, then I could be happy too.'

'Don't you know?' said the Guvnor, proudly. 'Then I'll have to tell you . . . Boris has passed his medical-student examinations and in three weeks he is going to an Anglo-Russian university.'

I congratulated Boris, and then the Guvnor said: 'We're all going to the theatre; you can come too.' I thanked him very much, and we all sat down to eat.

As soon as we'd finished dinner, the Guvnor called me to go with him to his study. I had not been in this room before, even though I had been living in the house for four years. It was a beautiful room — mirrors on the walls on both sides, comfortable furniture, and wonderful tapestries. Velvet curtains hung at the windows, in the middle of the room was a long table with eight chairs round it, and over the table hung a crystal chandelier.

Habinski sat himself down in a chair and gave me time to look round; he could see the admiration in my eyes, and that pleased him. 'Do you like this room?' he said, and I said, 'Very much.'

'Then sit down,' said the Guvnor. 'I want to talk to you. You're going away on holiday tomorrow, but I'll start your new wages right away, thirty rubles a month with all expenses paid. So you're having a holiday with pay. You'll have to buy a couple of suits to go with your job; you'll be mixing with very big business men. If you haven't any money I'll come with you to the shops and we will buy such things as you need to be properly dressed for the job. I'll pay for them, and we will talk about money another time. Do you agree with the terms for the job?'

I told him I certainly did, more than ever. And true to his word, the Guvnor took me out next day to an outfitters, and I picked out clothes that he thought were exactly right for his representative in Constantinograd. And next day when my holiday began I set off for Kremenchug to visit Hannah and Herscho again — although not before I'd called on Mama Marcovsky to say goodbye.

This second holiday in Kremenchug . . . it came pretty near disaster. But let me tell it as it came. For a start, the boat journey — that wasn't disaster, but maybe it will explain something of what the people were like, in my part of Russia, so many years ago. Friendly people, sometimes too friendly. Poor people and rich, but with kindness.

I'd had a pretty busy time, and I had to rush to catch the boat; my cab reached the quayside only just in time. I climbed up to the top deck and found a chair, sitting down and looking forward to eight hours' rest. But no sooner had I settled down when the man next to me offered me a cigarette. I thanked him but said I didn't smoke. Then he said: 'Well, we're both on this boat so we might as well be introduced. My name is Holubny and this lady is my wife.'

I replied that I was Moysey Levine and I was going to Kremenchug. So were they, he said. He was about fifty years old, and his wife looked a bit younger. They had children of my age, they said, we must meet, and they would be company for me. They had a daughter who was studying. . . . I must visit them in their home in Ekaterinoslav.

All I wanted to do was to sit back and doze in my chair, but this friendly couple wouldn't leave me alone. I got up to move around, and they followed me; I tried to break away to go and have some lunch in peace, but they said no, no, they had everything necessary, enough for all of us, we must all share.

I didn't want to be rude to people who were being so kind, but I began to feel like a prisoner. The man pressed a card on me: 'Buyer and seller of all kinds of grain,' it said. I worried in case he asked me my business; if I told him I was in the same line I'd never get any peace.

I made an excuse to get away for a moment, and shot off down below, looking round for someone nearer my own age who might be a shield against such friendliness. There was a vacant seat next to a young chap of about eighteen; I dropped into it, and we got talking, and I told him how I had been trapped by the couple on the upper deck and couldn't get away from them; how could I escape from being bored by them without being rude, I asked.

'Leave everything to me,' said this boy. 'Go back to them and take up the same position; I'll find a way.' So I returned to the Holubnys, and hoped he was right. Sure enough, I hadn't been sitting there long when the boy came rushing up, crying out a greeting to me like a long-lost friend: 'Moysey, I've been looking for you everywhere. My fiancée is waiting at the other end of the boat, I promised I'd bring you back.'

So we were both able to bid goodbye to the friendly Holubnys and walk away, pursued by their cries of, 'Don't forget to come and see us.'

Walking back along the top deck, I thanked the young man. He told me his name was Hymie Sekarov and his father was manager of the Russian bank in Verchneprovsk and I told him my name and that I worked for Habinski. I found myself blushing as I said it, because I didn't think there was anyone in Verchneprovsk who didn't know about Habinski and the parentless boy he took in. But all that Hymie Sekarov said was: 'Come to my cabin and have some tea.'

I explained I couldn't do that; I was travelling third-class and his cabin was first-class. He seemed to want to be friendly, but I tried to put him off; not for the reason that I'd tried to get away from the Holubnys, but because I thought we couldn't be friendly, not someone like me with the rich son of a bank manager. I told him I was grateful for his help with the Holubnys, but that his parents wouldn't like him being friendly with a boy who had no parents; I wasn't the sort of person he could introduce to their friends.

'What's happened, then?' he said. 'Have you killed anybody?'

So I told him all about myself. I didn't seem to be able to get away from thinking about this thing. I was a boy without parents. I had to keep telling people about it. All he said was, 'I'm sorry for your misfortune,' and walked away.

I thought: 'So that's got rid of someone who might have been a friend. Once you tell them the truth they don't want to know you.'

I was still sitting feeling very sorry for myself when he came back. 'Here,' he said, 'I've come to give you this. A first-class ticket. Now you can come and have some tea with me in my cabin.' And he picked up my case and made me follow him to his cabin. There was a table there, laid with all sorts of different things to eat, and we sat and ate and talked. He even seemed a bit envious of me. 'You're only sixteen and can decide things for yourself. I'm eighteen and a half, and I've always got to agree with my father,' he said.

By the time we'd finished our talk I saw through the porthole of the cabin that the boat was drawing into the shore for Kremenchug; he was going to Kiev, and we parted, after he had urged me to come and visit him and his parents. Rich and poor should share, he said, and forget the differences. 'Today my father in a banker, but what may happen tomorrow?' We waved a parting as I went ashore, and my cab headed towards the town while the steamer pulled out into the river, taking him on to Kiev.

It was getting dark when I reached Hannah and Herscho's place; I'd written to them so they knew I was coming, and Usher my cousin was there waiting. She was the first one to throw her arms round me and kiss me, and Hannah snorted: 'He's not your husband, why don't you leave him alone?' I kissed Hannah and shook hands with Herscho and brought out the small presents I had bought them. Usher was standing there too, so I had to give her something; I handed over a nice brush and comb which I'd really bought for myself. Then she wanted to kiss me all over again, but I bent down quickly over my case to dodge her. Hannah wasn't pleased, either, when Usher said: 'You'll both be out to work in the morning, but I'll look after Moysey.'

'Don't you worry, I'll leave everything ready for him when I go out,' said Hannah.

But next morning, it being a Sunday, Hannah and Herscho had to go out early to their market stall. I hadn't been alone in the house for long when there was a knock at the door. I didn't answer straight away, but the knocking kept on until I opened the door, wrapped in a blanket because I didn't possess a dressing gown, and there was Usher.

I hurried back to bed, but Usher followed me, and though I made out I was tired, she pulled up a chair and sat down and started talking. When I still didn't respond she put her face down against mine and began to kiss me; then she took her raincoat off and I saw that all she had on underneath was her nightdress.

I was frightened of a girl like this. I said: 'It would be a good idea if you went and made tea,' and as soon as she went into the other room I was up out of bed like lightning and got dressed. Then I went into the other room, and said, 'Tea?'

'Many people have tea in bed on holiday,' said Usher. I told her I wasn't people yet, I was a boy.

'You could play a game the same as any grown man,' said Usher. 'You should not be so stubborn.'

I drank the tea and swallowed some breakfast, thinking all the time that this sort of girl was dangerous to me; and then, to make an excuse to get away I said I had to go out and meet a man. Usher replied that she wasn't going to let me go until she had made a man of me.

'You can't make a man of a boy who is only sixteen,' I said.

'I can try,' said Usher. She dried her hands which were wet from washing up, and came up to me and began kissing me passionately. I stood there like a lump of wood, without a word.

'You can't go until you've kissed me,' she said, so I just touched her with my lips, and then said: 'I will have to be excused,' and went out. She followed me, very depressed, saying if I was going out she was going home, and when I called goodbye to her she didn't answer. I was relieved that she had gone; I didn't want to make a fool of myself at my time of life, and I hoped that after this she wouldn't bother me any more.

Having got away from Usher, the problem was where to go. I decided to call on the Komanievs, the landlord and his wife who had been friendly to me the year before. Madame Komaniev opened the door to me and showed me into the library; her husband came in stretching out his hand and greeting me, and we sat and drank tea and talked; I told him everything that had happened and the plans for me to go to Constantinograd for the Guvnor. When it was time for me to go, he invited me to stroll down to his stationery shop with him; he told me about his business and introduced me to his manager. He thought perhaps I wouldn't be interested in the stationery business, but as I told him, a businessman is always interested in anyone's business.

After that I went on to the market where Hannah and Herscho had their stall; but the same thing happened now as had happened the year before; Hannah wanted to show me off to everybody, and I couldn't stand people looking me over as if I was an animal in the zoo. I always wondered if they were thinking about me as the boy without any parents, the boy who was different, and it was more than I could bear.

There was Usher, too; in spite of what happened on the Sunday morning she wouldn't leave me alone, and was demanding that I escort her to work so that *she* could show me off to her girl friends.

Finally I couldn't stand it any more; there wasn't much to do with Hannah and Herscho out at work, except walk round the town, and in the evening I was finding Usher had accepted invitations to take me round to meet more people. So I went to the telegraph office and got a telegram sent recalling me to Habinski's; I didn't think Hannah and Herscho were bright enough to see through the trick; they'd never received a telegram in their lives, anyway. My telegram duly arrived in the evening, and I told them that I must go back in the morning. I had to go round to Usher's parents to say goodbye, and in front of them all Usher jumped up and flung her arms round me and kissed me. While they were looking on amazed, she took me to the door. I said good night to her and then told her: 'When you find a boy to marry, send me an invitation and I will come. Any time I will come — when you've found a boy to marry.' And I went home to bed.

In the morning I was up early and lit the samovar for Hannah and Herscho and laid breakfast; I couldn't be away too soon. I packed my case and at seven o'clock I said I must leave to catch the boat, and went out and called a cab and set off for the quayside. But once we were away from that part of the town, I asked the driver if he knew of a cheap place in Kremenchug where I could stay for a few days; for I didn't really want to go back to Verchneprovsk and Habinski, but just to continue my holiday in my own way without being shown off to lots of people.

'There's a good place in Station Street; I often take people there,' said the driver, and off he went.

XI. ADVENTURE
IN KREMENCHUG

We drove on for a good way before the cab slowed down and stopped outside a tall house in a wide street, the guest house the driver recommended. I paid him the fare and collected my own cases from the top of the cab, but he came into the house with me just the same, and said to the woman who met us and took my booking: 'I've brought you someone to stay for a while,' so I realized he probably got paid for bringing customers round.

The landlady was a woman about fifty, very strict-looking. She said a room would cost me a ruble a day, and when I agreed she rang a bell and from a side door there appeared a huge man dressed all in black. She said, 'Room Eight,' and the huge man picked up my cases and led me to the third floor, opening the door and handing me the key before he walked away.

It was a small room furnished with a little table with a few old books and magazines on it, two chairs, a washstand in one corner with a jug of water and a towel hanging on a hook from the side, and in the other corner a single bed with a heavy chest for clothes next to it. A little lamp hung from the middle of the ceiling, and there were very old curtains at the window. The first thing I did after I'd put down my case and shut the door behind me was to take out fifty of the sixty rubles I had in my purse and find a place to hide them; I didn't want to walk about with all that money on me. The chest was very heavy, but I struggled until I could lift one side and push the money under it; the heavier it was the better it was as a hiding place. Then I went out, locking the door behind me, and went downstairs to go out. As I passed the landlady she stopped me and said she had forgotten to ask for a five ruble deposit. I opened my purse, gave her the remaining ten ruble note and waited for the change — a mistake, because she could not help seeing there were only a few silver and copper coins left in my purse, and she asked: 'How is it a young man like you comes to a big town like this without extra money?' I told her not to worry; I might be trying to get a job, I said. So long as she was paid it didn't matter to her how much I had. I wasn't going to let her know I had fifty rubles more, for I'd read about people being robbed in places like this. I didn't like the look of her, or of the huge porter. There was a girl, Lisa, who worked in the house, too, I discovered, and she didn't look much more honest than the other two.

After paying the landlady, I set off to look at Station Street, which was a part of the town I had never visited before. It was a very long street, and wide, with trams running down the middle of it, and on each side ranks for cabs going to and from the station. On both sides there were shops, and further along a few more guest houses like the one I was staying in. There were a great many people about, including many beggars; so many people that if you weren't careful you would get pushed off the pavement; a much busier street than I had been used to.

One of the beggars stopped me. I thought I might as well give him a copper — I'd never given anyone anything before. But as I opened my purse to look for a coin, someone behind me snatched the purse from my hand. I whirled round, but it had happened so quickly that I couldn't see who had done it.

I went back to my lodgings, and I must have looked miserable, for as I walked in the landlady asked what the matter was: 'Can't you get a job?' she said.

I told her what had happened and realized at once that I shouldn't have told her. She would either soon realize that I must have some more money hidden away, or else she would try to get rid of me; but it was too late and I couldn't take the words back, so I went up to my room. I took five rubles from my store under the chest and went out again and found a small shop to buy myself something to eat — the guest house didn't provide meals. I bought some bread, a salty herring, and a bottle of milk, and took it back to my room, lit the hanging lamp and by its dim light sat down at the little table for my supper. I didn't eat all the food I had bought, but saved half of it for the next day. With five rubles stolen, it was sensible to economize.

Before getting ready for bed I went out of the room to go to the toilet. I don't think I was gone ten minutes, but when I came back the room was in darkness. I went downstairs and found the porter, to tell him my lamp had gone out and must need some more oil, but he said nothing could be done until the morning, so I went back to my room, locking the door on the inside and leaving the key in the lock. I felt there was something sinister about the house; the grim landlady, the huge porter in black, the lamp that went out leaving me in darkness. . . . I liked mystery stories very much at this age; Boris used to buy Sherlock Holmes and similar tales every week and pass them on to me when he had finished. Now I was thinking that something like these tales was happening to me in real life. With part of my mind I loved it, but the other part couldn't get to sleep; I lay there on the bed fully dressed, listening to the crackings and creakings of the old house — ordinary night noises, I kept on telling myself. I don't know how many times I heard the clock from the church chime — and then, suddenly, I heard someone touching the handle of my door.

I couldn't call out to ask who it was, because I was too frightened. I think I must have stopped breathing from fright. I stopped enjoying the idea of being in a mystery story. I was so scared I couldn't get up, but just lay there for a long time, listening but hearing nothing more, and in the end I must have fallen asleep, for I did not hear the church clock strike again until nine o'clock when I woke.

I sat up and saw with a great shock that the clothes chest was open and all my things were strewn over the room. And the door of my room, I then found, was closed but not locked. I thought it over and came to the conclusion that the only time anyone could have got in was the few minutes when I went down to complain about the lamp being out, leaving the door unlocked. And whoever it was must have been in the room all the time when I came back and lay down in the dark; and the sounds that frightened me in the night must have been someone trying to get out of the room. They would have waited in the end until I was asleep and then unlocked the door and let themselves out. Then I remembered my savings, and shot across to the chest and heaved it up to see if the money was still there. Thank goodness it was; whoever had been in the room when I returned last night had gone through my clothes but hadn't thought to look underneath the chest.

It was daylight now and I felt better; brave enough to decide that I must stay and unravel the mystery. I washed, and combed my hair, and then opened my door as quietly as possible and began creeping down the stairs like a cat, stopping every few steps to listen. When I got to the first floor I heard the landlady talking to the porter; she was saying she had taken all the clothes out and couldn't find any money, and the porter replied: 'He must have money; he looks prosperous.'

I went quietly back to my room, then banged my door and started walking sharply down. The landlady was still at the bottom of the stairs. She asked me if I'd found a job the day before, and I said I had the chance of one, so that she wouldn't start worrying me about money.

I spent that day going out by train to the railway granary, about five miles down the line from the town station. I introduced myself to the granary inspector as someone who worked for Mr Habinski, and that made him very polite to me. He showed me round, and we had a meal and a few drinks together. I could see he had no idea how young I was.

Back at the boarding house that evening I met the porter on the stairs. He told me he had refilled the lamp in my room. That wasn't the only thing he had done, I realized when I got into my room; I opened the chest and found that though my clothes were all in there, someone had been through them. But the money was still safely under the chest, and I was able to have a meal and lock my door and spend a comfortable night without interruptions.

The porter hadn't given up, however. Next morning I had just got dressed when someone rattled the door. I opened it and the big porter pushed in, closing the door behind him, turning the key in the lock. 'Now,' he said, 'this is your last chance. I know you've got money. Pay up if you want to live. I'm bigger than you, and we are high up on the third floor. I give you five minutes. Be sensible and do what is best for you.'

I was terrified. There was no way of getting out of the room past him. We sat in silence for what seemed a long, long while, and I tried to think how I could get out of this, but couldn't. Then the porter said, 'Three minutes are up. Are you going to give me the money?' He stood up from the chair on which he had been sitting and turned away, and like lightning I grabbed the chair, throwing it through the window, smashing the glass and calling for help. This was too much for the porter, who unlocked the door and ran out of the room. A moment or two later the landlady came panting up, wanting to know what was the matter. I told her the porter had demanded money from me and that I'd smashed the window to attract attention. I'd succeeded in doing that, all right; while I was speaking there was a knocking at the front door — passersby wanting to know what was going on. The landlady ran down to open the door, and from the stairs I heard her telling them that two guests had been fighting and one of them had thrown a chair through the window. While she was talking, I began gathering my clothes up and putting them in my case. Mystery stories were all very well, I thought, but I couldn't stand any more of this one. I was just going to heave up the chest and get out my hidden money when the landlady returned.

When she spied my clothes packed she said: 'Where do you think you are going? You can't leave here, I'm going to send for a policeman. You have to pay for the window and the chair.'

I didn't know what to think. How could people like this send for the police, after what had happened? I just stood there, while she went downstairs. The big porter was down there somewhere; I certainly wouldn't be able to get out past him if the two of them didn't want me to go.

A few minutes later she came back with the porter and a policeman. 'That youth threw a chair through the window and broke it,' she said. 'Then he wanted to run away.' I tried to tell the policeman what was going on in this house, but before I could utter a word he said: 'I don't want to know. Tell everything to the judge,' and took a little book out of his pocket and began writing down particulars. In a moment or two he asked for my passport. I gave it to him, and he began copying out the details. While he was writing I looked at

the number on the shoulder of his uniform, and kept it in mind:
171.

His uniform looked very shabby, and I was suddenly suspicious;
something was wrong about him. But he handed me back my passport, and said: 'Possibly in a day or two you'll get a summons,' and
shut his book, and away they all went.

After they'd gone some of my confidence began to come back. I
went downstairs and out of the house, leaving my baggage behind,
and nobody stopped me. I walked until I found a policeman. He
wasn't so shabby as the man who had come up to my room, and I
asked him the way to the police station.

When I got there I stood looking up at the big building, and I felt
frightened again, but I wanted to find out what was going on at the
boarding house and what these people hoped to do, so I plucked up
courage and went in, and up to the desk where an inspector was
standing. I asked if he had a policeman there with the number 171.
He wanted to know what my complaint was, and I told him I'd
seen a man in constable's uniform with that number, but the uniform had been very shabby and the trousers didn't seem to match
the jacket.

'You must have seen some play-acting policeman,' he said, and
took me through into a big hall where the men going on duty were
assembling. There were twelve of them, all very smart and clean,
and they stood to attention as the inspector came in. He asked for
No. 171, and a man stood forward. I looked him up and down, and
told the inspector: 'That's the number, but not the same man.'

He didn't seem very worried; perhaps I'd just seen a man wearing
an old police jacket, he said. I tried to explain that I thought someone was impersonating his policemen, but I could see the inspector
was not very interested, so I gave up and thanked him and walked out.

I didn't want to return to my strange lodgings too early, so I
walked through the town, looking at the trams — there were no
trams in Verchneprovsk — and at all the shops. The trams, I saw,
were used to deliver goods to the shops as well as to carry passengers.
I spent a long time looking at all the shop windows, including those
of a big jeweller's shop, and about one o'clock I went into a tea shop

for a glass of tea and two *beigels*. I sat there for a long while before going out into the street again. I didn't know where to go; I had nothing to do in this town of Kremenchug now. I didn't want to go to Hannah and Herscho again or let them know I was still here; I only wanted to find out what was happening in that boarding house.

Walking along, I saw a stationery shop, with Sherlock Holmes magazines in the window, so I went in and bought a couple of them and took them back to my lodgings and went up to my room and lay on the bed to read. The window had been put in and everything had been cleaned and tidied up.

I was so deep in the book that I didn't hear the door open. Then someone said: 'What, are you reading crime stories?' It was the big porter. He stood in front of me and said: 'Why don't you tell the truth? You have some money somewhere.' Then there came a knock at the door, and the same Constable 171 in the shabby uniform came in. He gave me a piece of paper, which he said was a summons, and made me sign for it. When he had gone I looked at it. It was a printed notice ordering me to appear in court next morning at ten, and then a list of what I had to pay: For breaking windows, 3 rubles 45 kopecks; for breaking chair, 4 rubles 50 kopecks; for two witnesses, 2 rubles 50 kopecks; for the summons, 5 rubles; for the attention of the policeman, 2 rubles. It was all added up: total, 17 rubles 45 kopecks.

As I finished reading it the porter said: 'You could afford to pay that ten times over if you wanted to. I will be one witness and the landlady the other one.' I was putting the piece of paper away with my other papers when he added: 'You don't need that now — you can tear it up.'

Then I knew I was right and that there was something fishy going on. So I picked up a paper and tore it into small pieces; the porter didn't see that it was not the summons paper. I could tell by the look on his face that he was pleased I had torn up the 'summons'. I looked miserable, and said: 'I am going out to get something to eat now,' and he followed me out of the room. I made the excuse that I had forgotten my book, and went back, picked up the summons from among my papers and tucked it away inside my vest, and went

5

downstairs again with my two books in my hand. The porter was standing with the hard-faced landlady as I went out; I suppose they were thinking what a big fool I was.

I went straight round to the police station, and asked for the inspector. The man now behind the desk told me I would have to wait, and showed me into the waiting room. I remember that waiting room in that Russian police station because of the books that were lying on the table there — books by Tolstoy and Gorki and Pushkin. I sat looking through them for half an hour until the door opened and the same inspector I had seen before came in. He said: 'You again? What do you want this time?' I began to explain, and at the finish he said: 'Have you still got the summons?' and I brought it out. He looked it through and said: 'This isn't a proper summons . . . very interesting. Tomorrow I will have the house watched by two men, and they will keep their eye on you. Don't worry, Moysey; we will catch these swindlers.'

I left him and went on my way, stopping to buy a bottle of milk and a couple more *beigels*. I felt very happy; it looked as if my own particular mystery story was working out. As I reached my lodgings, however, I took care to change my face and look miserable. The landlady wanted to know what the matter was, and I told her that tomorrow I had to go to court and I'd never been in court before. She told me not to worry; I wouldn't be hanged, I'd only have to pay, she said.

Up in my room I jumped on to the table and lit the hanging lamp and settled down to eat. Soon there was a knock at the door; the porter again. He was still on the same tack: 'If you pay now you won't have to go to court,' he said, and when I told him I had no money, even showing him my purse with only two rubles and a few small coins in it, he still kept asking: 'Where have you hidden your money?'

I told him to search me if he didn't believe me, and in the end he gave up and went out, saying: 'Tomorrow we will find out if you have money, when you appear in court.' I turned the key behind him, very happy to think that this little game would be stopped to-morrow; and I slept like a log.

Next morning the porter and the landlady would not let me go out of the house, even for a glass of tea, but insisted that I have breakfast there so that I shouldn't get out of going to court; and when it was time to set out for the court they walked out with me.

It was a long way, but the porter was very cheerful, joking: 'When you have to pay me my money in court, I'll be able to take a cab back.' On the way a man stopped the porter to ask him the route to somewhere. He glanced at me and caught my eye for a moment and I realized this must be one of the detectives who had been watching the house. His look seemed to say: 'Don't worry; I'm watching for you.'

At last we arrived at a big, old-fashioned house. It seemed deserted, but as we went up to the front door, the door was opened and a man stood there, asking for our papers. The landlady showed him some sort of form; he hardly glanced at it before saying: 'Go right in.' We were shown into a room with five rows of wooden benches. Opposite these was a table with three chairs; a man was putting papers on the table.

I looked round: the walls were bare and the only other furnishing was a big oil lamp standing on the table. Four people were sitting on the back bench. I suppose whoever fixed this place up thought that it was enough to impress whatever strangers from small towns came their way to be tricked, like me, and to make them think that it was a real court.

We waited for about ten minutes, and then a door opened and a tall man came in wearing a black cloak. Everyone got up, and I followed their example, and then as the cloaked man took his seat we all sat down. As we were sitting down the police inspector walked in very quietly at the door, with half a dozen of his men behind him. He came up to me and said: 'Good morning, Moysey. When we have these people under lock and key we will let you know what is going on.'

The big porter lifted his fist to give me a fourpenny one, saying: 'Take this, you bastard,' but before he could harm me one of the policemen stopped his arm in mid-air, took handcuffs from his belt and snapped them on to the big man's wrists. The landlady was crying that she knew nothing about anything and must get back to her hotel, but the inspector told her he was taking them all to the police station. Outside, a horse-drawn wagon was waiting for the prisoners, but I went in a cab with the inspector. At the police station the people from the bogus court were charged with demanding money with menaces, and after some formalities the police sent me back to the guest house accompanied by a policeman; I would have to stay in Kremenchug for a while, they said, until the details of the case had been sorted out.

I thought this was the end of the boarding-house mystery, but there was more to come. When the policeman questioned Lisa, the servant-girl at the house, we found there were five lads of about sixteen living in the house. They had all come there to stay, as I had done, and had lost their money or been tricked out of it, and the landlady had taken their passports and their best clothes and found them jobs so they could pay what they owed her, she had said.

'Now we are like prisoners, as every month she takes all our wages and just gives us back pocket money,' said one of them. They had all been unable to get away because they never had enough money, and they had been afraid to complain because the big porter had terrorized them. They had been earning sixteen rubles a month, all paid to the landlady, and getting only three rubles a month back from her. There was some arrangement between the fish merchant who employed the boys, and the landlady, and the police went off to inquire into this.

Day after day went past while the police inquiries went on. I was anxious to get away, because it was past the time when I should have returned to Habinski, but I couldn't do that; for one thing, the police were holding the passports of everyone concerned in the case. My only consolation was that the police were paying me one ruble twenty-five kopecks for every day from the time I reported the bogus summons, and I was staying free in the guest house along with the other boys, with Lisa looking after us — the landlady and the big porter were still in the cells at the police station.

Lisa was willing to look after more than the house. One night she came up to my room and declared: 'I'm going to sleep in your bed tonight . . . I've already slept with all the other boys.' I refused her offer, but all she said was, 'The others didn't complain any,' and plonked herself down on my bed. I slept on the floor that night; it was just like old times. In the morning, however, Lisa demanded three rubles 'because I slept in your room and if I tell my husband he will kill you'. I told her I didn't think she had a husband anyway, and she was just like the others except she didn't know when she was licked; and I didn't hear any more about the three rubles or her husband.

On one of my visits to the police station, I saw the landlady and the porter in the cells: it gave me some satisfaction to tell them they had been right when they thought I had some money, and to explain it had been hidden under the chest all the time. I also saw the inspector again and told him I must get home soon or I might lose my job. In the end I was taken in to see the town's chief of police. He seemed a very strict man, and I was a bit afraid of him at first, but eventually he agreed to let me go and he gave me a letter to take to my employer, and even arranged for a cab to take me to the steamboat landing at police expense. Not much more than eight hours later I was climbing down the gangplank of the river steamer safe back at Verchneprovsk.

XII. ON MY OWN

I was last off the boat that night, and all the cabs but one had gone. The couple who had hailed the last cab agreed to let me ride on top with the driver, however, and it turned out that they were going to the Habinskis too; the woman was Mrs Habinski's sister, on a visit with her husband.

The maid opened the door and we had started to take in the baggage when the mistress came out, and kissed her sister and brother-in-law. Then she saw me.

'The Guvnor doesn't want you any more. You can leave this house,' she said. 'You went away for a week's holiday and stayed three weeks.' And she went in with her guests, leaving me on the doorstep. I could hear her voice trailing away: 'Picking up a boy from the streets and letting him live in your house and this is how he serves you . . .'

I went into the office and waited for Mr Habinski to come home; there was nothing else I could do. Soon I heard the younger Habinski boy call out: 'Father wants to see you,' and I followed him into the dining room where everyone was gathered. I bowed to them and stood to attention like a soldier in front of an officer, waiting for the worst. But the Guvnor only shouted: 'Have you had any tea?' and when I said no, he shouted: 'Well, sit down and have some, and we'll talk later.'

Mrs Habinski didn't like it, but she handed me a glass of tea, and when the Guvnor shouted: 'Have something to eat,' she put bread and butter and some cake on a plate and pushed it across to me. The Guvnor went on talking to his sister and brother-in-law. It wasn't until we had all finished eating and drinking that he turned to me and asked why I hadn't returned on time. I began to explain, and soon I found everyone was listening and I was the centre of attention. But when I had finished the old grandfather cut in: 'He read all that in a book!'

Then Boris came to my rescue, saying: 'I've read hundreds of books but never one like that,' and finally I had my moment of triumph, dramatically producing the sealed envelope the police had given me and handing it to the Guvnor.

Old Habinski couldn't read, of course, but he gave it to Boris who opened the envelope and drew out a foolscap sheet with an impressive printed heading, Kremenchug Police, and began to read. The letter described what had happened, confirming all that I had told them, and ended by asking the Guvnor to be lenient with me for being late because it was the fault of the police that I had been kept in Kremenchug.

When Boris had finished reading I said to the Guvnor: 'Will you permit me to sleep here just for tonight? I will be leaving tomorrow.'

'Going away? Where are you going?' asked the Guvnor. I told him I didn't know where I would be going, but the mistress had told me to go. He was furious: 'I don't know where she gets her authority from,' he said. 'When you say you are going away tomorrow you are right — but you are going to Constantinograd for a while to buy grain for me.' Then he told me to see him about it in the morning and I thanked him and got up from the table, bade everyone good night, and walked off towards the office.

Boris came after me. He suggested that we go for a walk, and as we walked he kept urging me to write down all that happened to me in Kremenchug; I objected that I should be away in Constantinograd, but he demanded that I post it to him, and said he would pay for the stamp. So I agreed; but even then he wanted to hear the story all over again, and after I'd told it all through for a second time he insisted that we go on to the theatre to celebrate; even though the show had begun we could see the second half.

I was tired, and it was late, but I went. This time there was no more standing in the gallery for me while Boris went to a good seat, the way he had done in the past; there were two tickets for us together now. We left the theatre at about eleven o'clock, and still Boris didn't want to go home to bed. 'You can sleep in fifty years' time,' he said. 'Now come with me to the café — I know a new one.'

So we went there, and drank tea and ate pastries and listened to the band playing, and it was very late before we finally got home. When we did, there was a letter left for me on my bed, telling me to be in the office at six in the morning. What with going about with Boris, and worrying about the responsibility of the new job and being sent so far from home — further than I'd ever been before in my life — I didn't get much sleep that night.

All the same I was awake before six, and as I rubbed my eyes open and got dressed I was thinking that one day I would be my own boss and be able to sleep when I liked and as long as I liked.

The Guvnor was already waiting in the office for me. 'Good boy, good boy,' he said.

He told me to take a cab to the station at eight o'clock, and book myself a third-class ticket to Constantinograd; and not to forget that I had to make three changes of train. When I had got to the town and had found somewhere to stay I was to telegraph him and he would follow and make all the business arrangements. Then he gave me a hundred rubles for the train ticket, and two hundred more to put away for when I got to Constantinograd.

He must have seen that I was nervous, for he said: 'Now, be brave and don't worry about anything. It will all come to you.'

Then he looked me over as I stood before him, and said: 'You must be smart, so that people will think you are a great man.' I was wearing one of the suits he had bought for me before I went on holiday, and I told him the other was in my bag, and he said, 'Well, that's good' — and stretched out his hand to say goodbye. I was amazed; the Guvnor had never shaken hands with me before. It really looked as if he was beginning to think of me as a grown-up employee, and a person, not just an animal who had meals in the kitchen. I took Habinski's hand and thanked him and said goodbye, and left the office to see if I could get any breakfast from the maids and Vera in the kitchen. They gave me a good meal, and I wished them all well, the maids, Vera and the driver who had been my friends, and went out to the granary to say goodbye to my old friend Kovalevsky. He shook hands and said: 'Don't worry about the money I am saving for you; whenever you need it it will be handy for you.' I hoped that he was right and that I needn't worry about my thousand rubles, but I kept that doubt to myself and told the old man that I knew he wouldn't cheat me, and asked him to remember me to his family. Then I went out to the waiting cab, and the driver shook up his reins and we were off, out of Verchneprovsk, down the long road I had travelled so often as a carter's boy with Herscho and Anestrat, to the station.

I had never travelled such a long way on a train before, and I was worried about all the changes and connections I had to make; I kept asking different people where I should get off and what train I should catch when I changed. When we reached the big junction I got out and stood on the station like a lost sheep while everyone else went on their way; they all seemed to know where they were going but I didn't. In the end, I did find the right train and settled down in my seat, but I must have looked anxious still, because a gentleman sitting opposite, a man of about forty-five, leaned over and said: 'What are you so worried about? A young man like you shouldn't have worries.'

He brought out a flask and two glasses and poured tea for us both and we got into conversation, or rather, he kept asking me questions about where I was going and why. I was very cautious in answering — my experiences in Kremenchug had taught me that there were some bad people about, and I hadn't yet learned to judge strangers, so I was careful. I did tell him that I came from Verchneprovsk. He said he had never been there; then he asked: 'And your parents let you go from home all this way?' It was the same old trouble I had met before; you only had to talk to someone for a few minutes and they wanted to know who your parents were, where you came from, everything. I thought that this time I wouldn't bother to try to turn the questions away but would just answer them straight, and then perhaps the man would leave me alone. So I told him I had no parents and that gossip in the town said that they had run away to America before I was born. I was very upset to have to talk about it, and he saw it and apologized. 'There's not much else to talk about except your home and parents,' he said. Then I apologized too. It wasn't his fault I was a boy without a father or a mother.

5*

The man told me he was getting off three stations before Constantinograd, at a place called Karlovka. 'Get off the train with me and stay the night at my home and I will show you round a bit. You can go on next day,' he said. He took a card from his pocket and gave it to me. It said:

ZELEK PLOTNIK
GROCERY STORES
STATION KARLOVKA

I tucked the card away in my pocket, still not sure whether I ought to accept his invitation, and we went on talking.

The train reached Karlovka station some time that afternoon, and Mr Plotnik suggested that I get out, at least to have some food at the station buffet, for we had been travelling since the morning. The train would be waiting for some time because it took on water at Karlovka, he explained. So I got out, bringing my case with me for safety, and we had tea together. When Plotnik went off to see if his driver was waiting for him as he had arranged, I took the opportunity of asking the man behind the counter if he knew him.

'Everybody knows Plotnik,' he said. 'He has a big grocery business around here.' Reassured, I went to see whether I could travel on to Constantinograd the next morning on my ticket. I liked to see how different people lived and how they behaved, and what life was like in all sorts of families and places, and if Mr Plotnik was all right this seemed a good chance. He returned to see me talking to the booking-clerk, and said: 'Oh, you've decided to stay? The driver's waiting.'

I picked up my case and followed him out to his carriage. The driver, a chubby man with long high boots and a hat pulled right down over his ears, took the case from me and then bowed right down to me. People had never behaved like this to me before, and I said to Mr Plotnik: 'Why does he bow down? Does he think I'm a prince?' and he explained that village people always did that to someone from the town, clean and properly dressed. It was surprising what my new suits could do, I thought. We got in, and the chubby driver climbed into his seat; Mr Plotnik said, 'Home, Ivan,' and the driver whipped up the horses and we were trotting up the country road from the station.

After about a quarter of an hour we came into the village and stopped outside a big shop. I went to pick up my case to carry it in, but: 'My man will bring the cases in,' said Mr Plotnik.

Inside he introduced me to his wife Riffca, a slim woman with a rather pretty face and long black hair. A young girl was serving a customer; when she had finished he introduced us. She was his daughter Hilda. 'This is Moysey — I met him on the train and he is staying here until tomorrow,' he said.

I was taken upstairs to freshen up, and then handed over to Hilda to be entertained. She talked about books — I was surprised to see how many good books they had — and about places she had been, and she asked me about plays I had seen. I could talk about these; I told her I used to go to the theatre every Saturday, though I didn't know what I should be able to do now I was going to Constantinograd.

After a while Hilda disappeared, leaving me to look through some of their books, and a little later she called me into their dining room where a meal had been laid. The table was loaded down with food. Mr Plotnik came up from the shop, and we settled down to a proper meal together; and afterwards he invited me to come down with him and look round.

It was a very wide shop, really two made into one, and like a village store it sold everything possible — food, clothes, vegetables, boots. In one corner I saw a big scale of the kind wheat-buyers use, and when I remarked on it he said that he bought grain as well. I picked up a handful of the wheat he had bought, and examined it; a nice clean bit of stuff. Seeing me do that he asked if I knew anything about wheat, and I explained that I had been on my way to take up a position to buy grain for Habinski. In my bag at that moment, I told him, I had a small scale to test wheat to find out how good it was.

Mr Plotnik said his business was doing well. He had two assistants to work in the shop as well as his daughter and himself. One of the assistants was a married man with two children, and he earned twenty rubles a month, with all he wanted from the shop at cost price. And here I was, still only a boy, with no one dependent on me, off to start a job at thirty rubles a month! The comparison made me proud of myself, although when I thought about it afterwards I wondered whether it shouldn't make me sorry for the shop assistant.

The shop began to get busy now, with Mr Plotnik serving as well as the others, and I joined in and made myself useful. The daughter Hilda said I looked as if I was used to shop work; I told her I'd never served in one before (Habinski's granary didn't count) and that you didn't have to be very clever to serve behind a counter. Then I realized that this wasn't quite the best thing to say to a shop-keeper's daughter, and apologized, but she said: 'You're right — any fool can buy cheap and sell dear.' She asked me if I had done my military service yet. Everyone in Russia then had to do three year's military service, unpaid, when they were twenty-one, unless they could pay to get out of it. I explained that I was not quite seventeen yet, though that was a secret I didn't want people whom I would be doing business with to know. She reassured me that everyone would think I was at least twenty. Hilda said she was twenty-one; she had been engaged, but the boy had wanted the whole shop as a dowry so she had told him to get out, she said.

When evening came the shop was closed and we went upstairs again, where I was introduced to the rest of the family, a girl of eighteen who worked in the village school, and two schoolboy sons of twelve and fifteen. We sat down to eat again, and Mr Plotnik offered me a drink. I refused vodka but accepted a glass of red wine, and afterwards we went into the next room where there was a bowl of fruit and nuts on the table. I asked Mr Plotnik why he had taken the trouble to invite me to his home and treat me so well, and he said that his family didn't often meet people from the town and he thought it did the children good to meet someone else than the villagers they mixed with every day.

I slept that night in a spare bedroom that looked more like an office; there was a bed under the window but a desk and chair in it too, and papers lying around. Next morning I helped them in the shop again, and went round the village with Mr Plotnik to pass the time — there wasn't much to see — and finally Ivan the driver took me back to the station after I had thanked all the family for their kindness. At the station Ivan jumped down to carry my case; I gave him a silver coin but, like all village people, he seemed afraid to take money when it was given to him and I had to push it into his hand and grab my bag and make my way into the station.

There were only two more stations and then the train was steaming into Constantinograd and I was for a while very much a small-town boy in a big town. I'd never seen a station as big as this, and when I got out of the train I stood staring up at the terrific big building until a porter came up. He must have seen I was a country boy, for he made fun of me: 'What are you going to do, buy it?' he asked as he saw me gaping.

I said: 'No — I was looking at that bird up there — I've never seen such a wonderful bird before,' and I left him standing there looking for the imaginary bird and appearing just as foolish as I must have done.

Outside the station I was surrounded by cab-drivers all shouting: 'Where to, Mister?' I told one of them I wanted a cheap hotel to stay in, and he drove me to one called the Moskva — the Moscow. I said it looked a bit expensive, but the cab-driver urged me to try it, saying: 'I won't charge you if you book in at this one — I get paid by the hotel for bringing people here.' I thought that, since the Guvnor was paying my expenses, I would try it, and rang the bell. It was answered by a man in uniform, who showed me up to a room that to my eyes seemed fit for a prince. The bed was behind a screen; in the middle of the room was a table with four chairs, in the corner a washbowl, and there was also a small side table with a telephone and an electric bell-push.

I was thinking what would happen if my Guvnor could see this room — I couldn't imagine he had ever stayed anywhere like this in his life — when there was a knock on the door and the manager came in, welcoming me, saying he hoped I would be happy there, and asking how long I was going to stay? The room would be ten rubles a week, or thirty a month, he said, and I agreed to take it for a month. Only when I'd said this did he add that meals would be extra, but I decided, in for a penny, in for a pound of the Guvnor's money, and signed the register he had brought up with him, and paid him a month's rent in advance. He took it and went off, only to come rushing back with a receipt, and a little pad on which I could write down any orders. After he'd gone again I washed, and then pressed the button for the waiter and gave him the order for a meal which I had written down on the little pad — a couple of eggs, cheese, bread and butter, tea. He was back with it in no time.

After I'd filled myself up, I set off to find the post office and send a telegram to the Guvnor telling him my address. I also told the post office people where they should deliver any telegrams which came for us. Although I was now obliged to use the name Stocklinsky for official purposes, because Herscho had adopted it and he was my father, I couldn't get used to it, so for ordinary purposes I still used the name Levine, and this was the one I gave to the post office. Then, my business done for the day, I strolled about the town for a while and returned to my splendid room in the Moskva with its screened bed, its table and chairs, its telephone and its electric button to call the waiter. It was a great improvement on sleeping on the floor of Habinski's office or in a little lean-to room beside the house. I didn't know what the work would be like, but at least it appeared that my new life would be comfortable.

XIII.   THE GRAIN BOURSE

Next day the Guvnor reached Constantinograd after his journey from Verchneprovsk, and when he reached the hotel his first question was, 'Why do you want to stay in an expensive place like this?' I had an answer ready for that: 'Your name is involved,' I said. 'If I went to live in a little room somewhere, nobody would be able to get in touch with me. When I go to the grain market and people ask where I am staying it looks better for your name that I am here.'

The Guvnor nodded. 'You learn quickly,' he said, and when I pressed the button and the waiter brought in tea and cakes he added, 'And you live better than I do.'

He swallowed the tea down quickly and then set off with me to the grain market, the bourse. He seemed to know a lot of people there, shaking hands with everyone and when they complained that he hadn't been there for a long time explaining to them that he had brought someone in his place and introducing me. A lot of them looked at me and said: 'He's very young,' but the Guvnor wouldn't have that. 'After a couple of months you'll think differently,' he told them. 'I give him the prices and he just carries on.' He bought four railway trucks of wheat from someone while we were at the bourse, and then set out for the bank, explaining to me as we went how a grain merchant's dealings with the bank were arranged. 'Every truck of wheat I buy I give the seller a form saying how much I am paying for it. In return I get a document saying that a truck of wheat is deposited in the station granary. I take that document to the bank and on the strength of it the bank advances me money with which to pay for further deals.'

At the bank the Guvnor introduced me to the manager and got me to give him samples of my signature so that I would be able to sign things there in his place. I was told I could also draw up to three hundred rubles in cash if I needed it. I shook hands with the manager and then waited outside for the Guvnor to finish discussions of his other affairs. When he came out he told me that the bank manager had asked if he was going to rely on a young fellow like me to manage his business: 'I told him I was the best judge of that,' said the Guvnor, and I felt very proud that he had such faith in me. I thought to myself that I'd do my best not to let him down.

Back at the hotel we were too late to eat in the big dining room, so I rang for the waiter who brought up lunch for two, a beer for the Guvnor and lemonade for myself. After lunch Habinski explained that from now on he would send me my instructions by telegraph, telling me what to buy and at what prices. 'I can't telegraph you in detail because in words it would cost too much,' he said, and then made me write down the code he would use, each grain having a different number. When I'd taken all that down, he got up, saying it was time for him to go. 'Don't worry,' said the Guvnor. 'In a few weeks' time you will know everything.' I called a cab and rode with him to the station and watched him board the train before I set off for the grain market, very proud of myself.

The grain market was packed, with four different men buying and I made the fifth. Nobody took any notice of me at first, but when word got round among the people who were selling grain that I was there buying for Habinski, business became brisk — I bought fourteen different kinds of grain that evening.

At this Constantinograd bourse a lot of buying was done during the week, but most of all was done on Saturday evenings when the Sabbath was going out. I was there every day, and in two or three weeks I knew everyone and became friendly with other buyers who were there, like me, for their firms.

One of these buyers, a man named Ruchkovsky, said he'd always wanted to work for Habinski, and asked me how much I was paid. When I told him thirty rubles a month and expenses, he said: 'You must be mad. I get two hundred rubles a month, though not from my guv'nor. I make it on the side.'

Sitting in my hotel that evening — he had arrived uninvited and right away started to make himself look big, ordering drinks and saying they would be on him — Ruchkovsky explained how it was done.

'When you get a telegram in the morning telling you to buy say six trucks of grain at not more than one ruble twenty kopecks a pood,' he said, 'you tell the people who come to sell that the price has dropped to one ruble eighteen. But then you say you are willing to give them one ruble twenty, provided they'll give you back a kopeck a pood in cash for yourself. A railway truck is nine hundred pood, so you are making nine hundred kopecks a truck; nine rubles. Six wagonloads is fifty-four rubles. If you can do that three times a week, look how much you've made and nobody the wiser,' said Ruchkovsky.

I must have looked uncertain, because he explained: 'Your guvnor doesn't know. And the man who sells to you will never tell him, because he thinks he has made a kopeck a pood more for himself.'

I told Ruchkovsky I must think it over, because it was too quick for me to grasp. In fact, working it out, it seemed to me that every ruble I made this way would be by robbing a man who trusted me to buy the cheapest I could, and though my Guvnor cheated the peasants and underpaid his own workers, all the same I wasn't going to do that. Even if I had been tempted, I thought, I certainly wouldn't do it along with Ruchkovsky; it would give him too good an opportunity to tell the Guvnor and get rid of me any time he wanted to, with a chance that he might take my place. I wasn't stupid enough for that.

That evening a telegram arrived, telling me to buy twenty wagons of rye at not more than ninety-eight kopecks a pood. It was an urgent order, and I made up my mind to meet the train which arrived at Constantinograd next morning. A lot of people from surrounding towns would be on that train, bound for places further up the line to sell their grain; the train stopped about a quarter of an hour so I would have time to make deals before it moved on. So next morning I was at the station when the train arrived. Ruchkovsky was there, and introduced me to some of the people who had grain to sell, saying: 'Let's see what price he offers.' I thought, if Habinski wanted this rye urgently it was no time for haggling, so I said: 'Top price, ninety-eight kopecks.' In no time I'd bought twenty wagon-loads and had the necessary papers signed before the train moved away.

I was left with Ruchkovsky on the station, telling me I had made a very bad deal, and that I could have made a lot of money for my-self if I'd tried.

There wasn't much doing at the market, so I returned to my hotel, stopping on the way to telegraph the Guvnor saying what I'd bought, and then waited for the evening when business at the grain market would begin again.

By evening another telegram arrived, telling me to buy ten more wagonloads of rye. At first the market was very quiet, and I was sitting at a table when Ruchkovsky came up, asking if I'd bought anything — I couldn't seem to shake that man off. But he was useful to me in a way he didn't intend, for as we sat there the postman came up to hand him a telegram, and when selling began several buyers came to me asking if I had the latest prices — they must have thought the telegram had come to me. I took the opportunity and said that the price was down to ninety-five kopecks, although my last instructions had been to buy up to ninety-eight. I was able to buy six truckloads at ninety-five kopecks a pood straight away, and as I was signing the receipt for these six, a telegram really did arrive for me, telling me Habinski's ceiling was now ninety-five kopecks. The man from whom I'd just bought saw the telegram, though of course he couldn't understand Habinski's code; and I soon had people round me asking for the new price. I said: 'A kopeck down, to ninety-four,' and was able to buy eight more truckloads at that price before I finished for the night.

That was the way I earned my living, buying for Habinski at the grain bourse in Constantinograd, and you must imagine it going on like that, day after day, week after week. The regular buyers accepted me; strange ones wouldn't always believe that someone so young could be up to the job, but they learned — even the man who badgered me into playing dominoes for money, a way a lot of the buyers passed their time away waiting for business. I didn't want to gamble, but I let them teach me the game, and I even let them press me into one game for money; they offered me odds of ten to one in my favour, so I consented. They let me win that one; they weren't very pleased when I picked up my winnings and thanked them for the lesson, saying I'd decided I wouldn't try my luck any more.

I met all kinds of people including Vaskevich, a rich buyer, who took me home to meet his family and have supper. He dressed like a lord, and his wife, who was very thin and nice looking, had lots of rings on her fingers and wonderful big ear-rings on her ears, and they both spoke in very highbrow accents. Vaskevich seemed an unusual man; he was clean-shaven, for one thing, and in those days you hardly ever saw a man without a beard or at least a moustache. And another thing I found odd was that he and his wife never used one another's first names; it was always Dear and Darling. But it was interesting to see inside their house, beautifully furnished, and with every kind of drink and marvellous food — I had to pretend not to take any notice of it, because I didn't want him to think I hadn't seen such things before. He showed me to a chair, and when his wife entered the room he jumped up and pulled out a chair for her. The meal ended with fruit, cooked and fresh, and then we left the table; 'Come, my dear, let's go into the parlour; we will stay there for this evening,' said Vaskevich. They wouldn't hear of my going so early; Vaskevich said his driver would take me home when I had to leave.

So I followed them into this room, beautifully furnished, much finer than anything Habinski had; to me it looked like the room a millionaire might have. On the table was a bowl of fresh flowers, a box of cigars, a box of cigarettes, and matches. I didn't smoke, but Vaskevich pressed me into taking a cigarette, saying it was useful when talking to people and so it helped business; so I took one and lit it, and coughed and spluttered all over the place. I couldn't make out what they wanted to talk to me for, people like that with their house and their maid and their horses, but it seemed they were curious, just like other people, and wanted to know how I came to be grain-buying at my age. They obviously had a lot more questions they wanted to ask, but it was getting late so they called their driver to take me back to my hotel. The Vaskevichs were Russians, Christians, not Jews like most of the grain dealers, though I didn't realize this until I got into their house and saw the icon with a candle burning before it.

Then there was Vladimir, a young chap nearer my own age, who persuaded me to go along with him to a dance one Sunday. I couldn't dance and I was shy of girls, but I went along and bought tickets with Vladimir. We entered the hall, and when I saw all the girls I wanted to turn tail and run out. Vladimir got hold of my jacket, and if I'd run I'd have left half my jacket in his hand, so I had to stop. Three girls came up to us asking why he was so late, and he introduced me and then drifted away, leaving me with the girls, and more coming up like flies round a honey pot, I suppose because I was a stranger. When I told them I couldn't dance, however, they all drifted away except one, who said that she would teach me, and pulled me on to the dance floor and started telling me how to hold her and not to be frightened. But after a while she gave up, saying, 'I can see you're not a very good pupil, perhaps we'll try again another evening; come, let's see if we can find something to drink.'

We went to a buffet bar with about twenty small tables and chairs, and she called the waiter to bring tea and cakes. We had an argument about who should pay, and when I insisted she said, 'You are different from Vladimir — he never pays; all the girls pay for him.' I discovered her name was Anita; she was the daughter of a shopkeeper who bought wheat from the peasants. I told her I came from a small town; she had never heard of Verchneprovsk, and I told her, 'It is a town where you see more peasants than anywhere else, and not many people there can read and write.'

At ten o'clock she got up to go, and now I found myself looking at her for the first time with interest. Before, all girls seemed the same to me, but now, though I could not describe any of her features I realized Anita was beautiful. I held her coat for her, and she put it on, fluffing her hair out of the collar the way girls do. I had always determined to have as little to do with girls as possible,

but now I said to myself, 'Moysey, it is inevitable. What is the use
of struggling against maturity?'

We walked for a little way, until we reached my hotel. She asked
where I lived and when I said: 'Here,' she was surprised: 'What, in
this wonderful hotel?' she said. I called a cab and put her into it
telling the driver to take her where she wanted to go and to call at
the hotel for me next morning when I would pay for it, and I waved
as the cab drove away.

Next morning I sang as I washed, as I was so happy. The waiter,
coming in for my order, said: 'You are happy this morning,' and I
admitted it was over a girl; and realized, as I sat eating my breakfast,
that I was thinking more about Anita than about my food.

The Zlotniks were two more friends I made in Constantinograd.
They had written to the Guvnor at my hotel explaining that the
wife, Liza Zlotnik, came from Verchneprovsk, where her mother
still kept a fish shop in the market, and inviting Habinski to come
and see them and have tea. Their letter arrived after the Guvnor had
gone back to Verchneprovsk, so I answered it explaining that he was
away but promising to pass on their invitation when he was next in
Constantinograd. A little later they wrote back inviting me to go
in his place, and on the next Saturday afternoon I togged myself up,
even buying a walking stick so I should look older, and set off to
their house which was only a few minutes down the road from my
hotel.

Lev Zlotnik was a tall man with a ginger moustache, his wife Liza
was a short woman, and short-sighted too. She came to the door with
a baby girl about a year old on her arm. The Zlotniks were not more
than thirty-five, but they looked as if they had worked hard; they
were nicely dressed but not what I would have called smart. She
had a lot of rings on her fingers, and a bracelet on her left wrist; her
speech was very high class, better than her husband's or mine.

Lev left his wife to talk to me while he made tea. She asked me all
sorts of questions, but very formally and respectfully, as though I
were a lord, and I had to tell her not to be so formal but to call me
Moysey. All the same, I dreaded her questions. I was learning by
now that I could get on with people, but I had not yet got over my

old feeling that being a foundling was shameful. In my mind people looked at a chap with no parents as a wild one, a dangerous person, someone not to know. I didn't know how this couple would take it, but I thought I'd get it over and done with, so I told them. But Liza said: 'That's not your fault,' and then went on to tell me she knew all about me; she was seventeen at the time I was found. She knew that my first foster-mother didn't want to give me up, and that my second foster-mother wanted to take me to America but wasn't allowed to, and that my third foster-parents were the Levines; she knew all about the time I went to school and how I was always fighting with the other boys. 'We know all about it,' she said, 'but if it's any consolation to you we'd sooner have you here than the man you work for.'

I began to tell her I didn't want any of her pity, nor any parents either. Whenever I had to talk about this subject I got angry, and I couldn't keep my eyes dry. But she said: 'Now listen carefully — this might interest you. Many people in Verchneprovsk knew your father and mother. They were rich people; they were not married and did not want to bring shame to their families. They are in America now, and my mother knows the names of both of them. She could give the names to you, and you could go to America to see them.'

I told her: 'No money in the world would tempt me to go and see people like that who abandoned a baby, and I don't believe they could ever have any good fortune because of it. If they had come to my rescue, even when I was twelve and with my third foster-parents, I would be able to forgive them, but not now.'

Once I started, I told this couple everything about myself; of the harsh times I'd had with Herscho and Hannah, and how little protection the Jewish organization in the town had given me, and the miserable time I had when I first began working for Habinski. They listened sympathetically, and seemed to understand how I felt. When finally I got up to go they pressed me to stay to supper, and we finished the day laughing and joking, with me helping Liza with the washing up and Lev swearing that I was another brother to him.

I got on so well with the Zlotniks that not long after this they

suggested that I should move in with them. They had never let
their room before, so they did not know what to charge. I suggested
forty rubles a month, and for my washing I would pay separately.
As the hotel expenses were much more than forty rubles, I was sure
that the Guvnor would be pleased; I was getting forty rubles a
month now, but Habinski paid all my expenses including my board.
Next day I went to the post office to get a telephone installed in my
room; I had to have one, and I was lucky enough to get it quickly
because there was one only three doors away. I had telegraphed my
new address to the Guvnor and a few weeks after I settled in he
telegraphed that he was coming to see me. That morning I had
breakfast early, cleaned my boots, smartened myself up and went to
meet him.

I was not frightened of the Guvnor any more, as I had been when
I was younger. I knew he could give me orders, but he couldn't
compel me to do anything I didn't want to do. He could only sign
his name, he couldn't read or write, but I could, and I kept an
account of everything in a book, so that I was ready for him whenever he came. Whenever I received a letter or a telegram from the
Guvnor I imagined him standing in front of me, a tall man in a long
fur coat, with a long black beard. He reminded me of a big bear and
I would say to myself, 'Moysey, don't be frightened of a bear.' I can
see him now; his beard, his grey suit for weekdays, black one for the
Sabbath. Out of doors, in summer, he would wear a peaked cap, the
kind that policemen and soldiers wear now. Such caps were fashion-
able in Russia then, but a rich man like Habinski would have a cap
covered in silk. In winter, though, the Guvnor would wear a big hat
of fur; and summer and winter, indoors he would wear a skull cap.

On this visit, after a long talk about business, I told him that I
wanted to go to Kremenchug on January 23 and asked if he would
make arrangements for someone to take my place until I came back.
He said, 'Those two old devils Herscho and Hannah, have you forgotten the way they looked after you?'

I said: 'I will never forget them. If they had been nice people I
would be still driving horses. Look at me now — I've a wonderful
job. Do you know one wheat buyer offered me a hundred rubles a

month?' Habinski said he couldn't spare anyone from home to take over in Constantinograd while I was away. I suggested he hire a man at the bourse named Bechatsky, who worked for anybody on commission, but the Guvnor wouldn't hear of it. 'I could never give a man like that my business to conduct,' he said. 'He has so many buyers. But I have a new book-keeper at home and perhaps he could do it for a while.' We went off to the bourse then, and I introduced him to Mr Bechatsky, but the Guvnor insisted he would never trust such a man with his business, and would send his own book-keeper instead. It was a decision that cost everyone money and trouble, as you'll see.

When the train came in, Habinski took over the buying from me, and I just booked everything down for him. He bought a lot of grain, and then went on to the bank to check over my accounts with the manager; there were no faults to be found with my work. Then back to the station we went, for the Guvnor to catch a train on to Nikolaev for more business.

XIV. THE MATCHMAKER

January came round at last, and I returned one evening through the snow to find a letter from Verchneprovsk asking me to bring all accounts and statements from the bank to Habinski on the fifteenth of the month. It was signed: 'Lumsky, book-keeper for Habinski.' This time when I caught the train for Verchneprovsk I travelled first class, because I thought I would meet more interesting people this way. I had to change at the station called Lozovay and be smart about it, for on this station there were twenty different lines and the trains from here went all over the world.

When my cab from the station stopped at Habinski's granary in Verchneprovsk, everyone crowded round, and one joked, 'Be careful; the great Stocklinsky has arrived.' I took no notice, but paid the driver, and looked round for old white-bearded Kovalevsky. He wasn't in the crowd, but had stayed in his own department and he was looking very miserable. I asked him the trouble and he said the Guvnor had told him he was getting old and it was about time he retired. 'He told me he would pension me off with five rubles a month — what can you do with five rubles a month?'

'Never mind,' I said, 'your wife has a little shop selling needles and cottons and wools — that will help.' But he insisted she didn't make much there, and only went to the shop because she was so used to it. When I heard this I began to wonder if Kovalevsky was hoping to avoid paying me the money I had lent him twelve months ago. He didn't say anything about it, but this talk of poverty made me suspicious.

From Kovalevsky I went on to the office, and said 'Good morning' to the new book-keeper. Unlike the old one who had been there when I started with Habinski, this one tried to be clever at my expense. 'The Guvnor told me to get the accounts from a young boy of seventeen, but I can't believe it — who pulled you and stretched you so high?' he said. I ignored his funny remarks and said: 'I want these accounts done after lunch,' and left the office.

I spent the rest of that day with Mama Marcovsky and her family — my family, I always thought; and the next day, because the book-keeper still had not got round to my accounts, I went to the granary and offered to give them a hand. I spent some time talking to the foreman. 'Where have you been, what have you been doing?' he asked, and, joking: 'Have you found a nice, rich girl yet?' I said I was too young for that and asked him if his daughter was married. He said, 'No, she is waiting for you.' This upset old Kovalevsky who had been listening: he told me I should be careful about talking to men with grown-up daughters. 'They always entice you, and it is very hard to get out of trouble,' he said. 'I have seen clever chaps like you get trapped before.' I reassured him: 'People tried to marry me off in Constantinograd. The trouble with me is my size; I look older than I am,' I said. I wanted to talk about the money he owed me, but I didn't get a chance.

I took the opportunity, now I was in Verchneprovsk with nothing to do, to visit the Rabbi's son who had been my teacher and was now a doctor. A maid in uniform showed me in, and in a few minutes a tall distinguished-looking man came in to the waiting room. He recognized me immediately, and shook my hand with great enthusiasm, ushering me into the dining room and calling his mother to come and see me. He asked how I was getting on and I told him I had a wonderful position thanks to his help, and I opened my case and showed him the printed stationery with my name on it. And I said, 'For all this I thank you, for if I hadn't been able to read or write I couldn't have had such a job.'

The doctor had married since I had last seen him, and we all sat down to tea together. I noticed he still wore a skull cap at his meals, as a very religious man would, so I asked him if he could lend me one, and he found one and placed it on my head himself. His wife told me not to be shy, and to eat as much as I wanted. She smiled and said she understood a young man had a big appetite. Then she asked me when my birthday was. I told her it was very embarrassing to be asked this question — there were lots of times when I was having a good time and it would be spoilt by people asking such questions. She was upset about it, but I told her not to worry.

But I had already decided there was too much mystery about my age and birth, and after I'd said goodbye to the doctor and his wife I set off for the register office.

A young man in uniform showed me in and took my name and address, and conducted me into a big room where the Registrar was sitting behind a desk. I was surprised when this man got up from his chair and shook hands with me, saying, 'Moysey Stocklinsky? You were only so high when I last saw you with Herscho.' He offered me a chair.

I told him I wanted to learn all I could about my birth, and he looked at me over his glasses with his very bright eyes and said: 'I will get the book.'

He went out and came back with an assistant carrying the book, whom the Registrar dismissed.

'Now,' he said, 'you want to know your real age?'

'When I am in company, and I tell them my age they laugh at me,' I said. 'You can help me now to get things straight. I know that you often meet my guvnor in the synagogue and he talks about me, so I don't have to tell you where I work.'

He opened the big book, but just then the door opened and his wife came in. She said, 'Forgive me — I didn't know you had someone here,' but he told her to come in and said, 'Do you know this young man? This is the boy who used to live with Herscho and Hannah Levine.'

I was nervous enough and embarrassed as it was, and this seemed too much. I said, 'Don't worry about me. Tell her that I am the boy who was found in the synagogue, left there by his unmarried mother.'

The Registrar said gently, 'But you haven't done badly for yourself.'

'No, I haven't done badly for myself because as soon as I realized I was branded I made up my mind to fight my way so people should look up and respect me. I am not ashamed, only for my parents.'

The Registrar's wife said: 'I don't think you should worry about anything that has gone by. You are well and you are nicely dressed and you have a good position.'

I thought she was only saying that to be kind to me, and I told her so. She didn't answer but turned to her husband and asked him how long he would be, and as she walked out she looked at me and said: 'I will see you before you go.'

After she had gone he opened the book up and started looking through it for my birth date. He found the page and turned the book round to me. I read: On the twenty-third of January 1892, a young woman whom nobody saw (only the porter of the synagogue for two minutes) left a basket which contained a new-born baby in the synagogue. When people gathered for the morning service the porter told the Rabbi, who called a doctor. The doctor said the child was well and very expensively dressed and in his opinion it was one week old.

I closed the book. The Registrar said: 'And from that date we established your birthday.' I got up from my chair and thanked him. He shook hands and said: 'Don't worry; just forget the past and live for the future and perhaps one day you will be a rich man.'

Just as I was going out, his wife reappeared and insisted that I stay and have tea with them. I followed them both into the dining room. The furniture looked far more expensive even than Habinski's. I hesitated to sit down, although there were plenty of chairs. The Registrar's wife rang a bell and a maid brought in one glass of tea and some cake on a plate. I didn't touch it; I was still angry and embarrassed, and to sit there while they watched me eat and drink was too much. I said so, telling her I didn't want her pity. I could not understand, then, that they might be trying to be kind; I was looking for their pity so that I could spurn it. She was patient, though, this woman. She rang the bell again for the maid and asked her to bring in tea and cake for her husband and herself, and we drank and ate together and talked, though I was still impatient to get away.

Presently, their three daughters returned from school; the mother introduced me, and I rose from the table and bowed, and began to make my excuses, but still they wouldn't let me go. The Registrar said: 'What, are you frightened of girls?' I said that I wasn't, but he wouldn't want his daughters to entertain a boy like me.

He said: 'I thought you were a sensible boy, but I see you are a big fool. If I wanted you to go I would tell you so. You keep persecuting yourself and you must stop it,' and he made me stay and talk, and after a while he and his wife left me to talk with the two elder girls — two girls so nice looking, I didn't know which one to look at. When I finally left, my heart felt much lighter.

I made my way on to Mama Marcovsky's. I have never longed to see anyone as I used to long to see her. A peasant who knew my history once told me: 'You must remember the mother — not the one who bore you, but the one who brought you up,' and this was true.

There were photographs to see, of David the son who had gone to America. He had married there, and Vera was in the wedding picture too. We began talking of the chances of the whole family going to America, but Mama said, 'We will talk about that later. Let's have something to eat now. We have borscht and millett corn' — she knew that was my favourite food. I told Mama that I had been to the Registrar and looked up the record of my birth. She said she could have saved me the trouble, for she had all the particulars and papers put away in her trunk. She went out and brought back the papers in a box, and I went through them. One letter dated February 6, 1892, said the Jewish community was offering Mrs Marcovsky two and a half rubles a week for looking after a baby boy. I didn't quite grasp this, so I read the letter to Mama.

She said she had refused to accept any money because she looked on me as her own son. With that she burst out crying and I, like a big fool, followed suit; and while we were crying together Papa came in and said, 'Aren't you ashamed of yourself — a big boy like you?' And then he turned to Mama and said, 'What's the matter with you?' But they were not tears of real sadness, our tears.

That evening was very cold and when Mama had dried her eyes we sat round the table and Papa went out to get more wood for the fire, while Mama put on the samovar to make tea, and we sat and talked until Esther and Monica returned — they had young men to walk out with by this time — and we were all a happy family again. We talked and laughed and Papa fell asleep in his chair, and I said I must be getting back to Habinski's, but as I opened the door the snow was coming down very heavily in big flakes, so Mama put some blankets on the couch for me, and there, when everyone else had gone, I blew out the lamp and fell asleep.

Next morning, after saying my farewells, I went back to Habinski's house. The boys from the granary wanted to know where I had slept the night. I said, 'I slept in a house very dear to me,' and one of them said, 'In the bootmaker's house? No wonder; they have some beautiful girls there.'

The book-keeper now had to go away to Constantinograd to take my place while I had my holiday, and I looked in on him to help him get the accounts straight. I found he had called in the Guvnor. 'I can't make out why a young chap like Moysey has shown one thousand two hundred and fifty rubles expenses,' the book-keeper was saying.

The Guvnor looked at me and said: 'Is that right? Have you spent all that money?' I said: Absolutely right.' The book-keeper said, very sharp, 'What did you spend it on?'

I told him: 'I have bought eight hundred and sixty-five trucks of grain — that works out at one and a half rubles expenses a truck, which is very cheap.'

The Guvnor didn't need to hear any more. He said to the book-keeper: 'You carry on with your journey and when you come back, Moysey will check on *your* expenses to see how much you have spent.' Then he said to me, 'Now, Moysey, you are free to go on holiday and have a good time. But don't forget — only two weeks. I will expect you back the first week in February,' and he took out his wallet and paid me a month's wages.

I had not notified Herscho and Hannah exactly what day I was coming but they knew it was some time this week, and would be expecting me, so when the boat docked I took a cab to their apartment. They were not at home, so I took my case up the road to my aunt, Hannah's sister-in-law.

My cousin Usher was waiting; after everyone else had finished their greetings she came up to me and put her lips to mine and wouldn't let go. Her mother shouted: 'Why don't you leave him alone, you'll choke him,' but all Usher said was, 'I can't help it — I love him so much and when he is eighteen I'm going to marry him.'

Her mother snorted: 'Are you going to tie him up with string?' and Usher replied: 'I don't have to — I know he loves me too, but he is shy.' All this time I was standing there, in front of everyone, with Usher hanging round my neck, and to complete my embarrassment she said: 'Don't you love me?'

I said, carefully: 'You're a beautiful girl, but if you're waiting for me you'll have to wait a long time,' and then I made the excuse that Hannah and Herscho would be wondering where I was, and hurried off, with Usher calling after me: 'I'll see you later.'

I found Herscho much changed: he seemed to have grown suddenly older while I was away. He couldn't walk far without complaining, and he couldn't climb the three flights of stairs to their flat without puffing and stopping to sit on a step to rest and get his breath back. He was more slovenly, too. He no longer washed before meals, nor did he pray at meal times, and he mumbled excuses to himself for not going to the synagogue. 'I don't do anything wrong . . . I don't have to go there to pray,' he would say. He could still eat enormously, but when he had finished supper he would be so full he could hardly breathe, and would fall asleep in the middle of a sentence.

Hannah was the same as ever, as strong as she was wicked, I thought. They both seemed more anxious than ever to make me feel comfortable and welcome; from anyone else it would have been nice and I would have been pleased, but I did not trust Hannah and Herscho, and it wasn't long before Herscho let out what they had in mind and what must have been the reason why Hannah was taking so much trouble to serve me splendid meals and to make me comfortable. Herscho began by asking me how much I had saved up; I told him six hundred and fifty rubles, saying nothing about the thousand rubles that old Kovalevsky had borrowed from me. Then he said: 'When you have saved up a lot of money I'll open a big tobacconist's shop for you. You'll be your own governor then, and I'll manage it for you. Perhaps when you're eighteen we'll find you a girl and you might get a couple of thousand rubles dowry with her — you're a nice-looking boy.'

'What Papa says is very sensible,' Hannah chipped in. I thought to myself, very sensible for you — if Herscho gets his hands on my money he'll get himself out of his little tobacco stall in the market and into a big shop, but I'll be running after him like a little dog. But I said nothing.

Next day Hannah's part in the idea began to appear. She had made an excuse that she must go out to the shops; I offered to go for her, but she wouldn't let me. After she'd gone I glanced out of the window and saw her hurrying down the road; she didn't go to the shops but disappeared into a house near by. A quarter of an hour later she reappeared, a man with a long black beard showing her out, and hurried back to the flat. She said she wanted to introduce me to a man who taught the local Jewish children, and when I agreed she took me back to this same house, knocked on the door and asked for the Rabbi Rabinovich; the same black-bearded man appeared.

Hannah introduced me: 'This is my son, here on holiday. I'm going out and don't want him to be on his own; perhaps you'll let him stay and see how the teaching goes?'

The Rabbi said: 'With pleasure,' and invited me in. He asked me if I could read and write, and when I showed him, he asked if I could deal with one of his classes while he dealt with the other; if I took them through their lesson in Russian, he would be able to deal with the other class which was learning Yiddish. I agreed to this, though I didn't know what I should do as a teacher, and he took me into a room where about twenty children were sitting, tightly packed together. He divided them into two groups of ten, and handed one of them over to me, saying: 'I've got a Russian teacher for you now.'

It didn't seem so easy, now I was faced with the children. I whispered to the Rabbi: 'You know I'm not a teacher,' and he whispered back: 'They won't know,' and left me to it. I told the children to get out their exercise books, and wrote a few lines on the blackboard for them to copy, and then went round looking at each book, and getting them to read to me. They were very good and obedient, these children, I suppose because I was a stranger and they were frightened of me; just as well, for I wouldn't have known what to do if they hadn't behaved well.

At lunch time the children all ran home, but the Rabbi wouldn't let me go; he and his wife insisted that I stay and eat with them. It was a poor meal, and while we were eating it the Rabbi told me that the pay for teaching was very bad. 'I'm looked on almost as a beggar when I ask for payment. To scrape together enough to live on I have to go to the town across the bridge, Krukov, to do a bit of private teaching in people's houses in the evening,' he said. And indeed, he was so poorly dressed he looked like a beggar. He was very tall and his beard was very long; his eyes were bright and cunning. I wondered what was behind this meeting between us that Hannah had arranged.

He asked me if I had been to Krukov, and when I said I'd never visited that town he invited me to come along with him on his next teaching visit; he would introduce me to the pupils' parents as another teacher, he said.

That evening, Hannah wanted to know all about my day with Rabbi Rabinovich, and when I mentioned that he had invited me to go across the bridge to Krukov with him she said: 'Papa has a friend who goes to the market there once a week. Very rich people live there — they make their money in Kremenchug and go to live in Krukov where it's quiet. You couldn't go far wrong if you found a girl from there.'

On the Saturday morning, Herscho and Hannah slept late, and I got up and lit the samovar to make tea. If Hannah had been up, she would have gone looking for a Christian boy or girl to light it for her, not because she was truly religious but because it would give her an excuse to run about and talk to people. I didn't mind lighting it; I couldn't believe that striking a match on the Sabbath was a sin; it seemed to me that a sin was harming somebody. When the samovar boiled I made tea and woke them both up. The first thing Hannah said was: 'Who struck the match?' as though it was important. I said: 'An angel,' and she said: 'You didn't have to do it; the Konevs

6

have a girl working in their house who always lights it on a Saturday.' Herscho came in from the bedroom grumbling: 'What's the difference so long as it's lit? I want breakfast, I'm hungry.'

Later that day, Herscho had another go at me about getting married: I'd said it would be ages before I thought of such a thing, but Herscho began lecturing me: 'You are seventeen now and the bible says that when a boy is eighteen he must get married. That's the Jewish religion.' And again I wondered what was behind all this.

I spent the rest of that day visiting people I knew in Kremenchug. Next day, after lunch, I went to the park, just killing time because I'd nothing to do until four-thirty when I was to meet Rabbi Rabinovich and go with him to Krukov. While I was sitting there something happened; an unimportant thing, but worth telling, for perhaps it explains something of what it was like to be a Jew in Russia in those days.

I was deep in my book when I heard a voice say: 'Are you waiting for someone or can I sit on this seat?'

It was a boy of my own age; not so tall as me, but well dressed and very polite, and speaking Russian better than I did. He was wearing dark glasses, so I couldn't see his eyes.

I said: 'Certainly — sit down, I'm not waiting for anyone, I'm on holiday.'

He said: 'I'm on holiday too — I come from Kreelov,' and then we exchanged names — his was Stolchkov — and we chatted for a while, until he asked if I would give him the pleasure of my company for tea somewhere. Now, it didn't matter to me that he was well-dressed and well-spoken, but I wondered whether, if I told him I was Jewish, he would still want to take tea with me. I didn't look Jewish, and I did want company for tea, so I said I was Russian.

He said: 'What's the difference? It makes no difference to me,' and I said: 'I thought if I told you I was a Jew you would not want to walk with me.'

'Only ignorant people are prejudiced about nationality,' said Stolchkov. 'If I were to tell you I was a Jew, would *you* walk with me?'

I said: 'As a matter of fact, I am a Jew,' and he said: 'So am I,' and we shook hands and laughed and went off to a teashop together.

An unimportant incident, as I said. But such things didn't seem so unimportant, at that time, in that place.

We spent a couple of hours talking in a teashop, and then I hurried home to meet Rabbi Rabinovich.

When we went out into the street it was beginning to get cold, and in the side streets the snow was still lying very deep, so I offered to get a sledge, but the Rabbi said it would be much healthier to walk across the bridge to Krukov and feel the wind from the river; and so it was. We walked, and the wind made me feel fresh and good. On the way the Rabbi told me that a few years before the towns had been connected by a rough wooden bridge which had been falling to pieces, but English engineers had come and built this new one, of iron.

On the Krukov side of the bridge there were cabs waiting in a rank, and again I suggested that we take one, but the Rabbi wouldn't have it: 'Not much further now,' he said. We walked on for about a quarter of an hour, and turned into a road called Velensky Street. 'This is where the two boys live whom I teach,' said the Rabbi.

We knocked at one of the houses and a woman invited us in. It was a poor house, poorly furnished; she showed us into a room with a bare table and few chairs not fit to sit on, and I wondered how she could afford to pay for education when she was as poor as this. The woman was about twenty-five, not bad-looking, but her dress was torn and dirty and her hair untidy. From the next room came the sound of someone working with a hammer. She asked us to sit down and said the boys would be back in a moment, and she fetched a cloth and began wiping down the table and chairs.

The knocking with the hammer stopped, and a man came in, not very tall but very thin, with a large apron on; his hands were black as soot and his face gaunt and thin as if he hadn't had a meal for a month. The Rabbi introduced us, and asked the man how his cabinet-making business was doing. 'It's hard to make a living,' said the man.

There was a knock on the door and the two boys of about eight and ten came in; their clothes were shabby and their boots worn, and

they'd no topcoats on in spite of the cold. With them was a young
girl, whom they called Sonia. It seemed she was their mother's
sister, though the two didn't look a bit alike. She excused herself,
saying: 'I must go and tell my sister off for letting the boys out like
this,' and the Rabbi and I settled down with the two boys and their
books. I found it hard to keep my mind on the lesson. I was wondering about this family which couldn't afford proper boots and
coats for the children but was able to pay for private teaching. The
boys knew little more than their ABC, and they couldn't read Russian
at all.

I tried to coach them a bit, and after half an hour the Rabbi said:
'That's enough for tonight,' so we said goodbye and set off to walk
home. I was silent, thinking about those two boys. I didn't know if
I had been any poorer than they were, but I knew they were richer
than I'd ever been in one thing: they had parents to love them. They
had grandmothers and grandfathers and uncles and aunts . . . nobody would ever kick those boys or knock them about. I envied them.

The Rabbi asked why I was so quiet, and I told him I was thinking about the boys. 'The people we've just left — they can't possibly
pay you for teaching,' I said.

'I don't get anything from them,' said the Rabbi, 'but the grandmother has money and helps with the expenses. She's promised to
give her other daughter, Sonia, a thousand rubles for a wedding
present when she finds a nice boy to get married to.'

Now I saw it all, and I told him so. 'You took me there to show me
off and introduce me to Sonia, and if everything works out all right
the girl's mother will pay you for your trouble,' I said. 'You had it
all fixed with Hannah when she visited you!' The thought that
Hannah, after all the trouble she had made for me when I was small,
couldn't leave my private life alone even now I was grown up, made
me very angry. She had brought in the Rabbi as a marriage-broker,
and I didn't doubt that she hoped I would marry this girl and then
pass the dowry on to Herscho to look after, with his ideas of a big
tobacco shop.

When I got home I taxed Hannah with it. She denied it all, of
course, but she asked eagerly: 'Is she a nice-looking girl?' Grudg-

ingly, I agreed that this Sonia had seemed a nice-looking girl. But she was not for me, I said. I wasn't going to get tied up with any girl, not yet. And I complained that instead of showing me round Krukov her Rabbi had only taken me into one poor house.

Next morning Hannah and Herscho had already left for their stall in the market by the time I woke. I set out for a walk, and found myself heading towards the bridge across the river to Krukov.

The snow was very deep and frozen hard, so that you had to be careful not to fall, but I had taken my stick with me — in snow like that it isn't only the old who need to walk with a stick. After I had walked for about a quarter of a mile the wind from the river was beating in my face, and by the time I reached the far end of the bridge I was warm from the brisk walk. Once in Krukov I slowed down and began looking in the shops. One of them was a barber's saloon with a ladies hairdressers as well, and I stepped in for a haircut. While the barber was clipping away and dodging round me and talking, the way barbers do, I could hear women's voices from beyond the partition, chattering and laughing, and when the barber had finished and I'd picked up my stick and set out again, I saw two girls leaving just in front of me, and I recognized one of them as Sonia, the girl I'd seen the night before. I could only take off my hat and bow to them, and I finished up walking along the road between the two of them.

Sonia never said a word, but the other girl, whose name I discovered was Nina Lebedev, was very talkative; since I was rather shy, Nina had to do enough talking for the three of us, and she didn't seem to find that difficult. When I said that I wanted to find somewhere in Krukov to eat, she told Sonia: 'Let's go to your house — tell your mama that we met with my boy friend and you asked us in for a cup of tea.' And without consulting me, or even taking any notice of my polite refusals, they led me off like a lamb to the slaughter.

Sonia's house was not very rich, but it was clean, unlike her sister's. She left me with Nina and went off, returning with a tray loaded with boiled eggs and sardines and cheese and bread and butter; I was glad to see it, because it was two o'clock and I'd had no breakfast before I set off that morning. Between the three of us we got through the trayful, and Sonia went out again and brought in another tray of tea and cake and biscuits. They certainly ate well in that house. When we'd finished eating the girls began asking me questions. It was always like this; people seemed to think that I owed them something which I could pay by answering questions. They wanted to know where I worked, if I went to the theatre, if I had any close friends . . . and then the old business about my age came up. I told them I was only seventeen and a half, and Sonia said, 'You look at least twenty; you are tall enough for that.'

'I was born in a field so I grew like the grass,' I said.

We kept on this joking talk until we heard Sonia's mother come in. Sonia called: 'We're in the front parlour. Come and see what we've found.' Sonia's mother was about forty-five, and she looked as if she had done a hard day's work and was really worn out. She was about five feet four, thin, with very bright blue eyes. She didn't speak good Russian, and she said to me in Yiddish: 'Hallo, young man.' I jumped up and bowed and said, 'Good afternoon, Madam,' and she turned to the girls, joking: 'Where did you find him?'

'We found him looking in a shop,' they said.

'There's not much trouble finding a big chap like me — why didn't they find me when I was small?' I said.

'Your mother wouldn't have let them touch you then,' said Sonia's mother.

Sonia and her mother went out for a moment, and then the mother returned, asking me to stay for supper. I said I couldn't stay because Hannah and Herscho would be expecting me, but she wouldn't take no for an answer. 'Send them a telegram saying you've come across friends and will be home later tonight,' she said, and called out to Sonia who came in with a paper and pencil to write down my address. That surprised me; in those days you didn't expect to find many poor girls who could read and write. She wrote down the message and my address, and the mother wouldn't hear of my paying for the telegram, but sent Sonia hurrying off to despatch it.

I realized well enough what Sonia's mother had in mind. I was caught up in a match-making scheme. But having seen Sonia again, it didn't seem such a bad thing. She could read and write; she was sensible but shy; she knew how to dress. I thought about her: small, about five foot two, a good shape, her cheeks blooming with health, her brown eyes sad but warm. I didn't know much about girls, but I thought Sonia looked like a plant that needed watering to bring it to life.

When the mother went out of the room, I was left alone with the talkative Nina, who told me a lot about Sonia's family. She had one unmarried brother, Sam, who lived at home, said Nina, and I thought immediately that that was possibly why she was so friendly. Our conversation was interrupted by a banging on the front gate and the sound of horses' hooves clattering into the yard. 'Here he is,' said Nina. 'You'll soon see a ruffian come in.'

She was right. In a few minutes a man of about twenty-five came in. On his cheek was a two-inch scar, and I got the impression that he had taken a few glasses of vodka. He did not look at me as he entered the room, but went straight to Nina, saying: 'What are you doing here?' Then he went up behind her and put his hands over her breasts, saying: 'I'm cold — let me have a warm.' Nina broke away from him saying: 'Haven't you any manners when people are in the room?' and Sam turned and saw me and went red. I didn't like the look he gave me, but when he spoke he was friendly enough, saying he was a cab-driver and promising me that if I was a friend of the girls I could always ride with him for nothing.

He went off to wash, and Nina said: 'He looks a wild one, but he's a good-hearted chap.' She went on chattering without stopping, saying how she envied Sonia: 'She can read and write and I can't. If I get a letter I have to ask her to read it for me, and if I want to reply she has to write it, and I look such a fool.'

Just then Sonia returned. I jumped up to meet her. Her head was covered with a scarf. It had been snowing, and there was snow on the scarf. I remember even now how the flakes of snow looked like white roses on the scarf over her dark hair.

Sam returned. He had changed into trousers so tight I wondered how he ever got into them. Nobody could have bought trousers so tight, I thought; he must have pinched them. Nina must have been thinking the same thing, for she asked: 'Why don't you have your trousers altered, Sam?' but all he replied was: 'I like tight trousers. Why don't you go and give a hand in the kitchen while I talk to Moysey?'

The girls went out, and Sam produced a bottle of vodka from one coat pocket and a couple of glasses from the other, saying: 'We'll have a nice drink before they get back.' I refused politely, saying I didn't drink vodka, and this annoyed Sam. I got up and he got up, saying: 'Where are you going, friend? You don't want to drink with me?' I made excuses — I wasn't eighteen yet, I was too young to be drinking vodka — and Sam relapsed into muttering to himself and went off. I heard him telling Sonia she might at least have brought a man to the house, not a boy. 'I'll find you a man for a good husband,' he said. The mother returned, apologizing for her son: 'I want him to get used to people who don't like the bottle,' she said. Poor woman, she had to be apologizing again in a moment, for there was the sound of another horse's hooves in the yard, and 'That will be my husband,' she said. 'He's rough and he's probably drunk, but he won't touch you.'

'Why me?' I said. 'Why not let me go home?' but again she said: 'I want him to see that not everybody gets drunk,' and went to the door.

Sonia's father was a tall man; he must have been about sixty, and his hair was going white. His clothes were well patched, and he spoke in broken Russian. As he clutched a chair to place it next to me I noticed his knuckles were all swollen, and his breath smelt of vodka, and almost the first thing he did after I'd been introduced to him was to call to his wife: 'Hilda, fetch another bottle of vodka, I want to get more friendly with Moysey.' To me he said: 'Hallo, boy. My wife tells me I've got to be careful — what, are you a member of the royal family?'

Sonia's mother was very slow in bringing him his vodka, but she had to bring it in the end, and I saw from the label that it was ninety per cent proof. I told him I wasn't drinking; he filled himself a glass, saying, 'If you don't drink you're not my friend,' and swallowed it down in one go. It didn't seem to bother him, and I thought to myself his insides must be made of iron. 'Without this, I could not live,' he said.

When it came to the meal time, the old man, Sam and I sat at the table with Nina, and Sonia and her mother served the food. It was an embarrassing meal. The old man couldn't wait and, without washing his hands, proceeded to cut up the bread. He did not even keep the Jewish custom of saying his prayers before beginning to eat. He and Sam filled their plates, and they ate like pigs. Nina ate very slowly, her eyes on me. The old man got up, went out and brought in two bottles of lemonade with some glasses, and sat down again, saying to me: 'You can't get drunk on this, son.' I thanked him, and poured out lemonade for the women and for myself. I sat there, embarrassed because Sonia and her mother were embarrassed, and thought about the two men. They were from a different world; they couldn't understand me and I couldn't understand them. I looked round and I wondered how Sonia, with her sad brown eyes, and her mother so thin and tired-looking, fitted in with them. It was a relief when I could get up from the table, and soon afterwards go out with the father to help water his horses. Though I didn't work with horses any more I hadn't lost my love of them.

Back indoors I thanked them all for a wonderful evening, and went out into the cold, snowy street. Sam had his cab waiting to drive me home; he asked me to wait for a minute and went into the house, bringing Sonia out. He said she wanted to come for a ride. She climbed into the cab and I followed, and then Sam jumped up on to his driver's seat and away we went.

We trotted through the dark snowy streets, and all the way Sonia was saying how nice it would be if I would write to her from Constantinograd when I returned there, letters which she could show her friend Nina . . . though what good that would be to Nina, who couldn't read, I didn't know. I said that I would have written to her in any case, to thank her; but I added carefully that they were all taking too much notice of me and that I wouldn't be able to continue corresponding because I didn't have much time for girls yet.

6*

'You are jumping to conclusions,' said Sonia, quickly. 'I assure you I don't think anything about your friendship with me.' Perhaps she didn't, but Sam did. When we reached Herscho and Hannah's house I shook hands with him and thanked him, and turned to say goodbye to Sonia, when he said: 'Why don't you kiss her good night?' but we were both too shy for that, and I hurried in. As I climbed the stairs I heard the cab wheel round and the sound of hooves galloping away.

Girls — or their match-making parents — were really giving me a lot of trouble in those days. There was Usher, there was Sonia; and there was Marusa Konev, too. The Konevs were Herscho and Hannah's landlords; they lived in a splendid bungalow at the end of the street where their houses were, and I met them at Hannah's insistence — Hannah was forever showing me off to people now that I was grown up and doing well. I used to think, how nice it would have been if I had been able to feel it was a real mother's love and pride, but I knew it wasn't. I liked the Konevs; they were polite and friendly, and Mr Konev particularly took an interest in me and seemed impressed by the way I was getting on in Habinski's business. I liked their house, beautifully furnished, with an *electric* door bell and a uniformed maid; the bowls of fruit and nuts and sweets always on the table; and, best of all, a library; I could have spent days in that library. And it is only honest to say that I realized their daughter Marusa, although she was only fifteen, was very beautiful. I couldn't understand why a girl like that should want to talk to a chap like me, somebody without parents who had come from nowhere. But she did.

The Konevs had invited me to supper one evening while I was staying with Herscho and Hannah; I'd gone, and somehow found myself accepting that I ought to invite Marusa to the theatre. I did it very formally and correctly, writing to them and getting a reply back from Marusa, brought round by the Konev's maid, saying, 'Dear Sir, My parents have given me permission to go with you to the theatre.' We were formal in those days.

Herscho and Hannah didn't approve. Hannah liked showing me off, but she didn't like it when anyone else really took a lot of notice of me; and she felt I ought to keep to people of my own station in life. Herscho said: 'Moysey, you don't want to mix with these rich people. Mix with our own class of people — you'll be better off because they'll look up to you.' And Hannah, when she saw the note from the Konevs, sniffed and said: 'They *are* trying.'

Luckily the two of them had to go off to their market stall, so I had the day to myself. I had breakfast late, then went out and bought a newspaper to see what time the play started, and went to the post office to telephone the Konevs and arrange what time to meet Marusa — I didn't like to call on them again, even though their house was only just down the street. With this done I returned home, read a book until lunch time, cooked myself some potatoes and an egg, and then read again — time goes slowly when you've nothing to do.

I cleaned all my shoes and brushed my clothes, washed myself again, put on my good suit, looked at all my ties and tried them all on to see which matched the suit best. If anyone had seen me they would have asked if I was going to meet a princess. The only thing that disappointed me was that when I put on my overcoat I realized that though it was clean it was old. I was a bit worried about what Marusa would think of that; she was rich and used to having everything just right. She might even say she didn't want to go out with someone in an old overcoat. That would upset me terribly — not because of her, I told myself, but because of the principle of it. Then I had another thought; perhaps her parents really were thinking of finding a husband for her while she was young, as Hannah had suggested. If that was the case I'd have to tell them I was never going to get married. At the same time, I thought, it looked as if when my turn for marriage came there would be plenty of fish in the sea; and with that I picked up my stick and set off. It was one of those days when life felt worth living, provided you didn't think too much about shabby overcoats.

I was twenty minutes early but it was too cold to wait around outside, and I pressed the bell and the maid showed me in. In a few minutes Marusa came in. I'd never seen her dressed like this before. If my fussing with the ties had made anybody think I was

going to meet a princess, then they would have thought Marusa was
off to meet the czar. She walked over to me, her dress swaying, and
I said, 'Good afternoon, Mademoiselle,' and was rebuked prettily
for being so formal. 'It would seem funny if you called me Mademoiselle Marusa and I called you Mr Moysey in the theatre,' she
said. She wrapped herself against the cold, and we set out; I
striding along with my stick, with Marusa's arm in mine, and old
overcoats forgotten. She spent the time questioning me, mainly
about Usher my cousin, with whom she had seen me going about. I
said: 'She's my cousin and much older than me, and it's my duty
to go out with her because she's my relation,' which didn't seem to
satisfy Marusa but at least stopped the questions.

In the theatre she took off her coat and snuggled up to me like a
kitten with her arm still in mine; she kept her eyes on the stage but
she couldn't stop talking, until a woman behind us asked her to
keep quiet. Marusa didn't like that, and expected me to turn round
and defend her, and when I wouldn't she declared I was frightened;
but when I told her to keep her mind on the play and do her talking
afterwards she watched in silence except when people clapped and
called for encores.

When the show was over, and I was helping her into her coat, she
said she wanted me to take her for coffee somewhere. I said her
parents would be worried if we didn't get home, but she said: 'Don't
worry, if you can't afford to pay I have a few rubles.' After an insult
like that, of course, I couldn't refuse to take her. I wonder how it is
that girls know such things at such an early age. Marusa had it all
worked out; she knew precisely where to go to; a Greek place. A
waiter met us at the door and bowed us to a good seat, not far from
the band. In fact, I was worried; I didn't know what the prices
were in a place like this and I was frightened to order; it was a place
for people like Marusa's parents, not for me. I told Marusa so, and
asked her to come away, but while we were arguing a waiter arrived
and Marusa ordered some food and coffee, so that was that. I asked
her if the food was kosher, and she said: 'Everything is kosher to me
today, I feel so happy.' Then the band began to play, and she got
up and pulled me up, to dance. I couldn't dance, and told her so,

and that dampened her mood a bit, but all the same it was a quarter to twelve when we left the café, and Marusa wouldn't have left then if I hadn't picked up her coat and handed it to her. She snatched the bill the waiter brought, but I was quicker at the pay desk, putting a ten ruble note into the cashier's hand, and then we went outside into the snow and the darkness. Marusa said she felt very cold, and put her arm in mine; then she said, 'Hold me tighter or I'll fall in the snow.' And that way we walked all the way home; it must have been one o'clock before we got there. The house was dark — there wasn't a light to be seen anywhere. I took her to the door and said goodnight. 'To make the evening complete, you should kiss me,' said Marusa, and I kissed her politely on the cheek. 'That's not a kiss — haven't you ever kissed a girl before?' she said, and then, 'No? Well, I'll show you,' and she put her arms round my neck and kissed me hard on the mouth. When she let me go she asked: 'Did you enjoy that?', and I said: 'I don't know — I'll tell you next time,' and quickly pressed the bell-push. Marusa's mother came to the door, and I apologized hastily for bringing Marusa home so late, and said good night. At Herscho's house I found the key where they always left it, and crept upstairs and into bed. On the whole, I thought, it was a good thing I was going back to Habinski's the next day.

Next day, as I was packing my case, there was a knocking on the door and there was Usher, determined to see me off to the boat. She wanted to know if I'd booked a cab for the journey to the landing stage, and would not let me find one for myself but went off to find one for me. When she returned with it I said goodbye to Herscho and Hannah, ran down the stairs and piled my cases on top of the cab and climbed in. Usher followed me. I wanted to settle down and read a book, but she wasn't having that: 'You are going away for a whole year and you've the cheek to read!' she said. She wanted to know all about the Konevs and Marusa. 'She is younger than me but bigger — she looks like a big cow,' she said, and then: 'Were her kisses exciting?'

I told her not to worry, that I had no romantic intentions towards Marusa; and this pleased Usher. But when I went on to say, 'By the time my turn comes to get married you'll both be well and truly married with families,' that didn't go down so well.

At the boat station Usher wanted the cab to wait and take her back into town; the driver said he had another journey to make and refused to wait, although he told her if she liked to leave with him now he wouldn't charge her for the return trip. I told her there was no point in waiting, and after a little persuasion from the two of us she climbed in and I watched the cab drive away. It was just in time, for as I turned away another cab clattered up, and out got Marusa, calling my name. She wanted to see me off too, 'And I want you to stand and wave to me,' she said.

Marusa really was very beautiful, and I couldn't help taking her in my arms and embracing her, and whispering words of love; and she looked into my eyes and whispered beautiful words back.

We were so engrossed that we didn't hear the boat come in; we didn't hear anything until the 'passengers aboard' bell rang; and even then we didn't move until the second bell went, and I had to kiss her once more and run for the gangplank just as the two sailors were about to move it away. In a minute the ropes were cast off and the steamer pulling away from the shore, while I stood on the cold empty upper deck and waved and waved to Marusa until she disappeared from sight.

It was a very good thing I was going back to work for a whole year.

XV. THE MISSING BOOK-KEEPER

I spent the long boat journey reading and talking with a group of students who were travelling further on; they made tea over a little benzine stove and shared tea and slices of cake between us. The boat reached the Verchneprovsk landing stage very early in the morning, and a cab dropped me at Habinski's big house on the hill at six o'clock. Most of the household were asleep, and a sleepy maid let me in and lit the samovar. While she was getting some breakfast the Guvnor's driver came stamping in from the snow, cracking jokes about my looking a great gentleman these days. They were friendly people, the maids and drivers, and we talked and drank glasses of tea and I felt good and warm in the kitchen with them.

The driver told me that the Guvnor and his wife were worried over the book-keeper they'd sent to take my place in Constantino-grad while I was on holiday. The man didn't seem to be grasp-ing his work at all, and didn't seem happy at being sent to other towns; the Guvnor was afraid he might give up and leave, the driver said.

I asked him how he knew this, for he was a Russian and couldn't speak Yiddish, while the Guvnor and his wife, of course, would not be discussing business in Russian, certainly not in front of a driver.

He said: 'You forget, Moysey, I've been with Habinski for nine years. I can't hold a conversation with anyone in Yiddish but I can understand every word of it by now. I heard all this one night when I was driving them to the Jewish theatre . . . and I heard them say-ing how important you were to their trade.'

I'd finished one breakfast when the Guvnor appeared; he said his first 'Good morning' under his nose in the old way, but then he warmed up and said, 'Come on, Moysey, and have some tea with me,' and I followed him into the dining room. His young daughter followed us in; she was growing up now and in school uniform, so I said, 'Good morning, Mademoiselle.' They sat having breakfast while I drank another glass of tea with them; through the window I could see the driver standing waiting, with one horse harnessed to the sledge to take the daughter to school. She kissed her father good-bye and said, 'Goodbye, Moysey,' and hurried off.

The Guvnor turned to me. 'I want you to go back to Constantinograd by the eleven-thirty train,' he said. 'Here are two letters, one for the book-keeper there, one for the bank manager. Settle all the details completely before you send the book-keeper back; I don't want you writing worrying me about anything after he has returned.'

It seemed there was a girl who usually wrote the Guvnor's letters for him now looking after the books at the house, but Habinski needed the book-keeper back. The man was staying at the Hotel Moskva, where I had stayed when I first went to the town, and he wouldn't be expecting me because the Guvnor hadn't told him when I would be returning.

I had some hours before the train left, so I went to see the workers in the granary. The first one to spot me called out: 'Careful, chaps, Baron Stocklinsky is here!' but they all shook hands, very friendly, and asked how I was getting on. All except one; old Kovalevsky. He stood in the door of his department, never moving. I went up to him and asked how his family was faring, and he complained: 'Not very good,' and didn't seem to cheer up until I said I was leaving on the eleven-thirty train; at that relief spread over his face. It didn't spread over mine, because it seemed to me his happiness might have something to do with my thousand rubles that he was supposed to be looking after. But I couldn't stop, because I wanted to see Mama Marcovsky again before I left. 'You like that woman, don't you?' said old Kovalevsky, and when I said, 'I love her,' he said: 'And I think she loves you too.' And if I'd had any doubts about that, they would not have lasted long when I got to Mama's house. I'd had a lot of 'mothers', but the Marcovskys — they were my real family.

I was back at Habinski's before eleven, and the Guvnor's driver was waiting to take me to the station. He helped me with my case, and we drove off, talking all the way. I tried to tip him a twenty kopeck silver coin when we got there, but he wouldn't take it, so I dropped it in the sledge and made off to get my ticket.

At Constantinograd the grain-dealers were all round the train when I got out. One of them, Vaskevich, a rich man, took my biggest case while I handled the smaller ones. He greeted me like a long-lost friend, took me to have tea and pastries and asked how I'd enjoyed my holiday. Then I asked him how he was getting on with the man Habinski had sent in my place.

'That chap's no good for anything,' he said. 'He doesn't even bother to come and meet the trains — you can see, even now he's not here, and he should be. He's not liked by the other dealers. When he does come along he brings a woman with him, and she sits in the corner and waits for him. They leave together early — in time for when the theatre starts.'

I picked up my cases to go and find a cab, but Vaskevich offered me a lift in his sledge. We went out of the station, and his driver spotted us and ran up to take the cases.

I left my bags at my lodgings, promising Vaskevich I'd see him that evening when all the dealers got together, and then set off for the Hotel Moskva.

'Mr Hersch Lumsky?' said the manager. 'He has a double room — he has a woman with him. I've instructions to notify him first before I bring anyone up to him.' He went off to inquire, and presently showed me up. A woman came to the door, and called Lumsky, who seemed friendly enough, though he didn't invite me in; and when I said it was time to set off for the bourse he picked up a briefcase and came with me.

At the bourse the buyers crowded round. 'Where's your wife, Lumsky?' one asked. 'My wife? What, on my pay!' said Lumsky. 'I can hardly keep myself, let alone a wife!'

A postman came through the crowd calling 'Mr Lumsky,' and handed him a telegram. Lumsky opened it and said: 'No news, only that I'm to report back to head office. Mr Stocklinsky here takes over now.' A voice somewhere shouted, 'Bravo!'

Lumsky opened the briefcase, took out some personal papers and then gave the case to me. Then he left, to go and pack, he said.

I didn't wait long after he'd gone; there were no instructions for me and no business to be done. When I got back to my room I started looking through the papers in the briefcase. They didn't seem to be in very correct form, but I got so fed up with sorting them out that I decided to do it next day.

I was dressing next morning when the postman arrived with a telegram giving me the day's grain prices. He said he had been to the hotel for Lumsky first, but found Lumsky wasn't there any more. I was rather surprised by this, and wondered if anything was wrong, that Lumsky should go without saying goodbye to me. But the Guvnor would be able to sort it out when Lumsky returned to him with the accounts.

On the way to the bourse I called at the hotel again, to see if Lumsky had left any papers for me: there really wasn't enough in the briefcase to get everything straight. The manager took me up to his room, empty now. There were a lot of papers on the floor, but none of any use. The only other thing Lumsky had left, by accident I suppose, was an envelope with six photographs of him in it. I took them, saying I would send them back to him at Habinski's, and set off for the station. On the way a sledge passed me and stopped; Vaskevich leaned out and offered me a lift. I explained that I had been to the hotel looking for papers that Lumsky should have left, and he spent the rest of the journey telling me about Lumsky and the woman he was always with.

We arrived at the same time as the train, and for a while there was a rush of business. When it had calmed down, another grain-dealer, Malenkof, took me aside and, over glasses of tea in the first-class waiting room, asked me what had happened to Lumsky. I said he had gone back to Verchneprovsk, and asked what was the matter.

'I sold him three trucks of wheat; the papers were all filled in and he was supposed to bring me the money for them,' said Malenkof. 'Two thousand nine hundred rubles . . .'

I asked what rate Lumsky had offered, and he said: 'One ruble fifteen kopecks a pood.' That was impossible; no buyer could have seriously offered that amount, for wheat had been down to one ruble ten kopecks for the last two weeks, and I told Malenkof so.

'He was supposed to pay me two thousand nine hundred rubles now, and the rest when the wheat had been tested in Nikolaev,' said Malenkof. 'I have a copy contract from him and he has the original.'

I told him not to worry; I would write to Habinski about it straight away, and the Guvnor would sort it out. 'It's all right for you to tell me not to worry, but I depend on that money to carry on my trade,' said Malenkof and walked off very dejected and miserable.

I took a sledge to the post office straight away and telegraphed Habinski with details of what I had bought, and then went to my lodgings to write a letter explaining about the money Lumsky owed to Malenkof. Then I went on to the bank, to ask the manager about the transaction. He showed me the receipt Lumsky had received for the truckloads of Malenkof's wheat, on the strength of which he had drawn out the 2,900 rubles. I thought to myself, how could a man do a thing like that? There was bound to be a lot of trouble, and it would be bad for the reputation of the firm. I had put a few rubles on my expenses from time to time, but to swindle someone was different. And how would Lumsky hope to get away with it?

I got the answer to that when I reached my lodgings again. Liza handed me a telegram from Habinski. It began with the string of code figures which represented prices, and ended: 'Send Lumsky back. His services needed.' When I read that I realized that Lumsky could not have returned to Verchneprovsk, and that meant he must have run away.

Liza saw from my face that something was wrong, and I explained. She tried to cheer me up, saying it wasn't my worry but I did worry — it had happened in my territory.

That evening at the club where all the dealers met, everyone seemed to be talking about poor Malenkof and the way Habinski's man had made off with his money. I told them not to worry; Habinski was rich enough to look after such things, and was well insured anyway. When Malenkof came in he blamed it on to me: 'Why did you have to go away and your guvnor send down a swindler to work for him?' It seemed that Lumsky had become very friendly with Malenkof in the short time he had been there; Malenkof had a daughter and Lumsky had come calling on her — I suppose they hadn't known about the woman Lumsky was keeping at the Moskva hotel all the time.

I said: 'As far as that goes, you don't really know me. I might swindle you one day — though it would have to be for a great deal more than two thousand rubles. But when a chap comes to your house and is sweet to your daughter you don't have to trust him with all your money. When you've a lot more money to come I'll come round to your house and make love to your daughter and see if I can relieve you of it.'

That seemed to cheer him up, for Malenkof said: 'For you, I'll give my life, and you can have my daughter as well. Now, I've a wagonload of wheat. Will you buy?' So I fixed the deal with him, and he invited me to his house to meet his daughter.

Lumsky's swindle seemed to be the talk everywhere. Back at my lodgings Lev and Liza wanted to know about it. 'How do people rob one another?' said Lev. 'Don't you think you can see if someone is trying to swindle you?'

I'd been thinking about this, and I said: 'You probably never see it right away, but you find out later. People like Habinski, rich people like him, are always robbing the public, and nobody does anything about that.'

'How do you make that out?' said Lev, and I explained: 'My Guvnor has more than twenty people working for him. They're all married with children. What's their salary? So little that they have to come to work with clothes all patched and shoes all worn . . . because the Guvnor robs them by not paying enough for a decent living. I heard one of them asking for a rise because his wife was going to have another child, and what answer did Habinski give him? "I'm not keeping your children. You must carry on or find another job." Altogether we make six or seven hundred rubles a month for the Guvnor. He's got three children, and every year the missus takes them away for a month's holiday. The working people have to take their children on the lake for a couple of hours — that's their holiday. They work and slave to make Habinski rich, but they're as poor as the night.'

Lev said: 'You must be a Communist.'

I said: 'I don't understand politics. All I know is, if the poor are making money for the rich when they themselves don't have enough to eat, that's robbery just as much as what Lumsky's done.'

'That sort of thing has been going on for years and always will,' said Lev.

I disagreed with him. I said I was sure it wouldn't be long before the workers would get together to stop such exploitation; it might take twenty or thirty years but the rich man would one day have to share the profits he made.

Lev said: 'It's all right you talking. You are not a married man.'

That afternoon I changed into my best suit and hired a sledge to take me to Malenkof's house. Mr Malenkof opened the door, and took my coat, and showed me into the dining room where he introduced me to his wife. She was short and plump like most Jewish women, dressed in her Sabbath best, her hair tied up in a scarf. She had big hands with fat fingers, and her bust looked as if it was padded with wadding.

On the table there were a lot of glasses and saucers made from glass, there were biscuits and a home-made cake, a large box of chocolates with a pair of sweet tongs on top of it, and different kinds of nuts. There was a ring at the door and Malenkof went to open it. I could hear him shouting, 'Jacob, you also come late?' and 'Dora, explain why you're so late!' Then he brought them in, and introduced them to me as his wife's sister and his brother-in-law. He didn't have to tell me the woman was his wife's sister; she looked so much like her, though younger. The husband was very thin and bony. We all sat round the table for tea, and a maid brought in the samovar and placed it in front of Mrs Malenkof.

Glancing round, I noticed how expensively furnished the room was; there were beautiful curtains, and on the wall a full-size portrait of a young girl. Mr Malenkof saw me looking at it, and explained that it was his daughter when she was fourteen.

Mr Malenkof and Jacob were talking business, and they spoke in thousands, not hundreds—it seemed that Malenkof was not so poor. I suppose Lumsky's theft bothered him more for the harm it had done to his prestige as an astute business man than for the actual loss of the money. Mrs Malenkof poured out the tea and gave me the first glass, and began chaffing me, the way everyone did, about my age. Malenkof butted in, saying: 'If that young boy had not gone on holiday that swindler his guvnor sent in his place would never have wormed his way into my house and into my daughter's heart, and I would not have been swindled out of my money. My daughter was very fond of him and now we've found out he is a married man with a child, and he's run away with a different woman.'

About an hour after I arrived there was another ring at the door. Malenkof went to open it and returned with a good-looking girl, his daughter Manya. She greeted her aunt and uncle with a kiss and then her father introduced me. She gave me her hand and I said, 'Make no mistakes, I am a stranger.' She said, 'Don't worry; I know who to kiss.'

I looked at her, and thought, 'She isn't a girl to make mistakes with.' She was a tall, hefty-looking girl. With one swipe she could kill a man. I thought I was tall but she was a bit taller, and to get round her waist I would need another pair of hands. She dropped into a chair, and I thought it was going to collapse under her. Only now did I realize why Malenkof had trusted Lumsky: he wanted to find a son-in-law badly. He had told me Manya was nineteen, but I guessed she was at least twenty-nine. Her mother poured her a glass of tea, and Manya swallowed it in one moment, and came up for more.

When the time was coming up to six o'clock I wanted to get out, but Malenkof said, 'Don't go yet,' and the maid came running in and out, clearing the table and producing vodka and lemonade. Malenkof began filling up with vodka, and although I didn't usually drink vodka I got some down me. My glass was filled up again and I drank 'to the engagement of Manya and may it be soon'.

The chatting and drinking went on until seven o'clock, and then it was time to eat again. Manya started getting up from her chair, with some difficulty. When Mrs Malenkof began dishing out portions Manya took the first plate and brought it to me. She bent down to put the plate down in front of me, and I thought her breasts were going to jump out at me, they seemed to be leaving her blouse behind. When supper was over, the aunt and uncle started to get dressed ready for home, and I got up to find my coat too, but Malenkof said, 'They have to go as they have left a small child at home. For you, it is too early. It is only eight-thirty.' I did not like the way he stopped me but I was curious to know why he wanted me to stay.

Presently Manya returned to the room, dressed in a different suit of very good cloth. She sat opposite me and started asking me questions like all the other girls — where had I been and what plays had I seen? When I told her about the play where a Jewish girl married a Christian, she said, 'That is very sad,' and declared she would never allow a thing like that. I said, 'It would be much better if people mixed a bit more. A Jewish girl and a Christian girl are just the same.'

She said, 'You must be a Communist' — the second time that had been said to me in one day. Manya's mother got up from her chair and said goodnight to me, and asked me to come again, and went off to bed.

Manya said, 'Someone likes you.' I told her that all women liked me, because I wasn't interested in girls — 'I am too young,' I told her.

She said, 'It is very nice for young people to fall in love. It is better than falling in love when you are old.' Mr Malenkof said, 'I have heard this story before, so I am going to bed. Goodnight, Moysey. Come again,' and he went, too. When he had gone, Manya came and sat next to me. I said, 'It is getting late.' But she said, 'My people have gone to bed and it does not matter what time you go home,' and moved closer to me. I could feel the warmth of her thigh close to mine. I rose, saying I was not comfortable and walked over to the sofa where her father had been sitting. But this was worse; she came over to me and sat very nearly on top of me. She had taken her jacket off, and her blouse was so low it revealed almost all of her bosom. I would be telling a lie if I said that I did not enjoy looking at her. 'Now we have plenty of time to talk,' she said.

I struggled to my feet again, saying: 'It's too hot in here. I must be getting off home.'

'Take your jacket off,' said Manya. I was going to say, 'I can't in front of a lady,' but before I knew what had happened, she had her hand on my jacket and pulled it off. As I stood up to straighten myself, she grabbed me round the waist and started kissing me. I thought, 'No wonder Lumsky ran away.'

It was getting on for eleven-thirty when I finally got my jacket back to go home. 'Give me one more kiss and then I will give you your coat,' she said, and grabbed me so hard I thought I should be suffocated. She opened the door and the snow was pelting down, but I heard her mother call, 'Manya, has Moysey gone home yet?' and I said loudly, so that her mother would hear, 'Goodnight, Miss Malenkof,' and plunged out into the snow. There was no sign of any sledges around so I had to walk all the way home.

Next morning Lev and Liza wanted to know how I had enjoyed myself. I said, 'It was a very nice evening. They only had one daughter, but she is big enough for two. If she grows any more, her father will have to widen the doors.'

'Don't worry,' said Lev. 'A woman like that would keep you warm in the winter.'

It was too early for me to meet the Guvnor, so I went back to my room and tidied up my clothes. Then I took a slow walk to the station. I took my stick with me as the roads were still bad from the previous night's snow. As I got near to the station I could hear the blast of the train in the distance.

On the platform I saw Habinski alighting from one of the carriages. His black beard looked thicker than ever. If he could only have been turned upside down, you could have swept the snow away with him. He handed me a small case and we went out of the station to board a sledge which took us to the hotel Moskva. On the way he did not have much to say but when we arrived at the hotel, he told me that he had had a talk with Lumsky's father, a much respected man, who had been most distressed at what his son had done. Habinski had notified the police, who had circulated a description of Lumsky to the police headquarters of all the neighbouring towns. The Guvnor said he had to do this to show the insurance company he was going to do his best to find Lumsky. He had also advertised in the papers for information leading to Lumsky's capture, offering five hundred rubles reward. He said he thought Lumsky was still in the country, hiding somewhere. The police had told him swindlers often lay low in the same place for a few months, until the hue and cry had died down.

Then the Guvnor said: 'You don't do anything on Saturday. You could do something for me and also for yourself — you could earn five hundred rubles. Go to a second-hand shop and buy yourself an old pair of trousers and a jacket and some old boots like the peasants wear. Get yourself an old cap. Blacken your face and make out you are a coalman. Wander around all day in these rough cafés and mix with the customers. In the evening when you have some spare time, you could go round looking for information: you might get a clue to where Lumsky is hiding. Mix with a few girls, offer to pay for their tea. Make friends with one of the women and see what you can find out. Lumsky always liked women. Someone might have known him. But,' said the Guvnor, 'avoid actual fighting with anyone as you might get badly hurt and I don't want that to happen.'

I tried my best to get out of it. 'I don't want to lose my teeth at my age,' I said.

'You can look after yourself,' said Habinski. 'You are big enough. How long would it take you to make five hundred rubles any other way?'

I said, 'I don't want to be a cripple for life, and perhaps all for nothing.'

'Well,' said Habinski, 'see — I will pay all your expenses in buying tea and fares. And don't forget he might have had his moustache shaved off.' And that seemed to be that.

The Guvnor said he was tired from the journey, so he wouldn't go with me to meet the train at three o'clock, but he took out a paper and showed me some grain prices, and asked if I could buy him twelve wagonloads of rye. I told him I thought there was plenty about, and left him to have his lunch and a doze at the hotel, while

I returned to my lodgings, bolted my lunch and rushed off to the station. I wanted to buy the rye and surprise him with how quickly I could get it.

I met the train and found I could only buy five wagonloads of rye, but I did manage to get them for two kopecks a pood cheaper than the price Habinski had listed. I was happy because I had saved him eighteen rubles a wagon. So he had made ninety rubles in all, before he had even seen it. No wonder people like this get rich and could afford to say, 'I'll pay all expenses.' I wondered if I would ever be in that position, but dismissed the thought from my mind; I was very young and he was an old man and had been years at the trade.

That night I got a sledge and met the Guvnor at his hotel. We drove out to see the bank manager, and it was now arranged that in future the bank could give me up to five hundred rubles in cash, but should not pay me on the grain dockets. If this had been arranged before, the trouble would not have arisen with Lumsky. After we had finished talking, the Guvnor gave a big box of cigars to the bank manager, and we took a sledge straight to the bourse.

We arrived at about seven-thirty, and it was already full of people. Malenkof saw us come in, and I introduced him to Habinski, who assured him that he would not lose one kopeck of the money Lumsky had run off with. 'These insurance companies work very slowly, but if it takes more than three months I will see that you get interest on it,' he said. My Guvnor was determined to keep his good name at all costs. He spoke to one or two people he recognized, while I went off to mix with the dealers. I came across a man, Krotnik, who had ten wagonloads of rye to sell, and introduced him to Habinski, who clinched the deal there and then, and went on to buy more from other dealers.

When we had finished business, the Guvnor decided to walk back to his hotel but I didn't want to walk and put down the expense of a sledge when I got back to my room.

I told Lev and Liza the Guvnor's idea that I should go looking for the runaway Lumsky. He said: 'You know you are letting yourself in for a dangerous game. When is it to start?'

I told him I would wait to see Habinski off on his train in the morning and then see if I could get any suitable clothes in the market. And that I did.

I went round the market and picked up some very old clothes and a pair of high boots. I took them home and dressed up, making the old clothes look worse by tearing bits out of the jacket and tearing the peak off my cap. I dirtied my hands and face a bit, and then I went out to show Lev and Liza. When their little girl saw me, she fled screaming to her mother, so I judged I must be a success; Liza said I looked a real ruffian. So I decided to set out and try my luck. I went into one or two places and showed the man behind the counter the photograph of Lumsky; they would ask, 'What did he do?' and I would say, 'He ran away with my girl.' In one of the shops the manager said he had not seen him but called his assistants and asked them. One of them said, 'He looks like a Jew-boy.' I had been speaking in Russian, and I said, 'I think he is, but my girl is not. Just you wait until I find him.' But nobody remembered having seen Lumsky.

Well, I went on like this for two or three weeks. It was a lot of trouble to keep making myself up and then changing twice a day, and I thought I had made a fool of myself long enough. Every café I visited cost me three or four rubles for food and drink, and if I got talking to a girl as Habinski suggested it cost me double. Lev encouraged me to go on, but I thought I was neglecting my real business while I toured the town questioning people, and after another couple of months I wrote to the Guvnor telling him it was impossible to find Lumsky, and that playing detective was very costly.

The Guvnor wrote back saying I was very quick at giving up, and if he was paying, what was I worrying about expenses for? He wrote: 'I will tell you when to give up. You don't want to bother with friends or girls. I will let you know when the time is ripe for you to go with girls. I have a girl lined up for you when the time comes.'

It was now April, and the snow seemed to be clearing up, sledges were disappearing from the streets and it was not quite so cold. I was a bit miserable to think that the Guvnor expected me to give him all my time, now that the weather was better, because I'd have liked a weekend off from time to time. Instead he demanded my pleasure time and thought he could dictate to me when I should have a girl. I didn't know why he worried about Lumsky anyway, especially as he was insured. The money was only a flea bite to Habinski — but he plainly didn't like being fleabitten. And I had a pretty good idea of the girl he had in mind for me — his niece, who was ten years older than me. 'What does he think I am going to take — an old woman?' I thought. But I went on looking for Lumsky, even trying a new line, going an hour early to meet the train, and nosing around the third-class waiting rooms to see if I could find any trace of him. But I couldn't dress in my old clothes if I was to go on to do grain deals afterwards, and I got nowhere with my questions. Perhaps the third-class passengers would not talk to me because I was too well dressed for them.

I was still looking after the business very well, in my opinion. I got telegrams every day, telling me what to buy and the kind of grain the Guvnor wanted, and in the evening my time was occupied by entering details of all the sales in the books. When I had taken care of everything, I sometimes visited the theatre, but I did not go to dances or out with girls. And all the time I was haunted by the idea of Lumsky, and the five hundred rubles reward Habinski offered. That swindler, he filled up my leisure time, he interrupted my sleep, he made his way into my dreams. And even when I was at the bourse, he would interfere; I would be trying to bargain and would forget what I was saying while my eyes wandered, looking out for Lumsky.

One Saturday morning, Lev brought me a letter. 'By the looks of that printed envelope, it is from your Guvnor,' he said. I was rather surprised because I didn't get letters from the Guvnor often. The letter was typed, and, sitting at the breakfast table, I read it aloud to Lev and Liza. It said:

'These few wagonloads of grain you buy a child could do as well, after it had been shown how a few times. I do not think you are putting your knowledge to the best ability. You always seem to want me to tell you what to do. So, I am going to tell you. When you meet the train at eleven o'clock, see to your business and then board the train and travel on to the next station. See if you can do more business and buy more grain there. Carry on like this until you reach the end of the line. It does not matter if you don't return the same day as long as you do business for me. If you can't manage to buy a hundred railway trucks of grain a week, you will have to leave Constantinograd and come back for I shall have to close up that department. There are half a dozen firms buying grain and according to them, it is not difficult to buy a hundred loads a week. I have better prices than them, so if you cannot do this, I am afraid I shall have to dispense with your services. I know, however, you are capable of doing the job.' Signed: E. Habinski.

I was very upset about this letter; if I had been neglecting Habinski's business it was to try to find Lumsky for him. I told Lev and Liza that I was going to forget about this letter and go and have a look round at Poltava, the capital of the area, and see what jobs were going there in case I got the sack. I had been told that in Poltava there were good opportunities. And there was another attraction — it was said there were automobiles which could be hired for riding in. So I decided to have a day out in Poltava; I packed a small case and off I went.

Poltava was a wonderful town. I tried my best to see as many different places as I could. I even went up to the owners of the automobiles to see if I could have a ride in one. They wanted three rubles, a lot of money, but I thought, 'Why should I deprive myself?' and jumped in, telling the driver to take me to the zoological gardens. I had never been to a zoo before. It did not take ten minutes to get there, and when I said it wasn't far for three rubles, the driver agreed to take only a ruble and a half.

I spent a long time wandering through the park where all the different animals were, and it was only when I came across a big teashop that I realized I was hungry. What a price everything was! I ordered two sausages and boiled potatoes and after that boiled fruit, and the meal set me back one ruble seventy kopecks. It was a good job that they did not charge for bread.

Although I had made up my mind not to worry about Habinski's letter, I could not help thinking about it. I would have liked to have stayed in Poltava for a few days but when I thought of the letter and the expense, I took the train back to Constantinograd, arriving back at my lodgings just in time for supper.

On Sunday morning, I went to meet the train. I bought several trucks of grain and then I boarded the train, following the Guvnor's advice. I never took a ticket; the conductors all knew me and I tipped them well. At the first station, I left the train and went into a few grain-dealers' shops, told them where I came from, who I worked for, and left my name. Then I went back to the station. This is how I went along the line. In four or five days I had arranged to buy sixty railway trucks of grain, though many of the big dealers I met already sold to Habinski on their own, by telegram. With the grain I bought in Constantinograd, the amount I managed to buy was more than one hundred trucks.

I went on like this and I had no complaints from my Guvnor, and no more letters for some months. Then I received one from him asking if I was still looking for Lumsky, or whether I was afraid to blacken my face and look like a tramp. Did I forget that he had promised me five hundred rubles if I found Lumsky? 'You only have to find him, then telegraph me and I will do the rest myself.' The letter was signed: 'Written on behalf of Mr Habinski — Vera Krasilchicov, book-keeper.'

I had almost forgotten Lumsky and thought everyone else had too. If the Guvnor laid hands on Lumsky now, what hope had he of recovering the money he had stolen? And if he didn't get the money, he would probably refuse to pay the reward. I talked it over with Lev, and decided to write to the Guvnor, to get a written guarantee that he would pay the reward even if Lumsky were found penniless. And while I was thinking about money, I also wrote to old Kovalevsky, asking him for the money I lent him. He had been a good friend up till the time I entrusted him with my thousand rubles, but since then, though I had written to him I seldom got replies. I still wanted to be friends with him, and so in my letter I asked for only three hundred rubles now and the rest to be paid in another six or eight months' time. I wrote that soon I would be eighteen and I wanted to get engaged. This was not true, but it gave me an excuse for demanding the money without upsetting the old man, who, when I was thirteen or fourteen and a poor orphan, would share his tea and cake with me in the granary.

I sealed up these two letters and addressed them, and although by this time it was getting late, I started one to Sonia's family, the Brombergs. Sonia had written to me some time ago, asking if I would escort her to the great fair at Ekaterinoslav. I had had to refuse, because I couldn't take the time off from my job, but I wrote asking if I might visit her family in eight weeks' time when I should be taking my holidays. I went out and posted these letters.

Early in the morning I was up and trying to find some way of doing all the things Habinski wanted — buying grain for him and seeking Lumsky as well. I managed to find a chap to go round to the different stations and negotiate for me. Over the next three or four weeks, with his help, I was able to buy sometimes one hundred and ten, sometimes one hundred and twenty trucks of wheat as well as to go about in my old clothes making inquiries for Lumsky. This seemed too much for my Guvnor and now I got a telegram telling me to stop buying until further notice. I still had to go to the station however, for Habinski would sometimes telegraph an order for a very small amount of grain. But I had to put the chap off who was helping me, and put off customers who had wheat to sell.

I felt that something was up, and the only way I could get information was from Mama Marcovsky, so I wrote to her and asked her to find out what was going on with Habinski. At the same time, I asked her to find out about old Kovalevsky and his family — she knew I had left my thousand rubles in his care. I received her answer two weeks later. She said she hoped everything was all right with me, and that her heart ached for me. Then: 'Kovalevsky's grand-daughter got married and he gave her five hundred rubles as a dowry. Another important thing I found out, dearest, is that Habinski is planning to shut the office in Constantinograd.'

A second letter had arrived at the same time. This was from Kovalevsky. It said:

December 22, 1909

Dear Moshca,

I hope it is still all right to call you by this pet name for when I received your letter with the printed heading at the top, I could not help thinking what a great man you had become and yet you will always be Moshca to me. There were times when I gave you advice when you most needed it, and when you told me all your secrets. Now you have become very hard towards me. You demand three hundred rubles all at once — that is not the way to pay back a man when he looked after you and befriended you when you had no one. Now you have become a big man and I have become the little man. You just want to think back a few years ago, when you used to come round to me crying your eyes out and telling me that Mrs Habinski was treating you very badly. But let us come back to the money I owe you, which I am not denying. I would like to pay you twenty-five rubles every three months until I have paid all the thousand rubles back. You would not want your governor to find out where all this money is coming from. You just think it over and see what is best for you. You will collect one hundred rubles a year and nobody would know anything about it. I will send you the first payment on your agreeing to this with your letter. I am, your old friend,

J. Kovalevsky

Old Kovalevsky was sure that I would never take his IOU to the bank, but this time, I thought, he was going to be wrong because I would not wait ten years for payment. If he could give his grand-daughter a present of five hundred rubles, he could give me my own money back.

I wrote off to Mama Marcovsky again to find out if the little wool shop which Kovalevsky's wife ran in the market belonged to Kova-levsky or to his wife. I told Mama Marcovsky that if she went to the town office, for fifty kopecks the clerk would tell her who the shop belonged to. I do not know what I would have done without Mama Marcovsky: in six days she wrote back to tell me that it was only a little while since Kovalevsky made the shop over to his son-in-law, paying thirteen rubles fifty kopecks for the transfer.

I was very angry with Kovalevsky. Plainly now he was not my

friend; he was trying to rob me. I did not know much about legal matters, so I went down to the bourse that evening, and asked someone I knew what he would do if someone owed him a thousand rubles and he made over his business to a relative to avoid payment. The man reassured me; such a transaction could only be legal after three years, he said, and before that time the man owing the money was still liable.

Next morning before going to the station I went to a bank; not the one which handled Habinski's business, but another one — I did not want Habinski finding out about my personal affairs. I explained how Kovalevsky seemed to be trying to get out of paying me, and handed over the IOU. For sixty rubles the bank manager agreed to take over recovery of the debt. 'Don't worry, we'll see to it all,' he said.

The days had been passing very slowly, but now it was almost time for me to forget all about Habinski's telegrams and the grain business and go on my holidays. The next time I went to the post office, I drew out ninety rubles, and went off shopping. I bought two suits off the peg, a pair of shoes and four shirts, handkerchiefs and a pair of gloves.

This still left six hundred and forty-five rubles in my savings book, and since I wouldn't be staying much longer in Constantinograd, I transferred the account to the post office in Krukov.

Soon a letter came from the Guvnor telling me to settle up my affairs and to bring all the books back to Verchneprovsk with me for the book-keeper to check, because I wouldn't be returning to Constantinograd. I went round saying goodbye to everybody; I even took courage to say goodbye to the Malenkofs. Mr Malenkof was quite happy now because he had got all his money back through the Guvnor's insurance company. Manya was there too, bigger than ever, beautifully dressed but bulging out everywhere. I rose to greet her and when she took my hand I could hardly bear the squeezing of it. The maid brought in a meal, and while everyone was busy talking, I just watched Manya eating. I could see now why she was so fat; she ate more than anyone. She put four lumps of sugar in her tea, and she ate at one meal more than I ate all day

7

long. I felt very glad I wasn't the man who had to keep her in food.

At last the day came for me to say my last goodbyes to Lev and Liza, who had been so kind to me all the time I lived with them, and to kiss their little girl goodbye — she wouldn't be able to spoil my clean suits with her sticky fingers any more. Then I caught the train from Constantinograd to the junction at Lozovay, where I changed for Verchneprovsk.

It was good to be back in Verchneprovsk; the cab-driver recognized me and was friendly; there was Habinski's driver, an old friend, and Habinski's maid Sancha, joking and laughing as she always did. She hadn't recognized me at first — I had been away for a year — and when she did she said: 'Who would have thought it, the day you came here half starved. I thought you would have died from the cold that first winter, and you probably would if Vera and I hadn't fed you on the quiet.'

I heard the missus calling then, and went in and bade her good evening: she looked straight through me and muttered some kind of answer, before turning away and walking into another room. She hadn't changed either, except to get fatter. While I had been away these last two years, I had become more conscious of women's charms, and as I looked at Mrs Habinski she sickened me; she was so fat and out of proportion. I wondered to myself how the Guvnor could have married such a woman, but perhaps when she was young she had been different. Her daughter, who was there too, seemed to be growing into a nice-looking girl, but she also seemed to be filling out everywhere, and I hoped for her sake that she would not take after her mother.

I took my cases through to the bedroom that I occupied before, and washed, and combed my hair. I was going to join them when I remembered these people were a lot of hypocrites, but one thing they did insist on was the men wearing their skull caps, so I went back to put mine on. I went into the dining room and in a few minutes the Guvnor came in from the synagogue. He was the first person to say, 'Good evening, Moysey, how are you?' He spoke to me like man to man. 'Now everyone is here,' he said, 'we will have some supper,' and took his coat off and I hung it for him in the hall. When I came back, Habinski was sitting at the head of the table. There was no sign of the old couple, the grandparents. 'They don't live with us any more,' said the Guvnor. Boris was away too, continuing his education in Ekaterinoslav. The Guvnor filled up the glasses with wine and said a prayer over it and we all drank. Mrs Habinski couldn't miss the opportunity: 'I see you have learnt to drink since you have been away,' she said. I replied that for business purposes I had had to learn a lot of things.

The Guvnor wanted to know if I had given up looking for Lumsky, and I said I hadn't, but had asked someone in Constantinograd to keep an eye open for him while I was away. 'I'm glad you did that,' said the Guvnor, 'as I am not giving it up although the insurance company have paid out. I feel I must find that devil.'

Then he said that Kovalevsky had told him that I had found a nice girl and was going to get married. That brought Mrs Habinski butting in. 'What! He is going to get married? He can't even speak to people yet.' The Guvnor and I ignored this remark. I said: 'You ought to know me better than that. When I get to about twenty-four or twenty-five I might think about it.'

'Why tell Kovalevsky?' the Guvnor wanted to know. I told him it was a secret. He dropped it then, but when his wife and daughter had gone, saying good night, he tried again. 'Now,' said the Guvnor, 'do you mean to say it is a secret from the man who made you into a man? After all, I am the one to give you good advice.'

'I suppose you are right,' I said. 'I'll tell you, if you promise to keep it to yourself.'

'As the spirit watches over me, I will not tell anyone,' said Habinski.

I told him that two years ago I had some money saved up, and as Kovalevsky was my friend, and knew all about me, I lent him three hundred rubles and he gave me an IOU, saying that as soon as I wanted it, he would give it to me. I wanted it, so I told him as an excuse that I was getting engaged.

'Well, did he send it?' the Guvnor asked. I said, 'No, he promised to pay ten rubles a month, which would take thirty months, and that is no good to me.'

'You were always too friendly with the old man and put too much trust in him,' said Habinski. 'He is a wicked old man, and I'll tell you what has happened to your money. A few weeks ago, Kova-levsky's grand-daughter got married and the missus went to the wedding. Wine and vodka flowed like water everywhere. It was a wonderful big wedding and I heard that he'd given his grand-daughter a wedding present of five hundred rubles. I don't think you will ever get your money now, Moysey.'

Well all the same, next morning, when the Guvnor had gone to the synagogue, I went to Kovalevsky's house. Kovalevsky mastered his surprise and declared how glad he was to see me. 'Come up-stairs into my room to talk,' he said.

Once we were away from the rest of his family, Kovalevsky started to shout: 'I suppose you want your money, and I haven't got any. I can pay only little by little. If you present my IOU to a bank I won't pay you a penny. I haven't got any money in the bank. The little shop my wife works in does not belong to her. She only gets small wages.'

I knew this to be untrue, but I could not start arguing with him, an old man getting on for seventy, and I was only a youth of eighteen. I had thought that if he gave me a hundred rubles now I would stop the bank from taking proceedings, but from the way he spoke and shouted, I knew he did not mean to offer me anything. So I said to him, 'And you have just come from the synagogue,' and went down-stairs and out of the front door and walked off to see Mama Mar-covsky. She didn't expect me but there was always plenty to eat whenever I went to see her, and kisses, and a real welcome. Mama greeted me with 'My baby!' tears in her eyes, and my eyes began to get a bit watery too, until Father shouted, 'Come on, that's enough crying. Let's get some dinner.' And from then on it was eating and talking, and neighbours dropping in, like a real family, until it was time for me to return to Habinski's, pick up my bags, and catch the night boat to Kremenchug.

XVI. I PROPOSE TO SONIA

This visit to Kremenchug was very like my others; Hannah as cold-hearted as ever, though trying to hide it and then giving away her reason for pretending to be friendly by telling me a long story about the son of some neighbour of hers in the market who sent his wages to his parents every week to be looked after for him. I didn't rise to this; there didn't seem to be any purpose in quarrelling with Hannah or in trying to explain to her that I felt in duty bound to visit them during my holiday but that I didn't feel any duty to be such a fool as to trust them with my money. They had had their chance to earn my trust when I was a small boy, and hadn't taken it, and it was too late now.

Herscho was the same, too; a little older and a little shorter of breath, and a little more rambling and vague when he sat talking, and a little more ready to fall asleep. I bought a bottle of vodka for them, thinking this was a gift they would appreciate, and Hannah began by rebuking me for taking to drinking and ended by downing her share of the bottle. Herscho, at the sight of the bottle and the three small glasses, said: 'That's a very loud habit you've started,' but he had a few glasses too, and in the middle of supper he began to sing from the Hebrew service, so I guessed he was happy. Hannah seemed to be cheerful too, and so was I, yet all the time I was aware that there was no true love between us. Herscho went on singing until he fell asleep in his chair, and Hannah and I carried him into the other room and put him to bed; and then Hannah said she had a headache and thought she ought to lie down, and I saw no more of her, but got busy washing up and clearing away.

There was my cousin Usher too. Usher showed signs of being a nuisance again, as she had the year before, and from the start I found her very irritating. But in a way I was wrong to feel like that about her, for unknowingly she did me a very good turn, as you will see.

I met her the first day I got to Kremenchug, and decided that if I invited her to the theatre one evening, that would keep her happy and give me some time to visit other people I wanted to see without Usher hanging round me all the time. For a start, I wanted to meet the wealthy Konevs and their beautiful daughter Marusa again; and I intended to pay my promised visit to the Brombergs and their daughter Sonia. She was a quiet, shy girl, very unlike either Usher or Marusa, but she had been in my mind far more than they had.

So I called on Usher, and about twenty to six we set off for the theatre. Usher was in a stupid mood, acting like a helpless kitten, and that annoyed me so much I couldn't enjoy the show, and I was glad when it ended and we could come out into the cold evening about nine o'clock. Usher wanted me to go home with her for supper, but I knew that if we did that her parents would discreetly clear off to bed as soon as we got there, and I didn't want to be left alone with her! Instead I suggested that we go to a café for supper. We tried one, but Usher didn't like it, and there were not very many still open so late where the food was good, but Usher knew of another that would be open and led me there. I didn't like the look of this place much; twenty small tables crowded in, and a bar at the back, and crowded with a rough looking set of people, but if that was where Usher wanted to go I was willing, rather than returning to her house. We got a table away from the bar and a woman came up to take our order. As I looked at her I thought I had seen her before, but I couldn't remember where. Usher ordered some food and the woman walked away. I watched her as she went to the serving counter to fill up a tray, giving a ticket for everything she took, and as she returned to our table, suddenly I remembered: she was the young woman I'd seen in Lumsky's room at the Hotel Moskva in Constantinograd.

I pulled my hat down over my face a little and turned away as she came to our table with the food; and when she returned with our glasses of tea I had taken out a newspaper and was hiding behind that.

All this was very puzzling to Usher, of course, and she wanted to know who the woman was that I should be hiding my face from her. I told her to eat up and I'd tell her later, and as soon as I could I gave Usher the money to pay the bill and told her I would wait for her outside. When she came out I explained about the missing book-keeper and his girl; it seemed likely that if she was here in Kremenchug then Lumsky might be here too. It was a biggish town, and there were enough crooks and strange characters about for him to be inconspicuous. If he had shaved off his moustache he wouldn't be easily recognized from the published descriptions, and if he had lain low and not tried to pass the railway stations where the police might be on the look-out, he could well have been living safely for months. I told Usher all this, but I didn't tell her about the five hundred rubles reward Habinski was still offering.

Usher, of course, was thrilled; an evening at the theatre, a supper afterwards — even if it was a bit hurried — and a real-life detective story to follow made an exciting day for her, and when I reached her door and kissed her good night she was grateful enough to let me go fairly quickly. I hurried back to Herscho's house and crept into bed, but I could not sleep. I had almost given up hope of finding Lumsky, and now it seemed like fate that Usher should take me to the one place in all the town where I should see his woman. I lay in bed wondering what to do. I mustn't make any mistake that would warn her and — if they were still together — Lumsky. Five hundred rubles depended on it — more than a year's pay at my present rate. And apart from the reward there was the feeling I had that Lumsky had disgraced my firm on my territory, and even though I wasn't to blame it reflected on all Habinski's people that we should have a swindler among us. I lay thinking, and I heard the town clock strike every hour until three. Then, still planning how I could find Lumsky, I dropped off, and when I awoke it was nine in the morning and Hannah and Herscho had already gone off to their stall in the market.

I made myself some tea and cut myself some bread and cheese, and thought while I had breakfast. I'd arranged by letter to go to see Sonia and the Brombergs the next day, Monday, or the day after that, but I couldn't go visiting people while this business was un-settled, so now I wrote to them again asking if I might put off my visit until the end of the week. I was just sealing this up when there was a knock, and Usher was at the door. She was very polite this time, planting a kiss on my forehead instead of trying to browse all over me. She saw the letter and wanted to know who it was to, and offered to post it for me, but I wouldn't trust her with it. She couldn't read, of course, but she could easily get someone to read it to her, and I wouldn't have put it past her to destroy the letter. While I went out to post it she made more tea, and we talked again about the woman in the café and the chance of finding Lumsky.

Usher had a plan that involved us both dressing up in disguise and going round the low cafés which the shady characters of Kremenchug frequented. I'd had enough of dressing up in dirty old clothes when I'd wasted so much time looking for Lumsky in Constantinograd, and I didn't think much of starting again, but it was true that if I went in my ordinary clothes and Lumsky was about, he would spot me before I could spot him. And Usher was eager to come with me, and if I was in rags and dirt to match my low surroundings she couldn't accompany me dressed respectably. I suppose, too, that everyone likes to try to be an actor sometimes; we were both very young. It ended with my agreeing, and giving Usher twenty rubles to go and buy some old clothes for the two of us in the market.

Before she left, I showed her the photographs of Lumsky which I had found at the hotel in Constantinograd after he had run away. And here was the other amazing part of the coincidence; Usher, who had by chance led me to the café where Lumsky's girl was working, now thought she recognized the man in the photograph as someone she had seen around the town, and had even danced with at a fancy-dress dance a little while ago. If it was Lumsky, he had shaved off his moustache, she said. I wasn't sure if anyone could recognize him from the picture if he was now clean-shaven, but Usher was almost certain, and she went off to buy the old clothes for our disguise more excited than ever.

I was left to amuse myself for the rest of that day. I went to visit the Konevs and Marusa. Twelve months had made a big difference

to Marusa, she looked more beautiful than ever, and very grown-up
in high-heeled shoes and a Persian lamb coat. She was also engaged
now, to a rich young man named David. She wasn't very happy
about it, which worried her parents, but there was no doubt it was
a good match. And for a girl like Marusa, brought up with everything she could want, a rich man was much more suitable than anyone like me, and I wished them both luck. I spent some of the afternoon watching the performers around the bandstand in the park,
and then returned home early that evening, to spend some time with
Herscho and Hannah. But Herscho was falling asleep and Hannah
was out — she had gone to the public baths, for the poor tenement
buildings where they lived had no bathrooms, of course. So I had
to go to bed and try again to sleep, with my head full of hopes of
finding Lumsky and of fears of the mess Usher could make of it if
she said a word in the wrong place.

Next morning I awoke at nine again. Hannah and Herscho had
gone, and I was alone in the house again, and again there was a tap
at the door and I threw on some clothes and went to answer it, and
again it was Usher, looking very pretty in a black skirt and white
blouse with her long dark hair.

I must have looked alarmed, for she said: 'Don't be frightened,
you're a big boy now,' and came in, bringing the bundle of old
clothes she had bought in the market. I didn't want to get up, or go
out, but I knew it wasn't safe to be alone with Usher for very long so
I told her I thought I had a bad cold coming on, and crawled back
into my bed. But this didn't stop her; she asked if I had had tea,
and then rushed out to buy some lemons and returned to make me
some. I drank down three glasses of the strong lemon tea, and she
began to tell me that I couldn't have a very bad cold and that I'd
soon be all right. I told her politely that she was a good nurse, and
she said: 'Yes I am, but you're not grateful. You should be more
grateful to a girl who has saved your life,' and, cold or no cold, she
showed me how she thought I ought to show my gratitude. I said
that if I showed much more gratitude that way she would suffocate
me. But there was no putting Usher off; she declared that I must
really enjoy kissing her but just wouldn't admit it, and then said:

7*

'You are here for only a week and then you go away for another twelve months, and perhaps when you return I'll be married and never be able to kiss you again.'

There seemed no answer I could think of to this kind of talk, so I turned to look at the clothes she had bought. Suddenly she pulled me round towards her; her blouse had disappeared and she was half naked. Usher said: 'What a lucky boy you are — nobody's ever seen me like this before,' and tried to guide my hands over her body, but she could feel I was reluctant and she said: 'Why are you so obstinate — you're a young man; why try to fight against your will?'

I told her I was being sensible. 'I can't marry you, I can't make a good enough living to marry anyone yet, I can't afford to make a fool of myself,' and she let go, half apologetic and very angry at the same time, telling me that if I thought she was a loose girl I was making a mistake and 'Not one of my boy friends has seen me like this or had the chance you could have . . . but you're like a dead fish, your hands feel nothing.'

I said: 'I'd like to take you. But for a few minutes' pleasure someone may have to suffer for a lifetime. You know what happened to me — my parents had to leave me and run away. I'm not going to do that, I've been the victim. . . .'

Usher picked up her blouse and put it on, turning to ask me to button up the back for her. Then she picked up the bundle. 'Here's your clothes,' she said, and went out of the room.

That evening I dressed in the clothes she had bought, and with a little dirt on my face I felt I looked the part. I met Usher, who was dressed to match, and we set off for our evening of roaming the less respectable cafés of the town. I reminded her that we must remember to speak the way that peasants spoke; she must call me Vasil, and I would call her Martla.

We went from café to café, and it was getting late when we turned into one that seemed to be crowded with very shady-looking characters. I pretended to be drunk, which let me drop my head over the table so that I was less likely to be seen but could still glance round, and I called the waiter '*Tovarich*' and shouted for food. Usher

apologized for me and ordered something to eat, but while the
waiter was getting it I saw a man coming to help behind the bar.
And there was no doubt about it; although this man was clean-
shaven, it was Lumsky all right.

I risked raising my head for a second glance, and there was no
mistake. It was the man I was looking for. But now there was a
problem I hadn't really thought about; I'd recognized Lumsky and
if I stayed on in that small café it was quite possible he would recognize me, old clothes or no old clothes. And if he recognized me, he
would be off in a moment, and my chance to lay hands on him, and
on the five hundred rubles reward, would be gone. I had to get out
quickly and without rousing suspicion, even though I was leaving a
meal uneaten.

I began to rise, turning away from the bar where Lumsky was
busy, and mumbling to Usher that I must go outside. She came
with me, apparently holding me up as I slipped and fell about, and
a man sitting near us came to help. As we got outside the café I
started singing like a drunkard. Nobody would take any notice of a
drunk in that sort of place. Usher went back to pay the bill, while
I wavered about outside, singing, then Usher returned and we
moved off round the corner of the next street where I was able to
stop playing a part and explain to her that the man behind the bar
had been Lumsky and that it had all gone off very well.

It was late now, and we agreed that the first thing to do was to go
home, and change into our proper clothes, but we had to walk home
— none of the cabs would take us dressed as we were. The dirt and
the old clothes must have been a good disguise, for when I took
Usher to her door and her father opened it to our knock he quickly
closed it again, and wouldn't open it until Usher had shouted to
him: 'It's me — let me in and I'll tell you all about it.' I left her at
the door and returned to Herscho's house; they were already
asleep and I was able to wash, change and hurry out again to Usher's
house without having to answer any questions.

Usher had already explained how we had tried to be our own
detectives and had found the man we had been looking for; and
then I had to go over the story again, and even though I could

hardly keep my eyes open, sit and drink endless glasses of tea while everyone talked about it.

The first thing next morning I went to the post office and telegraphed Habinski: 'Lumsky is here — come immediately — meet you at boat station.' In two hours I received a reply: 'Coming by train — Habinski' which showed how eager he was; the train was quicker than the boat, but dearer.

When it was about time for him to reach Kremenchug I went to the station and hung about, until the Guvnor appeared, striding along, this time without his long fur coat so that he looked less like a bear than usual. He wanted to know all about how we had found Lumsky, and I told him, but he was being cautious; wanting to know if I was sure and insisting that anything which was done was done on my responsibility. We set off for the police station; I wanted to take a cab but his meanness had returned by this time and he said it was no good rushing things and we might as well walk. In the inspector's office Habinski began explaining, but then suddenly stopped, saying: 'I think my assistant can explain better than I can.' The Guvnor realized that he couldn't speak Russian very well.

I explained to the police inspector that Lumsky had disappeared with 2,900 rubles the previous January and that details of the theft and his description had been circulated. The inspector went off to look up the previous year's complaints. When he returned he had a detective and two constables with him, and we set off, the five of us. I persuaded the Guvnor to stay behind, because with his long beard he would be easily recognizable and might give the whole thing away.

It was getting dark when we reached the café. A cab was standing outside, and a woman was going in and out, bringing cases to load on to the cab. Then a couple emerged from the café and climbed into the cab; the man I could not see but the woman I recognized as Lumsky's girl, and just in time the detective stepped up and stopped the cab-driver, asking if he could be given a lift. A voice from inside the cab called: 'There's no room — drive on, we shall miss the train.' There was no mistaking Lumsky's voice. The detective swung up beside the driver and muttered something to him, and the cab drove off, the rest of us hailing another and following. It wasn't the railway station that we drove to, but the police station, and there I heard Lumsky's voice again, complaining that it was a scandal for him and his wife to be taken there.

Lumsky was ushered into one room and the woman into another. A sergeant began laying out the contents of her handbag on a table, and barked at her: 'If you don't tell the truth it will be the worse for you. What's your lover's name?'

'Lufunor,' said the woman.

'If you won't tell me I'll tell you — it's Jacob Lumsky and he stole 2,900 rubles from his employer,' said the sergeant, all the while picking up and putting down the things from her handbag. He picked up a large envelope and asked her what was in it. 'My money,' she said, and he emptied it out on to the table — six hundred ruble notes, ten notes of ten rubles, five of fifty rubles, and fifty rubles in small money.

The sergeant called in a constable to guard the money and went out, returning with Lumsky. He hadn't seen me up to that point, and I shouted, 'Good evening, Lumsky!' to him.

The woman was grabbing her things off the table and stuffing them back into her handbag, but the sergeant stopped her touching the money. 'We can't let you have that until we find out how you obtained such a large amount,' he said. He stirred the notes and from among them picked out a piece of paper and unwrapped it, revealing two railway tickets. 'Booked three days ago. Where were you going?' asked the sergeant.

'Those were to take my friend on holiday to Ramdin,' said Lumsky.

The sergeant wanted to know why Ramdin.

'I was told it's a nice place for a holiday,' said Lumsky.

'And conveniently on the frontier,' said the sergeant.

Among their luggage which had been carried in there was a large trunk, and the sergeant now told the constable to open it. The woman protested that it contained only her clothes, but the sergeant insisted, and the constable laid everything flat on the table; some clean towels, then two beautiful dresses, expensive ones; a great deal of ladies' underwear, beautiful shoes, stockings, handkerchiefs; then men's clothes, new ones, suits, shoes, underclothes.

'That cost a great deal of money — you can't make that sort of money working in a café,' said the sergeant.

The constable asked if he should repack the case, but the sergeant said it wasn't empty yet and took out some worn clothes. 'It's all empty now,' said the constable. The sergeant got out of his chair. 'Take that out too,' he said, pointing to the cloth which covered the bottom of the trunk, and pulled it out. Underneath was a large envelope, and when this was opened out came another eight hundred rubles.

'Now then,' said the sergeant, 'where did all this money come from?'

'What a silly question — you know where I got it from,' said Lumsky. 'I had the opportunity and handled a lot of money, and I showed that young upstart' — and he pointed to me — 'that I'm cleverer than he is. Altogether I've had nearly 2,750 rubles . . .'

The sergeant was writing this down, and gave the statement to Lumsky to read and sign. Then Lumsky and the woman were searched, and brought out another 110 rubles. The girl started to cry, and Lumsky said: 'Leave her alone, she had nothing to do with it. Give her that money back, it was our wages.'

'All right,' said the sergeant. 'I can give her that back, but I can't let her go until we find out whether she is wanted by the police anywhere. But you, Jacob, you've got to go back to Verchneprovsk on the prison train to stand trial.' And with that the woman was taken off one way, Lumsky the other, and I could go off to see the Guvnor back to the station. I felt satisfied now that Lumsky was under lock and key; not that I wanted him punished, but he had given people like me a bad name. He'd tried to rob one of the customers in my district, and it was a relief that I needn't go on looking out for him any more. And there was, of course, the five hundred rubles reward.

I walked with the Guvnor back to the station. He still wouldn't take a cab — this time he made the excuse that since it was the eve of the Sabbath he mustn't ride in a cab because that would be making the horse work, the old hypocrite. His religion didn't stop him catching the train back to Verchneprovsk.

When he had gone I had to return, first to Usher's house and tell them everything that had happened and to give Usher twenty rubles for helping me find Lumsky — she took it, and then demanded another eighty kopecks for the meal she had paid for. Then I went on back to Herscho and Hannah. They wanted to know where I had been and the whole story had to be told all over again. Hannah and Herscho were both sitting on the couch; the candles were alight because it was the Sabbath eve, and they were eating sunflower seeds, as all the poor Jews did at the weekend. They offered me some, and Hannah brought out some home-made cider she had been keeping, and we sat quite happily. Herscho tried to take some of the credit for what Usher and I had done, saying: 'I knew when you were a little boy you would grow into a great man — it was I who first sent you to school.' He was so happy that he rose from his chair and went out to the kitchen for a bottle of beer. I had always known that Herscho liked me, and in his way he wasn't a bad man, but he was afraid of Hannah and let her rule him even when he knew she was wrong, and now I pitied him, growing old with an evil woman like that.

It was because the happiness of the house depended so much on Hannah's temper that next day I thought I would try to make her a little softer, and so after dinner I helped Hannah wash up and then offered to take her to the pictures. There had not been a cinema in Kremenchug very long, and she had never been there.

To my surprise, something like a smile appeared on her sullen face when I suggested it, and she hurried to finish and get ready. While she was getting ready Usher arrived, asking me to take her to the pictures, and Hannah called out to her, like a young girl: 'Usher, you're too late — Moysey has asked his mother to go to the pictures!' Usher whispered to me: 'Aren't you embarrassed to go out in the street with an old witch like that? And on a Saturday when everyone is about and will see you with her?' I told her that I didn't know anyone in Kremenchug so why should I worry, and Usher dropped the cloth she had been drying the dishes with and ran off, very annoyed, which was a relief. I was willing to be friendly with Usher, but she was taking it for granted that I was her regular young man, and I wasn't. For one thing, I could never consider marrying a girl who couldn't read or write.

But Usher had been right about one thing, though I had denied it; I was embarrassed about being seen about with Hannah, especially when she was all dressed up She appeared from the bedroom in new dress, new hat, new shoes; but nothing fitted, everything was either too loose or too tight and she looked like a monkey dressed up. She asked me, 'How do I look?' and all I could reply was that she looked very nice, and set off with her. Hannah enjoyed the pictures, staring at the screen all the time, very excited and exclaiming with wonder how was it possible, and I took her home in a much better mood than the one she had been in that morning.

After tea I got ready to go out again, and they both said, 'Aha, Moysey's going out — he's got a girl somewhere in the town.' I didn't answer, and Herscho said: 'It's only right. But there's one thing you must remember, Moysey; if you've got the money you can go to the theatre but if you haven't you must sit in the dark at home. I wish you luck, but make sure she's a rich girl — I won't allow you to have a poor girl. You're not twenty-one yet and I can stop you marrying until that time.'

I knew exactly what he meant. It was the custom among Jewish families in this part of the world that if a boy married a rich girl the father had control of the money and directed all his son's affairs. But if Herscho thought that was going to happen with me, he was in for a surprise.

I took a train to the bridge which connects Kremenchug with Krukov, and walked across. It was getting dark and snowing lightly, but it was a pleasant walk; I was snug in a new overcoat with a Persian lamb collar and a fur hat; snug and pleased with myself because the year before when I had come that way I had been wearing an old cloth coat but now the Brombergs would see me in a new one, and a new suit, and even a new walking stick; with snow on the ground you needed a stick.

On the far side of the bridge there was a great crowd of cabs and I was surprised to see that many of the drivers were Jewish, even though it was a Saturday. They called out, offering me a cab, but I refused because I hadn't far to go, and then as I walked on I heard the noise of long boots in the snow and Sonia's brother Sam touched me on the shoulder; he had recognized me and realized I was going to his house and said he would take me; he ran back to the cab stand and came back with his horse and sledge and I got in. He did not drive right to the house, however, telling me that because it was a Saturday he didn't want people to see him driving the sledge.

Mrs Bromberg opened the door to us, and sent Sam hurrying away to find Sonia; she told me to come in and then ran to change from the old dress in which she had come to the door to a better one. I remembered the dress as one she had worn when I visited the house twelve months before, and I thought Mrs Bromberg looked worn out with hard work; if any money went on clothes it was on Sonia's, not her mother's. She sat down and made conversation, asking how I had been for the past year, and whether I hoped one day to have a granary of my own. In the middle of our conversation her husband came in; his wife went out to fetch a tray of tea and cakes, and he went out too, returning with a bottle of vodka and some glasses. I asked if he remembered me, and Mrs Bromberg said: 'Oh, him! He doesn't remember anything but his bottle. He's got a head like a horse.' The old man filled two glasses, tossed one straight down and offered the other to me, and when I refused it told me I was impolite. From then on he ignored me, but Mrs Bromberg kept refilling my glass with tea and hanging on every word I said, you would have thought she owed me money; and she kept looking agitatedly out of the window, afraid that Sam wouldn't find Sonia for me. All the while the old man kept drinking his vodka, and quite soon he was drunk and asleep. I'd heard somebody else moving about the house, and Mrs Bromberg explained that it was only their servant girl Herpina; 'She's been here four years; she's not very clever but she likes it here. She eats and sleeps here, and Sonia gives her a dress sometimes — we don't pay her anything.'

It's hard to say what Mrs Bromberg and I talked about; but

somehow I felt she was a person I could really trust, and who was worth listening to. And she must have felt the same, for she urged me to visit them again before I finished my holidays, and said she could talk to me as if I were her own son. I said: 'But you have a son and a daughter who must come first with you.' She replied: 'I have a daughter, but Sam is my husband's son, not mine.'

Now we heard the sound of someone in the hall knocking their boots to get the snow off, and Sonia came in with her friend Nina. Sonia said, 'Good evening,' quietly, and scolded her mother for not having prepared a proper supper for me, but Nina was as loud and saucy as I remembered her; when Mrs Bromberg said we'd been having an interesting conversation Nina said: 'What is important is, has he told you if he's learning dancing.' Mrs Bromberg and Sonia went out to prepare a meal, leaving me with Nina, who rattled on and on about things of no importance. Nina was a beautiful girl, but that is all you could say for her. Strangely enough, I didn't think of Sonia as being beautiful at this time, though she was sensible and quiet and intelligent and I even thought of the proverb: 'All that glitters isn't gold'; it wasn't until later that I was to realize she was beautiful too.

We sat down to supper, and there was no chance of real conversation with Nina there; for something to say I asked Nina if she lived far away and; 'Why, do you want to take me home?' she said playfully — it was all nonsense like that. The old man woke at one point, but only to say: 'Oh, are you here again?' and to go back to sleep. But at least before I left Mrs Bromberg had made me promise I would return next day, and I did this willingly enough. I finally left with Nina and Sonia, and soon we were picked up by Sam in his sledge. I said: 'I've almost fallen in love with Madame Bromberg,' and Nina, always ready, retorted: 'You'll probably fall in love with her daughter,' which made Sonia blush.

But before I was to see Sonia and her mother again, there came a bitter quarrel with Herscho and Hannah. A day or two before, talking to Usher, I had said lightheartedly something about going abroad. It was at the back of almost every Jew's mind, in Russia in my time. Emigration was the way out, if prospects were too poor, or if life was too difficult; if you could scrape together the money for your fare there was always hope of a new start in some other country. Anyway the words I had said so lightly, and foolishly, considering I was talking to Usher, got back to Hannah and Herscho. I had not been serious about it, at that time I had not been thinking at all seriously about emigrating, even though Mama Marcovsky's son and a daughter had gone to America, and I knew of many others who had done the same. I was sitting with Herscho the day after I had visited Sonia, and Hannah was preparing the evening meal, when Herscho began interrogating me about this talk of going abroad. He was very worried, not so much at the idea that I might go away, but because if a son did not do his military service his father had to pay three hundred rubles. Though Herscho wasn't my father, he had adopted me and so he was legally responsible for me. I tried to make him realize I hadn't been serious, and said that Usher was a fool to misunderstand me.

'Yes,' said Herscho, 'but fools often speak words of wisdom. You are planning something to get your own back on me, to pay me out for the suffering I caused you as a boy. When you run away I shall have to pay the three hundred rubles fine.'

I denied it again, but Hannah came in at this point and she was in her glory: 'I never trusted that boy, I never trusted that boy,' she said. 'You must watch him wherever he goes.' There was a row, and at last I could stand it no more. I had money in my pocket, and I didn't have to put up with these people if they didn't want me and didn't trust me. I packed up my bag, and — with Herscho protesting that I didn't have to leave — walked out.

Walking out was one thing, finding somewhere to sleep another. It was late, and though I knew plenty of people in the town by this time there was nobody to whom I could easily go and ask for a bed at this time of night, or whom I would want to know my family troubles. Except Usher's family. Then it occurred to me that Usher might well have passed on the story about my talking of going abroad, guessing that it would make trouble. There was nothing Usher would like better than for me to go to stay at her house, to rely on her family, to have her all round me, looking after me. Before

I knew where I was, I should find myself committed to marrying her. I decided that, even if I had to sleep under a hedge I would sooner do that than return either to enemies like Hannah and Herscho — or to friends like Usher.

There were no hotel rooms I could afford in Kremenchug. I hired a sledge and we went off, trying to find a room, and at last, well after ten o'clock, I came to a beer-house whose owner, a widow, I could see was Jewish. She didn't want to take me in, declaring that she wasn't running an hotel, but I dropped a word or two of Yiddish into what I was saying, and soon we were talking in Yiddish and I had paid the cab driver off — he asked three rubles, which was robbery, but it was very late at night — and was sitting down to a tray of fried fish and bread and a glass of milk before going off to the comfortable spare room of the house.

It was there that I stayed for the rest of my holiday, and each day I went to the Brombergs . . . to the great interest of my landlady, who knew them. 'She works very hard selling milk, so as to give her daughter a large dowry,' said my landlady. 'Her husband and her son are drunkards, no good; her daughter's a nice girl . . . she doesn't seem to belong in the same family with them. Are you after the daughter?' I didn't answer that question.

I filled up the morning with some business which Habinski had asked me to do, visiting a grain merchant in the town. I had been rather worried about meeting Mrs Bromberg out on her milk round, if I walked about the town early in the day; I thought she might not wish to meet me like that, but she didn't have that sort of vanity. When I did run into her, her can of milk in one hand and the measures for the milk in the other, she came up to me with her burden cheerfully and said good morning, and asked me to come for dinner at one o'clock. So, after my business was over, I looked into the shops to kill time, bought a pound of walnut halva in a confectioner's, and finally made my way to Sonia's house. As I walked up to the door, I could see heads appearing at windows on both sides of the street.

Mrs Bromberg was home, and everything was ready for dinner, with a jug and glasses for water on the table, and napkins and cutlery laid. On the walls were a few photographs I hadn't seen before, hung there I supposed to smarten up the room a little. Sonia appeared, bringing in part of the meal. She was wearing a beautiful lace blouse and a black skirt, and her hair was done in a new way, but it was still not her appearance that I found attractive, but something else about her. Unlike all the other girls I had known she didn't speak often, but when she spoke it was always sensible and worth listening to. We sat down to eat, the three of us — Sam and his father were out — and I don't think I had enjoyed a meal so much since I left Mama Marcovsky's. Afterwards I could hear Sonia and her mother arguing, each telling the other to leave the washing up and to sit down to talk, and in the end they both came back, Sonia carrying small plates and knives for the halva and her mother bringing some candied apples. It was very pleasant and friendly and homelike, and I was enjoying myself. But, because these people were still comparative strangers, because they didn't really know me, perhaps because I was enjoying myself, I had to bring out the thing that never quite stopped haunting me.

Into the conversation, I introduced a question, 'Suppose a few houses from you there lived a boy without parents. There are rumours that when he was born his parents weren't married, and afterwards they were frightened and ran away and left him. People call him bastard, and some say that such people are like an evil spirit, and should not have been allowed life. Do you think they are right?'

Sonia said: 'That's unpleasant, and sad, but people who say such things are savages. A child isn't guilty of his parents' sins.' And her mother said: 'If I knew of a child like that, I would give him a home.'

So I said: 'I'm talking about the person who looks back at me from the mirror. Decent-looking, a good position — but that stain on my character.' And I told them the story of my beginnings, the baby found in the basket at the synagogue in Verchneprovsk. At the end, Sonia went out of the room, saying nothing; her mother began to say how sorry she was, and I told her I didn't want pity; not now when it was too late, and I no longer had need of it. And I stumbled on, saying now she would be able to tell her husband all about me when he came home, and got up to collect my coat and go, stuttering that I must go home now that there was nothing more I could tell them that would be of interest. Sonia came back into the room, looking very miserable and upset; upset at what I had told them, I thought; upset that she should have been talking to someone like me; or that their neighbours might find out about the boy who had come calling on them, and I snapped at her that I'd better be leaving before her father and brother came home and I got thrown out.

Sonia was angry now, as well as upset. 'You are probably a good judge of grain but not of what is in anyone's heart,' she said. 'You can come here tomorrow. And don't think my father and brother are bad because they like to drink. They also have hearts. When you tell such a story, people's hearts are touched, and if you scratch a heart it is hard to heal, to forget in a moment. All our hearts are scratched,' said Sonia. And suddenly, all my bitterness was gone, and all Sonia's anger of a moment before.

She walked with me to the gate, and I plucked up my courage and asked her to come to the theatre with me that night. She asked me to wait, and ran in to tell her mother, and a moment later came back to say she would meet me at the other side of the big bridge. And with the thing I had to say all said now, with that ghost laid, I hurried off to my lodgings. There wasn't very much time, and I hurried to get myself spruced up — my landlady said there must be a pretty girl waiting for me somewhere, and ah! it reminded her of when she was young.

I got back to where I had to meet Sonia five minutes early. It was snowing, but not heavily, and soon I spotted Sonia approaching, wrapped in a big coat and with a gaily coloured scarf over her hair and her face glowing with the cold. I wanted to take a cab, but she asked that we walk, and we walked, slowly, talking all the way. We went to the picture theatre; I remember now how, when we got into the foyer, she took off her scarf and shook out her hair, and shook the snow from her coat, and how I looked at the colour in her cheeks and the brightness of her eyes and wondered if I might be lucky enough one day to kiss her lips; and how suddenly I realized that

Sonia was beautiful. And I remember how I bought the tickets and we settled in our seats; and how I bought a box of chocolates against Sonia's protests, saying it wasn't every day I took a pretty girl to the pictures. But what the pictures were we saw; that I cannot remember.

The pictures finished at nine o'clock, and I helped her into her coat and we went out. The snow had stopped and it was bright, but still very cold. I suggested once more that we take a sledge, but Sonia said, 'It's nice to walk on a bright cold night,' and so we walked. The bridge back to Krukov was slippery with ice, and she asked if she could take my arm because of that, and of course I agreed — willing, for once, to feel a girl's arm tucked into mine. The wind across the bridge was cutting our faces like a knife, and the long bridge seemed endless; there were sledges waiting on the other side, Sam's among them, but Sonia asked that we cross to the other side so that he shouldn't see us; and so we did. I saw Sonia to her home, and explained that I had to hurry back to my lodgings — it was getting late and my landlady wouldn't like waiting up for me. Sonia wanted to know why I was living in lodgings instead of with Herscho and Hannah; I said I'd have to tell her that tomorrow.

'I want to know everything about the life of Moysey Stocklinsky,' she said.

'Not just Moysey?' I asked, and she said that might come later. I said good night — unlike most girls, Sonia wasn't the sort who hung about waiting to be kissed — and hurried off. I'd a lot more to think about than I'd ever had before in my life.

Each day after this, until the Friday when I had to return to Habinski's, I called at the Brombergs' house, sometimes talking for hours with Sonia, sometimes with her mother. On one of these occasions, when Sonia was out, Mrs Bromberg said she must tell me the story of her life.

'When I was five years old,' she began, 'my mother died, and my father died not long after, and I was brought up by my brother, Matt Rabinovitch, who has a factory in Kremenchug making tobacco for the peasants — he is a rich man. I lived there until I was not quite seventeen when my sister, who was married to Mr Bromberg, died leaving four little children — the oldest only eight. Their father was already a drunkard, and every night I used to dream of my dead sister begging me to take pity on her children and look after them. Rabinovitch did not wish me to come to this house and take on the children and a drunkard, but every night I would dream of my sister, and in the end I came here. Bromberg stopped drinking at once, and the children were happy, and I got used to living here. My brother came in a cab to fetch me home, but when he saw how the children cried at the thought of my leaving, he left me here. On my seventeenth birthday I decided to marry Bromberg, and a few weeks later we were married. The next week he was drunk again, and my life became hard; I had to start trying to earn extra money to clothe the children. . . . I always bought new clothes for them, even if I had to buy second-hand ones for myself.

'I tried my best with the boy,' said Mrs Bromberg. 'I spent money on his education but he did not take to it — he is a drunkard like his father, and a hooligan. Two of the girls married and went to England; they live in London and are getting on very well — I've been to see them.'

I said, incredulously, 'You've been to see them, in England?'

Mrs Bromberg explained that when the girls left and Sam had begun working, life became a little easier and she had been able to save; and her father-in-law had given them the house where they now lived. 'He gave it to me, telling his own son that he could not be trusted because he was a drunkard.' By letting off part of the house, and selling milk, and from the gifts of the children in London, she had got together some money: 'I've saved a thousand rubles for Sonia's dowry, for when with God's help she finds a good-hearted man. I want you to be that man, my son and a husband for my daughter.'

'Someone like *me*?' I said, and my voice ran out of control with amazement.

'Why are you amazed? I have no real son,' said Mrs Bromberg.

I kissed her hands, and told her that I would like to be her son, and that I wanted that she should be a mother to me; but how could we tell what Sonia would decide?

'Just tell me if your answer is Yes,' she said, and I said: 'My answer is Yes.'

Presently Sonia came in; she looked beautiful in a black skirt and a Turkish blouse; I looked at her, longing to be able to take her in my arms but perhaps a little frightened at the idea of being hooked so young. I didn't know how I should say to her what I wanted to say, and as Sonia busied herself making tea and laying the table I worked my way round and round it. I asked if she remembered telling me, the year before, to write to her, and that I hadn't kept the correspondence up. 'Yes,' she said, 'she remembered.' I said I was going away this weekend, but would try to write regularly. But would I get a reply? Sonia, busy with the glasses and the samovar, said: 'Why ever not? But the only way to find out is to write to me.' All this while her mother sat watching us, a faint smile on her face. And I was just trying to think how I could say the next thing I needed to say, when Sam and his father came in, and it was too late, and I had to talk to them.

Sam was sitting with his back to the door, and at one point Sonia came in and stood in the doorway behind him, looking to see if anything had been forgotten for the table. Sam was saying something to me, and when I didn't reply he looked round to see what was distracting my attention. 'She's beautiful, isn't she?' Sam said. 'She wants a nice young man as a husband,' and looked at me very sharply.

I got a few minutes alone with Sonia later that evening. We were talking about some of her friends, and two girls who, she said, were nosey — 'They wanted to know if you are my young man.'

'Well, what did you say to that?' I asked.

'I told them you hadn't asked me,' said Sonia.

I went to touch her hand, but she withdrew it quickly. 'Supposing I did ask you, would you refuse?' I said.

'First you have to ask,' said Sonia, not very helpfully, and before I could open my mouth in came her mother again.

Sonia looked cross: 'How is it you always come in in the middle of our conversation?' she said, but I'd plucked up my courage and I couldn't wait any longer.

'Let me tell you whatever I have to say in front of your mother,' I said. 'I'm going away, and I'll be more comfortable in writing to you if you will promise to be my betrothed,' and we stood there, her mother and I, both waiting.

Sonia said fondly: 'My mother wants to get rid of me, so I've met a lot of young men. But none of them has ever proposed to me — you are the first. And I can't refuse you.'

I kissed her hand, and her mother kissed us both and asked God's blessing on us and so it was done.

I had only another day left before I must catch the boat back to Verchneprovsk, and I had to spend some of that saying goodbye to friends — among them the Konevs and their daughter Marusa. This wasn't easy, because Marusa was beautiful, lively, happy-go-lucky, as well as being rich; but now when I saw her the image of Sonia seemed to be beside her, and I didn't find it half so hard to be unresponsive when Marusa wanted to be affectionate.

I said my goodbyes to everyone, and hurried to Sonia's house; it was wonderful to feel that I had people there, two people at least, I could talk to and trust. Sonia came to the door, saying mockingly: 'I thought you might not be coming here any more, Mr Stocklinsky.'

'Mr?' I said.

'It's difficult to get used to calling a stranger by his first name,' said Sonia. 'Come in, Moyseyka, and shut the door.'

The whole family was in there; Mr and Mrs Bromberg and Sam, the married daughter who lived in Krukov and her husband, and their two small boys. The old man took out a large bottle of vodka, filled a large glass, opened a prayer book and said a few words out of it, drank a little vodka and passed the glass round for us each to sip in turn. Sam wanted to know what I had bought for Sonia as an engagement present. I explained that there hadn't been time, but that at Easter I would take Sonia and her mother into Kremenchug to buy whatever they wanted, and we could then celebrate our engagement formally.

Sam filled some glasses with more vodka and demanded that everyone drink to the engaged couple's health: 'You must kiss Sonia for everyone to see,' he said. But Sonia blushed, and her father broke in: 'That's not right, you can only kiss her when you are properly engaged, not before.' I protested that they were all embarrassing Sonia, and the old man replied: 'That doesn't matter — it has to be,' and I told Sonia I would make up the kisses at Easter.

After lunch the men drifted away and Sonia and her half-sister were washing up. Mrs Bromberg came in to talk to me, and told me about the other two sisters who were in London. 'The pay there is good — they wanted Sonia to join them there,' she said. 'She did not want to go without me; perhaps she will go with you.' I said I would need to learn some trade before I did anything like that, but, 'No — you will be a businessman there,' said Mrs Bromberg.

I told her all about my troubles with the money owed to me by old Kovalevsky; if I could get that back, and with the reward money and the six hundred and seventy-four rubles in my post office book, Sonia and I would have something to begin life with. Sonia and the other sister came in then, and we sat talking and eating sunflower seeds, until Mrs Bromberg thought she would go and lie down until it was time for her to see to the cows, and the sister at last seemed to understand that we didn't really want other people about, and said her goodbyes. I was left with Sonia all on my own; and I sat there thinking that now I would have all the family I ever needed, in her.

She misunderstood my silence, or perhaps she only pretended to, and asked why I was so engrossed in my thoughts. 'Have you so much trouble? Is it so hard to get married?' she said, and I said: 'It's something you have to go through — the sooner you get it over the better!' Then she wanted to know if I had had women during my life; I said that with all the troubles I had had, I'd had no time left for that particular trouble.

Too soon everybody began to reappear, and for the rest of the day I never seemed to have Sonia to myself for a moment, right until the time when I had to say goodbye and leave to catch the boat. Everybody shook hands; Sonia's mother kissed me and cried and wished me a good journey; and Sonia said: 'I kiss you with all my heart,' but she wouldn't kiss me in reality because all the family were watching. Even when she took me to the door we weren't alone; the two young nephews were watching us intently. I gave them a silver coin to say Goodbye Uncle and go away; but now it was too late, and Sonia only called after me that she would write, and I was hurrying down the street for my lodgings and then the boat.

XVII. LOSS AND GAIN

I slept soundly on the boat, until I was shaken awake and found a sailor standing over me. 'I thought you were dead — I've been shaking you for five minutes,' he said. 'We'll be at Verchneprovsk in twenty minutes.' It was time to think about work again. I'd had two weeks' holiday, and I thought: the first week with Hannah and Herscho seemed like two years. The second week with Sonia and her mother — every day of that seemed to have gone as quickly as an hour.

When the boat docked it was five o'clock in the morning. There were many sledges waiting, and I hired one. I didn't want to disturb the Habinski household so early in the morning, but I knew that Mama Marcovsky would be delighted to open her door to me at any time, so I directed the driver there. Early though it was, when we reached the house I saw there was a light in her room. I knew immediately that something must be wrong, and quickly paid off the driver and took my bags to the door.

Vera opened the door. 'Thank God you are here,' she said, 'Mama's very ill.'

I went through to Mama's bedroom, but she was too ill to recognize me. Grief seized me, and my tears began to flow. Papa was sitting crying in the next room: Marya stood there, tears running down her face, her fingers moving together ceaselessly. They told me the doctor had been there three hours before, and that the other daughter had gone with a prescription to the pharmacy.

Dawn wasn't far away, and as soon as it was seven o'clock I ran to their doctor, asking what could be done and if he would bring a specialist. He said that no specialist would come to such a poor home without being paid first. I opened my wallet. 'Ten rubles,' said the doctor. I paid him, and told him there would be more if only he could get the specialist there quickly. Then I ran back to the house, and we could only wait, and pray. I went into Mama's room again and tried to talk to her, but she stared at me unseeingly. It seemed an eternity before the doctor and the specialist arrived. They examined Mama briefly, and then consulted together. The only hope, they said, was to get her into a hospital; but even then there was little chance of her living more than three weeks at the most.

It was nine o'clock when they left, and arrangements were made for Mama to be taken away. Papa made us eat; 'Your being hungry won't help Mama,' he said. And presently the ambulance came, and took Mama, and there was nothing else that any of us could do.

I took myself off to Habinski's. Mrs Habinski was in the office; I said good morning to her, and to my amazement she answered, 'Good morning,' and began to speak to me politely. I told her I had been to Mama Marcovsky's, and she said: 'Yes, I know Hilda is very ill.' I explained that the specialist did not hold out much hope, and she said: 'She is still young,' cheeringly. She could see I was upset, and she told me I had done all I could, if I had paid for a specialist for her. For the first time, Mrs Habinski was talking to me as a person, not as if she were speaking to a servant. Habinski came in then, wanting to know why I was standing talking there, and his wife barked at him: 'His Mama's very ill.'

'Hannah ill and you worry?' said Habinski.

'Not her, fool — Hilda Marcovsky,' said Mrs Habinski, and the Guvnor said: 'Yes, I know what a good mother can be. I had a mother and father you know, but when the time comes we are all in the same position and there's nothing you can do about it except carry on. You must go and help old Kovalevsky, he's very busy this morning.' But then he turned to his wife and said gruffly: 'Give Moysey some tea and some breakfast before he goes.'

The machinery shop was crowded with peasants; this was the season when they would be buying ploughs ready for the ploughing of the fallow fields when spring came. I knew how to talk to the peasants, even better than old Kovalevsky did though he had been doing it for years, and I could sell to them, and as the morning went on we gradually dealt with them all. In the end I was left alone with old Kovalevsky, who began making tea as he always did. He was very angry, wanting to know why I had asked the bank at Constantinograd to demand the return of my money. I explained that I had now become engaged and would need all the money I could get for presents and clothes and such things; and this startled the old man into silence. At dinner time I returned to the Marcovskys — Mrs Habinski had even asked me to stay to dinner to save the Marcovskys trouble, but I couldn't wait, I would not be easy in my mind, I said. She said she wished Hilda a quick recovery, and let me go.

But the news was bad; news from the hospital was that Mama could not eat or drink and was being kept alive with warm glucose water. Vera asked me if I had eaten, and though I said I could not eat while Mama was so ill, she made tea and made me have some bread and cheese while we waited. And then Esther returned from the hospital, and told us that Mama was dead, and I wept and covered my face with my hands. I was a grown man now, but I could remember when I had been ill and she had neglected everything else for me, and I had slept in her arms.

I had to go to the hospital and get a death certificate so that she could be buried in the Jewish cemetery; and I telegraphed the news to her eldest son in America, though we could not delay the funeral for him to be present — it took six weeks in those days to get from there to Verchneprovsk. There was a prayer to be said at the graveside by the eldest son, but I said it instead, with great difficulty, for my heart was breaking. From that day onwards for twelve months a prayer had to be said in the synagogue early in the morning and again in the evening, and this I never missed.

For the next week or two I was working at Habinski's and could spend the evenings with the Marcovskys; after that Habinski decided to send me back to Constantinograd. I attended the bourse and met the trains and bought wheat in the old routine, and as time went by my sorrow healed a little as sorrows will.

I wrote to Sonia twice a week, and there was one piece of good news to tell her — the bank had got my thousand rubles out of old Kovalevsky after all, despite all his pretences of poverty, and this made our prospects of marriage much brighter. At Easter I took eight days off and rushed to Krukov to see Sonia. I greeted her with a kiss on the cheek; and she blushed and said it was the first time in her life that a man had kissed her; I said it was more than that — it was the first time her future husband had kissed her. Mrs Bromberg had begun preparations for the formal engagement party, and I wanted to get this over before I returned to work again. But a formal engagement was much more important than our private agreement that we should become engaged, and I took Sonia's hand and asked her if that was what she really wanted.

She began to hesitate, the way girls will, saying things couldn't be decided quickly, so I said: 'I'm only here eight days. Yes or no?' and Sonia said, 'Yes.'

'Now why don't you kiss her,' said Mrs Bromberg; Sonia said she was shy, but I was tired of waiting and I took her in my arms and kissed her; and it being done, shy or not, Sonia responded with kisses.

Her father and Sam returned from work soon afterwards, very dirty from dealing with their horses, and while they were washing Sonia said how tired she was of keeping the house clean when they were always coming in and dirtying it; and I told her that soon I would be able to take her away from that, away with me to Constantinograd where she could have a maid, and we should show people how to live.

Nina arrived too, and we told her that the formal engagement party would be on Sunday. She congratulated us, and we said that perhaps in a few weeks we would be going to her engagement party, but 'That won't happen,' she said, 'I'm poor and nobody wants me. A lot of boys want to marry me at first but when they find I've no dowry they leave me.' Sam got hold of her playfully round the waist and said: 'Why don't we get engaged on Sunday too?' Sonia asked if he meant it, but Nina said: 'You know your brother. He will never marry — his life is vodka and billiards.'

Before the party there were certain formalities. I had to go to Hannah and Herscho and invite them; not that I wanted them, but since I was under age they would have to sign the betrothal. They were taken aback when I told them I had found a girl I intended to marry but when I pointed out: 'You arranged it with the Rabbi last year,' and told them that the dowry was a thousand rubles, they cheered up. 'That's a fine sum,' said Herscho. 'You'll be able to buy a nice shop with that.' Hannah tried to be difficult, saying, 'Well, you're sold already — you don't belong to us any more,' but I told her not to be ridiculous: 'The world gets married,' I said. She did insist, though, that I must observe Jewish custom and while I could stay with the Brombergs for the next few days I must return on the day of the betrothal so that I should set off to the party with her and with Herscho. I promised I would do this, and went off to issue invitations to other people we knew in the town.

It was past midnight when I returned, only to run into more trouble. Sam and his father were hanging about, and Mrs Bromberg said that Sonia had gone to bed with a headache from too much excitement, and was asleep. Then Sam and his father cornered me. Sam said: 'It's not excitement, it's because Mama forced her to get engaged, that's why Sonia's not here waiting for you.' And the old man said: 'If you are really a good friend you will leave now and not come back — it's no good marrying a girl who has been forced into it, not even for the money. You must tell Sonia that you've decided you can't marry a girl whose father and brother are always drunk in the street.' Sonia's mother couldn't get a word in: 'I'll get rid of him,' the old man kept saying.

I had begun to protest that I wasn't marrying Sonia for her money when Sonia herself appeared at her bedroom door in a dressing gown, very angry and rounding on her father and brother scornfully. 'You'll get rid of him, will you?' she said. 'Two grown men behaving like hooligans, treating someone like this. Go to bed!' And she drove her father off to bed, looking as stunned as if he'd been hit on the head with a hammer, while Sam slunk out saying he had to get back to his sledge, there was good money for working at night.

While the old man was grumbling off to bed, Mrs Bromberg said good night and we all went to our rooms, but in a few minutes when the old man was asleep she called me again, and there was Sonia, fully dressed now and looking so beautiful I fell in love with her all

8

over again. She said that she had made tea and she thought we could all do with a glass, and we sat round the table to drink it.

'Those two men are wild,' said Sonia. 'They say they are upset because I told Nina you had no parents and now everybody knows and people come up to them in the street and ask about it. But really they are afraid that Mama intends to sell this house to get the money for my dowry — they don't know she has saved up the thousand rubles, and more beside to pay for the wedding. That's why they wanted to get rid of you.'

I told Mrs Bromberg that rather than have trouble in the family I would not take any dowry; I wasn't marrying Sonia for a thousand rubles, and she ought to spend the money herself, because she had worked for it and needed it more than we did. But she replied: 'The money is not because you are marrying my daughter, but because you are now both my children and I'd like you to have it — I'll get my enjoyment seeing you make use of it.' And so that was settled.

In the morning both Sam and Sonia's father came round, apologetically. Sam admitted the trouble was over their fear of losing the house, and the old man confessed that, though he didn't like people talking about his getting a son-in-law who had no parents, he was more afraid what his wife and daughter would say to him than of anything the neighbours might say.

The rest of the day I spent going about the town with Sonia; and all the way it was: 'Is this your young man, Sonia?' from passers-by, or long searching glances through windows. In the shops it was the same; people coming to serve me and I saying, awkwardly: 'I'm waiting for my fiancée,' and Sonia blushing. 'Mademoiselle Bromberg, you have been coming to my shop since you were five,' said one shopkeeper, 'And you are shy to tell *me* you have a fiancé?' We walked across the bridge to Kremenchug because Sonia wanted to stroll and swing her umbrella, and everyone saw us and we were without a care in the world. The weather was pleasant that day, and I felt it was a pity the bridge wasn't longer; if the walk had taken a month it would not have been too long.

In Kremenchug we went into a printer to choose engagement

cards, and then on to a high-class teashop — Sonia said she had always wanted to go into that one, but Nina had never had the pluck to go with her. We ordered our tea and pastries, and then went out to stroll again, window-gazing in the finest street of the town. It was too early for the theatre, so we took a tram to the town's art gallery — Sonia had never been there before, but it was her idea. Then we strolled back to the theatre to see Valsova the great soprano. Sonia asked me to let her choose the seats, and got two for five rubles fifty kopecks — she said that we must take care of our money now, and I wasn't to throw it away showing off to her. It was a big theatre, and a good class one; when the curtain went up you could have heard a pin drop — it seemed ruffians didn't come here, although there were no notices to keep them out, only a few forbidding smoking.

When the play ended I told Sonia that it was a pity to spoil a pleasant evening, but we had a duty to perform — to visit Hannah and Herscho. She said she didn't mind, and I called a cab and said 'to the cripple Baron's house' — they all knew it as that. It went off easily enough, Hannah kissing and shaking hands with Sonia, Herscho replying to Sonia's 'How do you do?' with 'I always do well when I meet a beautiful girl', and the four of us sitting round eating sunflower seeds; Hannah apologized that we could not have tea because it was Friday evening and so, as a religious person, she could not light the samovar, and Herscho brought in lemonade instead.

I spent the Sunday morning before the party at Sonia's house, helping to get everything ready, and finally everyone was dressed up and I had to set off to meet Hannah and Herscho. I hesitated, looking round for Sonia, and she came out of her room dressed for the party; each time I saw her she seemed more beautiful, and now I had no doubts at all that I wanted to be engaged to her. She saw me watching her and said: 'I think I can read your mind — you want me to come with you to meet your loving parents,' and she grinned. But she had to stay to greet the guests, so I set out alone.

Hannah was wearing a new dress and new shoes, and Herscho had a new pair of high boots. I introduced them to Sonia and her mother and father, and then shouted to everyone in the room: 'I'm the intended bridegroom and here are my father and mother,' and everyone answered back 'Good luck to you!' and the two hired waitresses began handing round the drinks so that people could drink our health.

At six oclock the Rabbi arrived, carrying a briefcase; he began a speech, saying: 'We are all gathered here together to betrothe Sonia Bromberg to Moysey Stocklinsky,' and then sat down and started filling in his forms, asking all sorts of questions. He wrote down that on the fifteenth day of April, 1910, Sonia and Moysey became engaged according to the Jewish law and religion; and then asked Sonia how much her intended dowry was going to be. She said one thousand rubles. Then he asked what present I had for Sonia, and before I could answer Sonia said, as we had arranged, 'He has given me three hundred rubles to buy a present because he came here too late to buy something and must go back soon to Constantinograd.' I had to fill in the intended date of the marriage, and wrote, '15.4.1911', and then Sonia and I had to sign, and Herscho and Sonia's father, and a copy was given to me and another to Sonia.

'Now,' said the Rabbi, 'everyone enjoy themselves — I have to run off to another engagement,' and we all filled our glasses and drank and sang. Except for Hannah; she sat there like someone with a gun in her back, though Herscho was happy enough. I was pumped with questions by various aunts of Sonia's, until she rescued me, and we ate and drank and ate and drank. At half-past ten Sonia and her half-sister tried to tell their mother not to bring in any more food or drink, but she replied: 'I've only one daughter to marry, and everyone must be happy.' Mrs Bromberg had had a few drinks too. At half-past eleven the guests began to go, and at last only Hannah and Herscho were left. Herscho was too drunk to get out of his chair so I pushed him on to a couch and left him there, and Sonia let Hannah share her bed for the night. (She complained afterwards that when they got into bed Hannah touched her breasts, saying, 'They are real, then? I thought you had padded them to impress the boys,' which upset Sonia.) In the morning Sam took Hannah and Herscho home in his cab, while I helped Sonia and her mother clear up the house; Mama Bromberg (for so I was now to call her) was singing and when Sonia asked why she was singing so early in the morning she replied: 'I've a daughter and a son now. I've had a struggle in my life but now God has repaid.'

I asked Sonia if she felt as happy, and she said she was happy for her mother but 'about me, I shall see later'. Then she explained: 'I am thinking of what will happen when Herscho decides he won't let you marry me because you are under twenty-one. He will make us wait until you have done your three years military service.' I told her not to worry. 'God will give us the day and the necessities for that day,' and she smiled and came up to me and I put my arms round her and kissed her.

For myself, there was happiness even though I had to leave Sonia so soon after the engagement party. I had found a house, a home which I could call my own, somewhere I could return to, to people whom I really loved. The wishes of all my life were satisfied. I was totally happy.

XVIII.   MARRIED

I had taken these few days' holiday without telling the Guvnor, and
my punishment awaited me when I got back to Constantinograd, in
the form of a pile of telegrams. I put off opening them as long as I
could, but finally I took them up to my room and began opening
them one by one and with each one I opened the more worried I
became. Each of the telegrams was an instruction for me to buy
grain and grain and more grain; I should have bought forty truckloads if I had followed the telegrams' instructions, and now there
would be no chance to buy so much. But it was over and I could do
nothing about it except go to bed and try to sleep. And in the morning there came a letter from the Guvnor. It was written, as usual, by
the girl he employed, and she, knowing that he could not read,
would always write to me very nicely regardless of what the Guvnor
dictated. The letter read:

'*I have sent several telegrams to you during the last few days and
I am writing this letter hoping that you will reply. In this way I
may be able to pacify Habinski. I must inform you that the grain
business is very bad and prices are dropping daily. The next few lines
are as Habinski wants me to write:*

'*These few telegrams to which you did not reply means that you
have not bought any grain, and I am very grateful for this, even
though I was angry at first. If you had bought the grain I would have
lost a lot of money. You have not sent an account of your expenses
for a long time. Do so soon for it is more convenient to have accounts
settled.*'

And the girl signed it, Tania Markin.

It was too good to be true; I couldn't believe my luck.

Soon I was back into the routine. There was little business to do
at first, but after a while it picked up and soon I was getting the
usual stream of telegrams, meeting the trains, going to the bourse. I
got from the bank the money that Kovalevsky had repaid me, and

sent it to Sonia; I got a letter signed by all the employees at Habinski's, wishing me luck on my engagement; I sent little presents of
silk handkerchiefs and fancy combs to Sonia and her mother, a tie
to her brother, and a postal order, the price of a bottle of whisky, to
her father.

And then, when I had been back in Constantinograd about eight
weeks, I received a very distressed letter from Sonia saying that her
brother was dangerously ill, and then a telegram asking if I could
come to Krukov. I telegraphed my Guvnor, and caught the train.

As I neared the Brombergs' house I noticed a lot of people standing about, and a little girl told me: 'Mister, don't go in there, someone is dead.' I pushed through the crowd, into the house, and saw
Sonia sitting on the couch being comforted by a neighbour. She told
me that Sam had become ill and had been taken to hospital, where
they discovered he had an incurable disease; he had died that day. I
thought to myself how strange life was, that only a couple of months
before he had been so strong, and now he was dead.

I took Sonia in a cab to the big hospital where her parents had
been for the past three days, and we fetched them home. Her father
began straight away to drown his sorrows in vodka, and I went
through the pantry to find some food — cheese, herrings and bread
— and lit the samovar, and made them eat and drink. The next day,
at the father's request, I made the arrangements with the under-
takers to bring the body back to the house and the funeral was fixed
for six o'clock that evening. (This was one Jewish custom I did
agree with — that the dead should be buried within twenty-four
hours. For thus all the crying and misery is done and suffered in the
one day together.) Sonia and her mother were very miserable, and to
make things easier for them I insisted that we must clean out the
front room before the funeral service — it gave them something to
do and stopped them thinking. Then the body arrived, and the
Rabbi, and the service with its wailing and crying; it was a long
service but at last it was over. I annoyed the father by staying at
home to look after Sonia and her mother — it isn't the Jewish custom for women to go to burials, and I thought I could do more good
with them than at the graveside. But the old man forgave me when

he returned from the burial — he went straight to the cupboard for his big bottle of vodka — and asked me for a favour. 'As you know, the Jewish religion demands that when a parent dies the son has to go to the synagogue and pray every morning for a year. I have no son now — when I die I want you to do that for me.' And I promised, while the old man sat there swigging away until he fell asleep with his face on the table. Sonia was ashamed at the sight, but I told her not to worry because soon I would be able to take her away from such things, 'And we'll live like ordinary people live,' I said.

I stayed with them for a day or two, and though it was a house of mourning, at least I was with Sonia. Each day, according to custom, the Rabbi came and blessed everyone and wished them long life, and got paid for it. He wanted to arrange for the special low chairs to be sent from the synagogue for everyone to sit on during the time of mourning; it seemed to me to be just nonsense, not religion but merely tradition.

Mama Bromberg didn't want me to go; now that she had lost her son she was eager for me to be near at hand, and she suggested that we should bring the marriage forward, and that I could buy a grain shop in Krukov. I asked if Sonia agreed, and she said, 'It is up to you.' I kissed her, and thought that this would be better than waiting the long twelve months to marry. But first there was the question of Herscho's permission; and that was difficult.

I crossed the bridge into Kremenchug to visit him, and explained what we wanted to do. He was very quick to remind me that I could not marry without his consent, and he rubbed it in; 'Although you are a big tall chap, right now I've got you like a little dog on a chain.' I was angry at this, and told him that it might be true but he hadn't got a whip any more as he used to have when I was small. He softened after that, and promised that he would sign the papers to allow me to marry, and I thanked him and shook his hand, and kissed Hannah before rushing back to the Brombergs. And that day I went out with Sonia, and we walked arm-in-arm across the big bridge again, and I sang her love songs, which she seemed to like very much.

I had now to go back to Verchneprovsk, both to tell the Guvnor that I would be leaving him and starting up on my own, and also to give notice to the Registrar in Verchneprovsk so that the marriage could be arranged. Before I left, Mama Bromberg took me aside, and asked me if I would visit a man who had always been her friend and her legal adviser, who had often helped her during the troubles of her hard life. He might be able to give me good advice for my future and Sonia's, she said; so I agreed at once. I didn't feel quite so happy about it when she went on to tell me that this man was the town's chief of police; I didn't like the idea of telling him my plans and ambitions, and it seemed as though I might be put through a very searching examination to make sure that I was really a fit husband for Sonia. I must admit I slept badly the night before, twisting and turning and watching the hours go by, but in the end I had to get up and have breakfast, to kiss Sonia goodbye and set off.

I was walking into the police station when a policeman asked me what I wanted, and when I said I had an appointment with his superior, Mr Evonov, he showed me in and went back to his post at the door. I saw a big office with a few desks in it, and a grey-haired man — tall and very slim and delicate-looking, in a black suit with a few medals dangling on one side, more like a general than a policeman. Every time he wanted to look at some papers he fixed a pair of glasses on his nose and when he had finished he left them dangling on a black cord which hung round his neck. Two other men were sitting at a desk, busy writing. The grey-haired man opened an adjoining door and we went into a smaller room. He sat down at the desk and asked me to sit opposite him. 'Here we can talk without anyone hearing our conversation, so there is no need to be afraid to talk,' he said. 'Don't hide anything from me. You can talk to me openly; I am here to help you, not to do you any harm. I have been here twenty-eight years in this office and I don't think you will find one person who can say I have been unfair to them. I've also known your future wife since she was a baby, and if I can help Madame Bromberg's daughter in any way I will.'

He asked me my name and when I told him 'Moysey Stocklinsky', he said, 'I will call you Moysey as it will be easier to talk to you.'
8*

Then he said, 'We won't waste time, I will come to the point. Have you got a passport?' I gave it to him, and he looked at it saying, 'According to the date on this you only have five weeks to run. Leave it with me and I will get you a six months' extension on it.' He looked at it again. 'By the look of it you have got to put yourself forward for military service in eighteen months' time,' he said, and I agreed.

He answered: 'But you have planned to get married in three months' time and then you will have to go away for three years. Do you think you are going to leave that poor girl here to struggle alone for three years? I don't think I can allow that. Did you know that your future wife has two step-sisters abroad, why not go there?' I looked up at him in amazement and hesitated before answering. You do not expect to hear a chief of police advising someone to break the law. He said, 'Don't hesitate in your reply. I am here to help you, you must trust me otherwise it is no good. Your intended mother-in-law has had a lot of aggravations from her family. She had a lot of trouble with her husband's children before they went abroad, and with her boy dying. Now you come along and want to give her more trouble. It is time she had peace and happiness from her only daughter.'

He thought for a moment and then he said: 'I don't want you to come here after this, but I will get you to sign a paper, and when you get married I want you to leave this paper with your wife.' He walked out of the room and after a quarter of an hour he returned with a foolscap paper in his hand, and told me to read it. This is what I read: 'I Moysey Stocklinsky permit my wife Sonia and any children she may have to go abroad whenever she wants to.'

I signed this paper and he did the same. He placed it in an envelope and gave it to me saying: 'Keep it until you are married, then give it to your wife. If I require to give you a message, I will communicate with Madame Bromberg.' He stood up with me, shook hands, and wished me luck. I was about to say something when he said: 'I don't want any thanks or payment. I have enough money and I am getting old. I would not know what to do with it. I have no children myself and you both deserve happiness.' He squeezed my hand and I could tell by the pressure of his grip and the look on his face that he meant everything he said.

I said goodbye and went out of the door past the saluting policeman, and I made my way home. I told Sonia and her mother what a good-hearted chap that chief of police was and that he had advised me to go abroad. I noticed as I was talking that Sonia had an envelope in her hand. She said, 'This is the reply from the invitation we sent to London to my two step-sisters, Dora and Lily.' Mama Bromberg said, 'How nice it would be if you and Sonia could go to London, and live all in one town. I have been to visit London once to see Dora and Lily; I think you should write yourself to them and find out if they would like you to go there. Father and I could follow you in a year's time.'

So after dinner, I sat down to write a polite letter to Sonia's relatives in London. I addressed the letter to the oldest son-in-law and asked him if he thought it worth while my coming there. '*At the moment I have a good position,*' I wrote, '*but soon I will be drafted into the army. I don't mind that, but your step-sister will not be allowed any money — as you know, over here dependents are not considered. And Sonia would be left alone for a long time. Sonia would like to live near her sisters, I know, all in one town together. If you think I will be able to get a living in London, I will come and bring Sonia.*

Yours truly,

Moysey Stocklinsky'

I put my letter into an envelope and Mama said she would stamp and post it when she went out. And that was how this next great step in my life was taken.

I told Sonia that tomorrow I was going to Verchneprovsk to settle up with Habinski and tell him I was leaving, and to see the Registrar about our marriage. Sonia didn't like the idea of me going to Verchneprovsk; I think she was a bit afraid I would not come back again. She even said: 'I suppose you will be seeing more of your girls again.' I told her I did not want to go but I had to, and early next day I set off.

On arrival at the Verchneprovsk boat station, I noticed Vassil, the cab man, whom I promised long ago that I would visit his family.

When I had got off the boat he came up and said, 'It is four o'clock — get in my cab, we are going home to have something to eat.' I couldn't argue so I got in the cab and he drove me to his home, and rushed into the house to warn his wife to prepare extra food as he had brought a friend home. I waited for him to unharness his horse and put it into the stable, then we both went into the house. Vassil was a well-built man with black eyes and a black beard, and a huge moustache. To look at he was frightening, but really he had a heart of gold.

It puzzled me why he bothered with me — he was not Jewish and he knew I was. Yet he would do anything for me.

He shouted out, 'Marie, look, I have brought Moysey for dinner!' A woman came, she had a beautiful face but her body was so enormous that it spoilt her beauty. I bowed down to her and said, 'Good afternoon' and she told me to sit down, and brought in meat, potatoes, fresh baked bread, and curd dumplings. Vassil put on the table a bottle of vodka and some glasses. While we were eating and drinking I took from my pocket one of the small cards Sonia and I had had printed, announcing our engagement, as was the custom then. I told him I did not know his address but I intended to send him a formal invitation when I had the chance. He took it and read it, and he looked amazed: 'So young,' he said. His wife could not read, so he read it to her, and we all drank to it. We were all happy but I noticed she had her handkerchief to her eyes once or twice, I did not know why. She took out the plates and came back with two water melons. She left them on the table and she said to her husband, 'I am going to the shops before they are closed.' She must have put her coat on outside; then we heard her calling, 'Vassil, I have not got enough money — give me a few more rubles.'

Vassil said to me, 'Women! They never have enough money. When you get married you will find out what expense is.'

Just then his wife came in, a scarf over her head. I looked at her, with the scarf on her head, and suddenly I was a little boy again, sitting shivering on a car in the snow and bitter cold of the square at Verchneprovsk, my frostbitten hands hugged under my ragged coat to try to keep warm, and a woman with that same scarf on her head stopping to talk to me and getting me taken off to hospital. I felt so moved I went up to her and touched her and said, 'Please, don't go out anywhere.' Vassil came up to me and said, 'What's happened, why are you so pale?'

'You knew all the time — why did you keep it a secret from me?' I said. He said, 'I don't know what you are talking about.' I said, 'Well, once upon a time Mama here saved my life.' And I told him how she had been the one kind person who had noticed me and had bothered to tell the authorities when I was an ill-treated child. And all this time I had been sitting in her house, eating a meal with her, and not recognizing her until she put on a headscarf. If she had not prepared to go out, I would never have known. Tears were rolling down her cheeks as I talked. I got out my clean handkerchief and gave it to her, and said, 'Why are you crying?' She said they were tears of happiness, and I went down on my knees and kissed her hands. I did not need any more proof that she was my guardian angel.

We spent a long time talking over old times. Their daughter Anita came in while we were talking, and the evening ended with my taking Anita to the theatre. From the time I got engaged to Sonia I always liked to compare other girls, and Anita was beautiful, a happy girl and full of life with not a care in the world.

There was extra excitement in the play that night, because in the middle of the performance there was a commotion: a police guard came in, and arrested one of the actors for 'insulting the police force' — in his part he was accusing the police of corruption. Anita did not want to stay until the play started again, so she suggested we go out for a walk. Walking her home I found out she was not only a happy girl, but she was also a naughty one. I suppose she was spoilt, being the only child. It took us a long time to get home. Her mother was waiting for us, although she did not admit it — she said she stayed up late to finish her work.

They persuaded me to stay the night, and I settled down on the sofa, but I could not sleep straight away so I lit the lamp again and decided to write to Sonia. I told her all about how I met Vassil and how I had supper with them, but I did not mention that I took his daughter out.

Next morning I set off for the granary to see the Guvnor. Everyone there congratulated me on my engagement, but when the
Guvnor heard he said, 'These boys grow up so quick,' and began
lecturing me. 'How come you got engaged without asking my
advice? You are still a boy.'

I said, 'Would you mind going through all the papers to see if
they are correct, because I terminate my services with you today.'

'You can't do that,' he exploded, 'you have to give me six months'
notice.'

'If I stay here another six months it will not do you any good,
because my mind is not here. It will be much better for me to leave
at the end of the week,' I answered.

The Guvnor was determined to be cross whatever I said, and
slammed out of the room into the office, ordering the girl book-
keeper to go through all my accounts and ordering me to stay and
give her any help she needed. We began going over my books, and
after a few minutes there was a tap on the door and the maid came
in with a glass of tea for the girl who handed it over to me asking the
maid to bring another. But it was Mrs Habinski who came in with
the second glass, much more friendly than usual. I jumped up and
bowed to her and offered her my chair. 'The maid told me there
was a nice young man in here — perhaps you will join us for lunch
when you've finished your business here,' she said.

Apart from one or two small things the accounts and the papers
were all correct, and the girl said I was entitled to a months's pay
and gave it to me; then she wished me luck — and kissed me, which
I didn't expect.

Habinski spotted me as I came out of the office and called me
over to where he was sitting with his daughter; I remembered her
as a little girl in a white dress but she was fourteen and growing up
now. She was curious and asked questions like a grown-up too;
what did Sonia look like, was she beautiful, and how much money
had I been offered for her dowry? I had to ask her parents politely
if they could make her mind her own business. The Guvnor had
been sitting all this time without saying a word; suddenly he got up,
went to his wine cupboard and brought out a bottle of vodka. He

must have got over his bad temper and decided to accept that I was right about leaving him, for he said more cheerfully: 'Come, enough of this arguing. Have a drink. Let's all drink to Moysey,' and we drank, and in this more cheerful mood sat down to lunch. Afterwards the Guvnor said that, though I officially had twelve more days to work for him, business was quiet and I could leave earlier if I wanted to with his full approval. I thanked him very much, and said I would like to leave that afternoon to visit the Registrar of Marriages; the Guvnor agreed, and I walked out feeling for the first time free of every care in the world. On second thoughts I decided I wasn't as free as all that, because I was getting tied up in marriage, but that kind of tie didn't matter; perhaps it made life all the sweeter.

At the Registrar's office I found that I had first to get a special paper from the Rabbi, so I set off again to find the Rabbi: I had to wait a long while to see him, but when I finally got in and told him my name he said that he had already had a letter from the Rabbi in Krukov wanting details of my history. 'She is a respectable girl and great care has been exercised to see that she marries the right person,' said the Rabbi. 'I have not answered the letter yet, but as you are here we will see to it now.'

He called to his assistant, who brought in a great book and went out again. The Rabbi began turning the leaves, found the page he was looking for, studied it a minute, then looked at me and studied it again. Finally he said, not very happily, 'I have to tell every detail of your birth, every detail.'

I said: 'What can you tell them? I was born. I wasn't a thief or a cheat when I was born, so what can you tell them?'

'I have to tell them that you were left an orphan at the synagogue, that your mother was unmarried and ran away,' said the Rabbi heavily.

'Oh, that,' I said. 'I've already told them that. I thought it best to tell them before they found out for themselves.'

The Rabbi wanted to know how I could tell people such a story about myself without being ashamed. I had worked this out for myself since I had met Sonia, and I told him that to try to keep things dark and to be ashamed of things was foolish; it was to behave like my own real parents had done. I could understand now that they must have been very young and silly, and perhaps as they got older they had understood better what they had done, and had been sorry.

The Rabbi filled in his forms, and made me stay and have a glass of tea with him; but I was glad to get away as soon as I could. My next visit was a more cheerful one; I was walking past the shops and had reached the place where Herscho used to buy his horse-feed when the shopkeeper stepped out and called me to stop. 'Are you going to pass by without coming to see me?' this man said. 'Because you dress like a lord you don't want to know me?' and he pulled me inside to show me to his wife.

I remembered his name; Mr Malach — a very big fat man but with thin legs, and his wife was tall and thin and flat-chested — if she'd have dressed in men's clothes I swear no one would have been able to tell who was the husband and who was the wife. She said she remembered me as a pale, cold underfed little boy, 'And now a tall, strong lovely man!' I told them I was getting married, and they brought out the vodka and talked of old times. Malach mentioned that Herscho left town owing him sixty rubles. I said that since it was over the scandal of my running away that Herscho had to leave, I felt it was my fault, and I would pay him back, but his wife said: 'That's a silly thing to suggest. Don't go round offering to pay Herscho's bad debts — we're not the only ones he owed money to.' And they asked me to send them an invitation to the wedding: 'We've not been away from the shop for a good while and it will do us good to come to Kremenchug,' they said.

Next morning I completed my business in Verchneprovsk, and said goodbye to the Guvnor, thanking him for all the years he had looked after me. Mrs Habinski asked me to stay on to lunch, and the Guvnor said they wanted to buy Sonia and me a wedding present: 'It is unlucky to buy it before the wedding, but send us an invitation and we will post a present to you.' So when I walked for the last time out of Habinski's house, to which I'd come as a small boy, I had kindness to remember as well as the hardness of the early days.

On the boat I curled up in a chair and went to sleep, sleeping right

through until the boat was pulling in to moor at Kremenchug. I
took a train from the boat-landing to the bridge, and walked across
to the cabs clustered, as always, on the Krukov side. When I asked
a driver to take me to the Brombergs, he remembered me and when
we arrived he wouldn't accept his fare but drove off calling: 'I'll
have an extra glass of vodka at the wedding.'

Sonia was still asleep, but her mother told me that Herscho and
Hannah had been to visit her while I was away, and had been
friendly. Herscho had agreed to sign the forms permitting me to
marry, provided I settled in Krukov; and Mama Bromberg had
heard of an old man who had a grain-shop and who wanted to sell
out. When Sonia woke I discussed it with her, and we agreed that I
should try to buy it from him. It would be a bit hard for me to deal
with peasants when I had been dealing in railway truckloads for the
past few years, but it would keep Herscho happy, knowing I was
living near by, and ease his fears that I might run off abroad somewhere.

I decided then and there to go and talk to the old man about his
granary. When I got to the shop he was on his own, but he insisted
I wait so that he could fetch some friends to advise him. He returned with four men, and after talking together for a few minutes
we fixed on a price of two hundred and twenty rubles for the
business — a bargain, I thought, as there was only a small rent to
pay and there were scales and sacks ready for my use thrown in. I
promised to return in the afternoon with my father, for I was under
twenty-one and I couldn't complete the sale without his signature.

From the shop I went on to the market, to find Hannah and
Herscho at their stall. They were very pleased at my news; Herscho
agreed to return to the shop with me, but he said he couldn't turn up
to make a business deal in his working clothes so I took him to his
home to change, and then in a tram back to the bridge. Herscho was
getting old; it was a job for him to walk across the bridge, and so on
the other side I took a cab to Sonia's house and then, after he had
had a rest, on to the grain shop.

As we walked in I could see from his face that Herscho felt a
great personality. He told the old man that when young people

wanted to get married it was the duty of all parents to try to help them out — as if it were his money and not mine that was going to pay for the business. Then he started haggling over the price, even though the old grain-dealer pointed out that we had already agreed on that. After a great deal of argument Herscho got twenty rubles off, and I paid a small deposit — ten rubles, all I had on me — and got a receipt, and we returned to Sonia's house where Herscho bragged endlessly to Mama Bromberg about his cleverness in getting the twenty rubles.

Sonia brought out a bottle of vodka and some cakes to celebrate, and Mama Bromberg said she would get the police chief who advised her on all legal affairs, to draw up the documents to make sure there were no mistakes.

That couldn't be until next day, but early next morning we got the papers from the police chief — I gave him five rubles for his trouble in drawing them up — and asked Sonia to come with me to pay the grain-dealer and take possession of our shop. The old man counted the money carefully, signed the papers, and handed me the key of the shop. And there we were, Sonia and I, very proud of ourselves, standing in our own shop, a shop I owned.

Two days later I opened for business. Sonia came round to the shop, and we made plans for our wedding — there was plenty of time to make plans, because I didn't buy more than ten bags of chicken food all day. I wasn't worried about this, because I thought that I had only to offer the peasants a better price for their wheat and the news would soon get round and the grain would begin to arrive. We went home that evening and told Mama Bromberg that we had decided the wedding should be on August 15. Mama got busy next morning; she hired a hall on the edge of the town for the reception, and soon the house was humming with Mama's sewing machine preparing sheets and pillowcases and such things. Sonia was getting clothes ready; I ordered a new suit and an overcoat.

I had been right about the peasants; when word got round that I was offering better prices they began to flock round my shop, and soon I had it filled with all the different grains. The big dealers who visited all the small grain shops to buy up what the small dealers had accumulated soon came to me. They asked where the old man had gone, and I explained that I had bought the business from him and invited them in to look round. They thought my stock looked good, and offered me prices I knew to be fair — I could always check in the grain trade magazine. The only worry I had was that even though the prices were fair I couldn't make a good profit: I couldn't and wouldn't cheat the peasants in the way that Habinski had taught me; and it was this cheating which made the difference between a very small profit and a good living for most of the grain merchants. But I couldn't do anything about it now except take the price the big dealers offered me.

Three weeks before the wedding I closed the shop one afternoon, putting up a notice CLOSED FOR PERSONAL REASONS, and went off to collect Herscho and arrange for him to come with me to get the marriage licence. He had agreed to the marriage and had raised no objections, but now he changed his mind. 'I won't permit you to get married,' he said. I asked him why, and told him that Mama Bromberg had made all the arrangements, even to paying for the hall, and begged him not to torment me like this, but all he would say was, 'I don't care what expense has been incurred — I won't allow the wedding.' There was nothing else I could do but go home to the Brombergs, very sadly.

When Sonia's father heard about it he was furious. 'I'll see about him stopping the wedding. We will visit him tonight — I'll take a pal with us who will deal with him!'

'What pal?' said Mama Bromberg, and he replied: 'Slomer!'

When the old man went outside to see to his horse I asked Sonia who Slomer was. 'A very fierce man,' she said. 'I don't like him, but he's been very good to our family. His wife is my mother's niece — he practically forced her to marry him under threats of killing her. He's always involved in fights.'

Mr Bromberg and I took a cab to a place across the bridge; a little street of small houses. The old man knocked on a door, a very good-looking woman opened it and said, 'Hullo, Uncle, come in.' We went in and were introduced to her husband, Slomer. He was an enormous man; I was pretty big, but even I was frightened to look at him. I turned to Sonia's father and said: 'Do you remember when you wanted to get rid of me? If you'd shown me this relation of yours you would have succeeded!' The huge man laughed. 'I may look like a killer but I like to distinguish between right and wrong and look at both sides before striking,' he said.

I explained to him about Herscho agreeing with the marriage and then changing his mind now that time was running short. Slomer listened and said: 'Don't worry, Moysey. The wedding will be on the day arranged.' The three of us went outside and climbed into the waiting cab, and off we went to Herscho's house.

Hannah opened the door; she didn't see that I had anyone behind me at first, and she began: 'You back begging again? You'll get nothing from us until you've done your military service.'

Slomer's voice came from behind me. 'You will help him, if you and your husband want to stay in one piece and if you don't the boy won't need any permission to get married. . . .'

Herscho came to the door, and hastily took Mr Bromberg aside. Sonia's father told him: 'If you'd decided from the start not to let Moysey get married until he had done his service, that would have been all very well. But you gave him permission to marry and now you change your mind. You know my wife and I must get our daughter married, and you are not being very fair.'

Herscho thought he could deal with Mr Bromberg. 'You go home and I'll have a talk to Hannah and we'll let you know tomorrow morning,' and it looked as if Mr Bromberg was going to accept that. But Slomer said: 'You aren't going to leave it till tomorrow. We want the answer right now.'

Herscho was brave enough. He told Slomer: 'I'm not frightened of you, even if you are a killer, a gangster.'

Slomer said: 'I may be the things you call me, but I know what is right and what is wrong. You can't play with this boy like a toy; you can't make these people waste a lot of money that they've spent for the wedding. I want you to know *I* will come round here on Monday morning and we'll all go straight to the Registrar. Monday morning, ten o'clock,' said Slomer.

He must have guessed what was going through Herscho's mind,

because he added: 'If you happen to have the police here on Monday, they may take me away. But don't forget that I've got friends. And they *are* what you call gangsters. And your little tobacco shop will be broken to pieces and so will you. Good night,' said Slomer. And we all went down the stairs and back into our cab. I wasn't very happy about this; Herscho was an old man and for all his awkwardness and even remembering the way he had treated me in the past, I wouldn't want anything to happen to him. But it was all arranged now, and I couldn't draw back, only hope that he would be sensible.

He was. Ten o'clock on Monday morning saw us all standing outside Herscho's shop, and it seemed that Herscho was ready because he was wearing a new suit and hat. But even at the last moment he tried to be difficult; he began to walk away, until Slomer grabbed him by the lapels of his new jacket and asked where he was going. Herscho said he was going to get a cab, but Slomer wasn't taking any chances: 'Do you think we've come here to play hide-and-seek?' he asked. 'You'll come in our cab.'

I was frightened, but Herscho didn't try to resist; he climbed in with us and the cab moved off.

We reached the Registrar's office at about ten-thirty, and Slomer said he would wait outside. Herscho was very upset. 'Did you have to bring that killer here?' he asked me, but I told him Slomer was a relation of the Brombergs, and that there was nothing to be frightened of; Slomer wouldn't hurt him now.

The interview with the Registrar was very embarrassing. The Registrar asked: 'Herscho Stocklinsky? Have you and your wife any children? Have you legally adopted this one?' — pointing to me. 'Do you realize he is not yet of age? Do you realize that if by the age of twenty-one he has not presented himself for military service you will have to pay a fine of three hundred rubles or go to prison for six months? Do you permit him to get married?'

Herscho answered: 'Yes, I realize all this, and I give my assent to the marriage,' and signed the certificate, which the Registrar stamped and handed to me. He asked me for three rubles fifty kopecks, which I paid him, and we went outside. Slomer asked if everything was all right, and I waved the certificate in front of him, and we all climbed into the cab and took Herscho back to the market, where Slomer told Hannah: 'Congratulations, now you have a married son.' I called out to them: 'Don't be late for the wedding!' and the cab wheeled round and trotted off to the Brombergs' house. I got out ten rubles and offered it to Slomer, asking if it was enough for his trouble, and he said, 'More than enough,' and I climbed out and rushed in to Sonia while Slomer went on his way.

I showed Sonia the certificate and told her that now we were already married, but she said: 'No, we're not married until we get a certificate from the Rabbi.'

But even that wasn't quite true. The next day Sonia and I took the certificate to the Rabbi, who gave us a marriage contract written in Hebrew which both of us had to sign; then the Rabbi signed and stamped it and I paid him one ruble seventy-five kopecks for his trouble, and he said: 'The ceremony in the synagogue will finally mean you are married.' And that was five days off.

Meanwhile the tenants who lived in the Brombergs' house came from upstairs to congratulate us, kissing Sonia (who was very shy and blushing) and congratulating me, while Mama Bromberg gave them drinks and they wished us long life and happiness together.

I had been staying at the Brombergs, but the night before the wedding I took my necessary clothes to Herscho and Hannah's, so that I would not see the bride before the wedding. In the morning we all got ready and called a cab to take us to Krukov. Hannah and Herscho were all dressed up in new clothes, which didn't seem to fit them, and at last I was getting out of the cab with Herscho on one side of me and Hannah on the other. It looked as though the whole of Krukov was out in the streets and in the gardens of their houses and around the synagogue, and I wondered what important event was happening — until I realized that they had come to watch the wedding. As we walked through the crowd up to the synagogue I was puzzled at the way people spoke their thoughts out loud, so that we could all hear what they were saying about us: 'Nice-looking boy, but no parents,' and things like that.

Sonia was already standing under the wedding canopy, and my

parents led me up to her. The Rabbi said the service for the marriage ceremony, and the glass of wine was passed from hand to hand, and then I was handed a glass wrapped in a napkin which I had to stamp on, in the Jewish tradition, and when it shattered under my heel all the people shouted 'Maseltov!' — congratulations — and called to me to kiss the bride. Sonia was very shy, but I said we must oblige the onlookers, and persuaded her.

The crowd outside was so large when we came out that policemen had to make a pathway for us through them, and there was so much confetti that it looked like snow. And after the wedding came the reception, walking the red carpet from the street to the entrance of the hall, and the music playing. So many people kissed us that it seemed as if we were drunk with affection. Mr Bromberg was soon drunk the more usual way, and so was Herscho, though not so badly; in fact at two o'clock in the morning, when the party finished, Mama Bromberg was the only one who was sober.

When we finally got back to the Brombergs' house, Hannah and Herscho fell asleep on the couch, and I gave them a pillow and left them there. Mr Bromberg woke up and asked for a drink and then went back to sleep again. Mama Bromberg, though she was very tired, lit the samovar and made tea, and I sat with my arm round Sonia; we really were married at last.

But Sonia was so tired that I took her to her room, kissed her, and went back to help Mama Bromberg wash up; and then went off to my old room and fell asleep too; a married man.

XIX. THE ROAD TO A NEW LIFE

When the excitement of our marriage and the troubles with Herscho were over, I began to worry over my new business; with fourteen other grain-merchants in the town, trade was not very good.

One morning when the peasants had finished their trading and had gone home — and not many of them had come to me — I had an idea, and set off to see the owners of the other fourteen grain shops. To each of them in turn I explained my idea; we could all get a good living, I said, if we fixed one price for the grain instead of all competing with each other; why didn't we get together and agree? Five of the merchants were willing, but the other nine told me I was only asking for them to agree on fixed prices because I couldn't make a living in the town against their competition. I confessed that this was true, but I still asked them why they should want to be fighting one another, and when they still held out against my suggestion I threatened that I would explain to the peasants how the grain-merchants cheated them in weighing the grain. The merchants weren't worried by this threat; the peasants would never believe me, they said.

And it looked as if they were right. For when it was clear that they wouldn't agree to my scheme, I did go back to my shop and for four weeks I did my best to explain to the peasants how they were cheated, but none of the peasants would listen to me. They didn't seem able to understand what I said.

At the end of the month, I was very depressed; my share of the grain trade in the town was bad, my scheme for fixing prices had failed, the peasants wouldn't listen to me . . . and if something didn't change soon my hopes of establishing a prosperous business were gone. Then I had another idea. I closed the granary and put a notice on the door saying it would be closed until further notice for personal reasons, went home and told Sonia and her mother that I

THE ROAD TO A NEW LIFE

must go to Verchneprovsk for business reasons, and took the next train back to the town where I had been brought up.

There I took a cab from the station to the town, and another out to the village where I had sought shelter when I ran away from Herscho. I paid off the cab and walked through the village looking for the house where Ivan the peasant lived; I still remembered it, because although a lot had happened since, it was only six or seven years ago that I had been a ragged boy running away across these fields.

A young man was working in the garden; Vassil, Ivan's son. I told him I had important business to discuss with him, and he invited me into the barn and told me to take a seat on one of the sacks of grain. I asked him if he remembered a young Jewish boy he had caught in the wheat-field and accused of thieving: 'You must remember because you sent your dog after him,' I said.

Vassil said: 'What happened to that boy?' and I said: 'He is here,' and introduced myself. He was amazed, and shook hands and invited me into the house. As we went in he told me his father had died and that his sister Tatania was married but still lived in the house, as did his mother; and Vassil himself was married. Inside he shouted: 'Mama, come here,' and when his mother came I recognized her, though she was not so fat as she had been a few years ago; and I took off my cap and bowed to her. She was very curious to hear what had happened to me all this time; and while I was explaining to her a young peasant girl came in, nice looking but very fat, whom Vassil introduced as his wife Horpina, and we had to go over the story yet again.

I told Vassil about my opening a granary of my own, and how I found it impossible to compete with the other merchants because I refused to cheat the peasants; I had been well-treated by the peasants when I was poor and hungry. I explained to him how the grain-merchants cheated when they weighed the grain, and then cheated by short-changing the peasants, and then tempted the ignorant peasant children to cheat their own fathers by keeping false account of the sacks weighed.

I explained: 'I must have an assistant who can explain this to the peasants when they come with their grain to Krukov. I want you to come with me so that you can explain to the other peasants. I'll give you a room, and I'll pay you five rubles every week.'

Vassil was eager to come, but his mother told him it was impossible for him to leave the farm with only two women to look after it. She went out, saying she would find someone else for me. About fifteen minutes later she came back, and took me along to a neighbour, an old man with a grey beard who sat beside the fire in his hut. He had four sons, and I could take the youngest, Alexander, who was eighteen, he said, provided I gave him twenty rubles, paid the boy twenty rubles a month, and taught him to read and write. The old man was smart; though he couldn't read he demanded that I put all this down in writing and sign it, and when I scribbled a few words down on paper thinking it wouldn't matter because he wouldn't understand, the old man said he would take it to the police station in the village to be read to him, so I had to write it all down again just the way he wanted it.

It took him half an hour to take the paper to the police station and return; then he pulled out the cross which he wore round his neck, called the boy to him, and told the boy to swear to obey everything he had told him. The boy promised and kissed the cross and that was that; no Russian peasant would break his word after such an oath.

I wanted to be going, but the father said it was too late and insisted that we stay for supper and sleep the night there, and the mother who had been packing Alexander's things, brought out food and laid it on the table. It was not the first time I had eaten in peasant houses, and I enjoyed peasant food very much, so we stayed on. After the meal the eldest son's wife was left to clear the table while the others all went to bed, and Alexander led me to a small bedroom, lit by a small dim oil lamp. The bed was just a wooden bench and we both sat down on it. He told me that under the bed he kept a small gramophone, and he asked if I would like to hear some music. I couldn't believe my ears; you didn't expect to find a gramophone in a peasant cottage, but Alexander pulled the machine out and played a record, and it was very nice to listen to it.

He told me he didn't want to be a farmer all his life, but wanted to be properly educated so that he could one day become a village administrator, and I promised him that before he had finished with me he would be able to read and write as well as I could. Then he went out and fetched in two more boards to make another bed for me and filled a sack with straw for a pillow, and put some more straw on the boards; and so we went to bed. It was a long time since I'd slept on straw over boards, but all the same I slept through the night without interruptions.

We lay talking for a while before going to sleep, and Alexander told me more about himself; how his mother had died when he was five and the woman I had seen was his stepmother. His eldest brother's wife looked after them all, he said, and the family stayed close together because they knew the old man had a lot of money put away; they all worked for him for food and shelter but the father would not give them any money; it was very hard even to get clothes out of him. Alexander didn't want to be like the others, tied to the old man and waiting for his money; he wanted to get out and get educated, he said.

After breakfast — and after the old man had reminded me to pay him the twenty rubles — they harnessed up the horse to a two-wheeled cart, and drove into town, and so on to Kremenchug. Alexander took one look at the town — he'd never been to so big a place before — and wanted to go back home. I assured him that after he'd been here a few days he wouldn't want to go back, and persuaded him to carry on. It was all strange to him; as we crossed the big bridge over the river he exclaimed in wonder that anyone could make a piece of iron so long, and I had to explain to him that it wasn't all one piece but had been made from bits and pieces held together with nuts and bolts.

When we reached the other side of the bridge I took a cab; I wasn't a snob but I didn't want people to see me taking a peasant boy into my house. I was feeling nervous; I hadn't told Sonia I was going to be away overnight, and I hadn't told her I would be bringing anyone back with me; what's more I'd forgotten our young maid who slept in the house, and it now entered my mind that if we weren't careful Alexander might finish up in the maid's bed.

I'd been right to worry about Sonia; she was very cross and upset, complaining that she couldn't even understand what Alexander was saying; but her mother took her off into the kitchen and I heard her telling her that if she wanted me to get a living she mustn't interfere and that she must trust me to know what I was doing. Sonia was not convinced, but we all sat down to a meal together, and afterwards Sonia's father arrived, and when I introduced him to Alexander he said he liked village people better than townsfolk, and assured the boy that he would be all right and wouldn't be sorry that he had come.

After I'd taken Alexander to his room, and warned him not to try anything with the maid, I went back and tackled Sonia; she was still miserable and worried about the maid, but I promised her that I would see about getting lodgings for Alexander so that he wouldn't be in the house and in temptation, and we kissed and made up. Then she wanted to know all about the village, and if I remembered it from the days when I had run away from Herscho; and I told her how I had slept the previous night on straw spread over boards. She said: 'And don't you think it is better here?' and I said, 'Of course, with you here it is like heaven,' and so we fell asleep.

All the same, I didn't have as good a night's sleep as I'd had in the peasant hut; at one o'clock and again at three I woke and began worrying whether Alexander might have got up and run away, and couldn't rest each time until I'd gone to see. Each time I was re-assured to find him asleep, lying there like a sheaf of corn.

In the morning I showed him where to wash. I don't think he had ever washed himself before, and it occurred to me that I might have a difficult job making a gentleman out of a ruffian like this, but I still thought I could do it. I showed him the bowl on a table in a corner of the hall, with a large jug of water and a piece of soap and a clean white towel, and stood aside to see what he would do. He washed, but without touching the soap, and then was afraid to use the towel because he would dirty it. So I made him start again, using soap this time, and this time he felt able to use the towel.

We had breakfast together, and then went off to the granary. He proved to be very alert and bright, and as the days went by he soon found his way around the place. I was hoping that I wouldn't have to use my plan to warn the peasants about the other grain-merchants, but business still didn't improve, even though the peasants could see that I had a Christian working for me; I hoped this by itself would be enough to bring them to me. Each day I took three hundred and fifty rubles with me to the granary ready to buy grain, and each evening I was bringing the same amount home again because there was no business; and I had Alexander's wages to pay. And every time I came home with Alexander, Sonia would be upset because I had a Christian assistant.

At last I had to go to Sonia and ask her if she had any more money left, and she told me there was just eight hundred rubles she kept by for emergencies. So I told her about my plan to warn the peasants and keep them from going to other merchants; she said it wasn't a very nice thing to do, but I explained it was the only way if we were to keep the business going.

Next morning at the granary I explained to Alexander the various ways in which grain-merchants cheated the peasants, ways I had first discovered when I went to work for Habinski; I explained about the unjust scales and the short-change tricks which all enabled the cheating merchants to offer the peasants what looked like a few kopecks over the price for their grain but was actually several rubles lower.

Alexander listened carefully, and said: 'I understand, Guvnor.' I told him from then on I wasn't Guvnor, but Moysey, and that it was now up to him whether the business prospered or not, and if it did I would give him five rubles a week as well as the five I was sending to his father. Then I got him to change into his old peasant clothes, and he went off to talk to the peasants as they came into the town on their carts with grain to sell.

Where I had failed, a few weeks before, to convince the peasants that they were being cheated, Alexander certainly succeeded; they trusted him more because he was a peasant and a Christian, as they were. In two hours there were eight or ten carts round my granary, full of grain. Alexander came to help, and explained to the peasants that, just to show there would be no cheating by miscounting the sacks, we wouldn't count them by twos but would stack them all up together at the same time so that everyone could see them. The peasants were all interested in the way we worked, so different from other grain-merchants they had dealt with, and in no time at all I had filled my store, and had run out of cash too; I had to send Alexander running home to Sonia to get some more money.

On Sunday I had to go to Kremenchug to sell my grain to the mills, to get enough money to carry on the business. Everyone was happy now, because Alexander was plainly earning his keep, and Sonia realized that, and could see that he was fitting in with us and learning quickly and behaving just like a town boy.

He was very eager to help, and became devoted to us. One evening over our meal Sonia suddenly asked: 'Have you got the granary insured? Now you have got so much trade you will have made enemies — you know how people are. Someone may even set the granary on fire.' I had to confess that I'd had so much to do that I'd forgotten about insuring the granary. Immediately, without being asked, Alexander said to Sonia: 'Madam, I'll go and hide myself near the granary and guard it all night and every night until the place is insured.'

I told him I couldn't force him to stay outside all night, but he laughed that aside: 'It's not winter, and you're not compelling me to do anything — I'd love to catch someone if they try any villainy.' And as soon as it began to get dark he went off on his self-appointed guard duty.

I saw to it that he didn't have to stand guard more than one night, for early next morning I went off to Kremenchug to get an insurance policy. I found a Christian insurance company, because I thought under the circumstances that would be best. When I paid my premium they gave me a metal disc to hang outside the granary, so that the police should know which company insured the building. When I got home Sonia told me that Alexander had returned after daylight, and had had his breakfast and then gone to sleep, very pleased with himself for being able to help.

The next weeks went by smoothly, and I sent off five rubles a week to Alexander's father and gave Alexander another five rubles a week for himself as well, which made him very pleased. In the granary trade was good and I was able to make an arrangement with a company in Kremenchug to come and buy my grain whenever I let them know. I was able to go home for lunch, leaving Alexander in charge of the granary, knowing that I could trust him with the money there as well as I could trust a brother. After I'd eaten I would return to the shop and Alexander would go to the house for Sonia to give him a meal.

One day when I returned for lunch, Sonia handed me a letter. I asked why she hadn't opened it, and she said it had been addressed to me. 'Perhaps,' she added with a smile, 'it's from one of your girl friends.' I handed it back and said: 'Then you open it.' She did so, and said, 'It's from the President of the Synagogue. He wants to see you at six o'clock on Tuesday evening,' I said: 'I know just what they want. They want me to send Alexander away, and this I will not do.'

I kept the synagogue elders waiting for a week, to show them that I did not think it important, and told them I would turn up the following week with Alexander; I knew when they held their regular meeting. Sonia and her mother and father all said that the elders would never let me in to their meeting in the synagogue if I was accompanied by a Christian, but I said that if they wouldn't let Alexander in I wouldn't go in either and we'd both come home. I told Alexander to dress up as smartly as he could, and we set off.

The meeting was in the synagogue hall. The doorkeeper there — a Christian — knew me but didn't recognize Alexander, I said he was a friend, but the doorkeeper went and fetched the President, who was polite and bade me good evening, but declared that since this was a Jewish organization no Christians could be present. I could see through the open door that the town's grain-merchants were inside, so I told the President that if the organization was connected with the grain trade then my assistant had a right to be present. 'But if those people want to see a newly-married couple turned out into the street to beg, then they are not my people,' I said. 'Come, Alexander, let's go home.

When the President saw that I was determined he asked me to wait and disappeared into the hall. In a few minutes he was back. This time he asked: 'What's the use of your assistant coming in — he doesn't understand Yiddish.' I said: 'We all buy grain from Christians, so we can all speak Russian.' He gave in, then, and let us enter. As we went into the hall I gave Alexander a little notebook and told him to write down as much as possible of what they said so that there would be a record of what went on.

All the grain-merchants were very polite as we entered, saying: 'Good evening, Mr Stocklinsky,' in unison. I answered them suitably, and then shouted — for the hall was very large — 'This is Alexander Dobrovsky, my bodyguard.' They all laughed at this, but I warned them it wasn't a joke. 'I know you would be happy to see me begging in the street so you can continue with your cheating, but you won't have the chance,' I said. 'You are supposed to help a newly-married couple but you saw me for three weeks with no peasants near my door, and you waited for me to shut up shop and leave.'

One of the grain-merchants jumped up, interrupting me and shouting: 'We didn't ask you to come here and make a speech.' I shouted back: 'If you don't like my speech, you'd better leave.'

After a long argument, the President said: 'Gentlemen, there are fourteen people here, all of whom have a granary, and you all seem united. He is only one. Is it not possible to make peace between you?'

This was my chance, and I took it. I put forward again my plan for setting up a grain-buyer's union to fix prices. 'If everyone tries to outbid the other there is trouble, even fighting between you,' I said. 'If there is one price for all of us as a union there will be no fighting and we can share the profits between us, and we can sell together and so get a better price.'

This time, my plan got a better reception; they agreed at least that I should write out my plan and get leaflets printed so that they and the other grain-merchants of the town could study it, and that way the meeting ended, better than it had begun.

In the next day or two I drafted out a leaflet, with Alexander's help, and sent it off to the printers, and the President of the Synagogue circulated them to all the grain-merchants.

Alexander was proving more and more useful; he was very quick and intelligent, and learning fast to read and to write well — he had more time to learn now that he wasn't working in the fields all day like the peasants, and there were quiet times at the granary when there were no peasants selling grain, but even so I was amazed at how much he had improved. He could speak well, too; he could still talk like a peasant, but he could speak like someone brought up in the town as well. And in spite of our fears there had been no trouble with the maid, Sanca. He had got used to us and to our way of living, and to our food which was different from peasant-style food, and Sonia and her mother had grown to like him. As for Mr Bromberg, Sonia's father, he liked Alexander better than any of us.

We saw this one evening when the old man arrived with the news that the Rabbi who had married Sonia and me had died. The whole town, he said, was talking about the fact that when Moysey had dealings with young Sam Bromberg, Sam had died; and now Moysey had had dealings with the Rabbi, the Rabbi had died, though he wasn't an old man, and that Moysey must be some kind of devil. He was half serious, too, for when I said: 'Do you mean you believe what they say?' he muttered: 'The whole place is talking about it, not only me . . .' It didn't seem to matter what I said about it, but when Alexander stood up for me the old man quickly quietened down. And when I slipped Alexander a few coins to go out and get a bottle of vodka for Mr Bromberg, that settled it completely; whoever bought his vodka was the old man's best friend, devil or no devil.

Business was better than ever, and Alexander was a help here in another way; with so many peasants coming to trade I would sometimes run short of cash to pay them, but they believed in Alexander so much that they would accept a signed receipt instead and take the money next week. And it was quite a big thing for a peasant to accept a signed piece of paper he could not read instead of solid coins. About this time Alexander asked me to stop sending the five rubles a week to his father. 'I am not a slave — that is over now,' he

9

said, and he declared he would never go back to the village to live. He asked me to pay him monthly, too, so obviously he was saving his money up; he said that he only wanted the same amount, twenty rubles a month, but I increased it anyway.

By now the President of the Synagogue had sent out the leaflets and had received the replies from the grain-merchants to my plan for a grain-buyers' union. They had agreed to try it for a year to see how it would go. That evening Alexander and I closed the granary and went round to all the grain-merchants, collecting ten rubles from each for expenses. With this money I rented a large room for an office, and hired two girls as book-keepers, and in eight days we were ready. At our first meeting as a union, I wanted the merchants to elect some elderly man as chairman, but they insisted that I must be chairman because I had started it all, though I was not yet twenty years old. I agreed, and I appointed Alexander to go round to all the granaries seeing that the scheme ran smoothly.

We bought at one price, and when it came time to sell we were able to speak as one merchant making one big sale instead of as a number of merchants who could be set one against the other. After our first sale this way there were six dealers dissatisfied, but the others all declared it was a wonderful idea and were very pleased at the way it had gone. Now that they were not competing against one another all the time, there was no need for anyone to be cheating the peasants but all the same Alexander got to hear of one merchant, Mischa Zaudskym who was still at his old tricks. So he put on his old peasant clothes, and went out to talk to the peasants as they came into town with their grain. He told me afterwards how he had got into conversation with a boy and girl who were looking after three carts while their father was off somewhere. He turned the conversation to money, and the girl told him that she got fifty kopecks from her father and her brother forty kopecks, 'But when we go to sell the grain the merchant gives us fifty kopecks each.' Alexander thought at once that no grain merchant, especially a Jewish one, would give away a ruble for nothing; and sure enough when he went idling along to watch, it turned out to be the old trick of giving the children a small coin to mark each sack of grain as it was weighed and then persuading them to keep a few of the coins for themselves. Every coin that the peasant girl kept back meant a loss of six or seven rubles for her father.

Alexander said nothing, but came back and told me all about it. It was an old story to me; I'd seen it happen time and again when I worked for Habinski. Although I'd told Alexander about it, he'd never seen it worked before, and he was very angry. He wanted to write to the peasant and warn him what was going on, but I stopped him. 'He can't read, so he'll take the letter to the village policeman to read for him, and the policeman will spread the story through the village and then there will be a riot against the Jews,' I said. 'Don't forget I also am a Jew.'

'But how can I stand by and see one of my fellow-countrymen robbed every time he brings grain to town?' Alexander asked, and I promised that I would think of a way to warn the peasant without making trouble.

I felt very contented with life at this time. Business was good, I had a good wife, and a mother-in-law who was more like a mother to me, and even though my father-in-law wasn't quite so friendly, he never got in my way. Only one thing worried me: the time when I must do my military service was drawing near. I wasn't so much worried at the idea of being conscripted, but I didn't like the thought of leaving Sonia alone, and for three years. No money was provided by the Russian Army for conscripts' dependants, and Sonia was now expecting our first child. We had often talked about going abroad, and Sonia had urged me to go to England, to her two sisters who had settled in London; she would be content to wait and to follow me later.

If I left Russia before doing my military service it would have to be secretly, illegally; and Herscho as my father would have to pay a three hundred ruble fine. But I was not so worried about this. Since my business had begun to prosper he was always coming to the granary and borrowing money from me, fifty rubles here, seventy-five rubles there, on one pretext or another. Once he said that he needed money desperately because his tobacco stall in the market had been broken into, the door smashed and the stock stolen; I gave him the money he asked for, but I sent Alexander round to check, and Alexander found no sign of any breaking-in — it was just another story. I didn't tell Sonia about these loans I was making to Herscho, but I totted them up, and I reckoned it was getting very near to the three hundred rubles Herscho would have to pay if I fled the country.

The baby arrived one afternoon when I was at the granary. Alexander came rushing back from the house where he had been having his lunch, saying that Madame Bromberg had told him to send me home quickly. I dropped what I was doing and hurried home, to find the midwife already there and the door of Sonia's bedroom closed. After a time, and it seemed a very long time, she came out smiling and congratulating me on being the father of a wonderful big daughter. She told me I could go in and see Sonia, but not to talk. I went in, and Sonia was looking wonderfully well, and very pretty, with all her frilled things — pretty things she must have bought without my knowing for I'd never seen them before. I bent down to kiss her, and she said: 'Don't you want to see your daughter?' so I sat down by the bed and looked at them both and thought how wonderful it all was.

In two weeks' time I went to the synagogue to give our daughter her name — Riva, which in English would be Rebecca. Coming home, I walked into our dining room and there on a chair was a basket with our baby tucked up in it, her little face looking up at me, and suddenly I thought about another baby in a basket at a synagogue, and I could only stand there looking at her, tears rolling down my cheeks. Mama Bromberg saw me standing there and joked: 'What are you staring at? You've seen her every day.' Then she saw my tears, and she must have realized what I was thinking for she said: 'Haven't you forgotten it yet?'

I said: 'How could a woman be so bad as to take a baby out into the cold and leave him and run away?'

Sonia came over, wanting to know what was happening, and her mother said: 'Just look at that man, crying worse than a woman,' but Sonia came to me and put her arms round me, saying, 'Don't get upset . . . forget what happened years ago and think of the present,' and then Sonia's father came in pulling a bottle of vodka from his pocket and shouting for his supper and a celebration of the day, so all of us, and Alexander too, joined the old man in drinking Riva's health.

It was Sonia who settled the business of Mischa Zaudsky the cheating grain merchant, and the peasant he had robbed. She told Alexander to pick the peasant up on the road into town and take him for a drink, and explain it to him there, getting him to promise in return for the advice not to make a fuss about it but simply to take his grain elsewhere in future. This Alexander did; he was even able to persuade the peasant not to punish his son or daughter for their part in the trick — they had not seen through the trick, though the peasant did as soon as Alexander told him; there was nothing stupid about him even though he couldn't read or write. Alexander was pleased about this; I think he liked the peasant girl. He told me she was very beautiful.

About this time Alexander ran into a bit of trouble. He had gone to Kremenchug on business for me, and did not return. It began to get late, and I was worried. When I set off from the granary for home he still had not returned, and when I got home Sonia told me that the police wanted to see me. I hurried off to the police station, and there I was shown into the office of Sergei Ivanov, the inspector who had given me advice about leaving Russia when I saw him a year or so before. He told me that one of his men had arrested a boy who gave his name as Alexander Dobrovsky and claimed that I would vouch for him. He pressed a bell and Alexander was brought in. It appeared he had been walking back from Kremenchug when a policeman had stopped him and asked for his passport; Alexander hadn't got one.

'You can't live in this town and not have a passport,' the inspector explained to Alexander. He would release him if I promised to be responsible for him, but we must send for a passport for him at once. We gave the police the details necessary for a passport, and then Alexander was given back the personal property the police had taken from him when he was arrested, and they let us go. But that was what life was like in Russia; if you didn't have the proper papers, and were a stranger, you were liable to be arrested, and you couldn't stay in a town without those papers.

Perhaps it was this incident which helped to make up my mind; perhaps it was the letter from Sonia's sisters which arrived, along with some clothes for the baby, inviting me to go to London to join them. Anyway, I decided that I should stay in Russia no longer; like thousands of my people I would leave behind all the places that I knew and the people I knew, my home and my friends, pull up my roots and set out for a new life far away.

We talked it all over, Sonia and I, in the evenings when we were alone together. I told her that Alexander would make a good grain dealer on his own when I went; I would give him the business for nothing because of all he had done for me, but he would have to pay for the stocks of grain, and if he hadn't enough money to pay cash for it he could pay her in monthly instalments. I would get a contract drawn up for that, and Sergei Ivanov, the police inspector, could deal with the legal side of it, as he had always dealt with the Bromberg family's legal problems.

We wrote to Sonia's sisters in London, and in a few weeks I received from London a boat ticket to get me to England. There were other arrangements made so that I could get past the frontiers and the customs. I went to Sergei Ivanov and told him what I was doing, and I told Alexander that I was going to Ekaterinoslav soon to see about a new grain business and possibly setting up a new grain merchants' union there, and offered him my present business. He was delighted. By spreading this story I thought I would be able to stop people wondering where I had gone, at least for a while. I took Alexander to Sergei Ivanov to get the papers signed for the transfer of the business and to ensure that the money would be paid regularly to Sonia. And I went off with Sonia and the baby for a last visit to Herscho and Hannah. They were getting very old now, and I knew it would give them pleasure to see their baby granddaughter; Herscho loved little children. We had a pleasant evening, and when we were going I told Herscho that he need not return the money he owed to me, and that soon I hoped I might be able to send him a few rubles every month.

At last the day was fixed; it was to be on a Thursday that I left — for Ekaterinoslav, so far as Alexander and anyone else outside the family knew, but in reality for London. I told Alexander that from Friday he would be on his own, his own boss with his own business. On the Wednesday I got out a little plaited raffia bag, and packed it with some underwear and one spare suit, and took it to the station at Kremenchug, and then returned to Krukov; I had lunch with Sonia in my own house there for the last time, and went off to spend the afternoon at the granary with Alexander; all the granary owners would see me there and this too would relieve any suspicions anyone might have.

That night I almost changed my mind about going; Sonia was in tears and I could not bear to see her crying; and I looked at Riva our baby again and again and again. It might be a long time before we were once more a family together. I would have dropped the whole plan, I think, but Sonia's mother insisted that it would be best in the long run for all of us if I went. And next morning I kissed them all goodbye, and walked out of my house, and down to the station.

I took a ticket to Romodan, and changed there and caught a train for Lublin in Poland, which was part of the Russian empire then; and as the journey continued I realized that I was not the only one taking this sad secret way out of Russia, for people got into conversation on the train and when they asked one another where they were going they all seemed to say 'abroad'. At Lublin I had to meet an agent who smuggled people across the border from Poland into Germany; and sure enough it was a mass exit which was going on, for outside the station at Lublin were three farm carts, the big farm wagons that usually carried hay but could take maybe thirty people each, and we filled all three carts uncomfortably full. Everybody seemed to be, like me, without a passport for travelling abroad, and the three drivers were no ordinary country people but very shrewd-looking men, picked, I guessed, especially for the job. They drove us through Lublin and turned into a large yard with a barn. The gates were closed behind us and we were told to climb down and go into the barn, which was full of straw and had a loft with steps leading up to it. In this barn, bedded down in the straw, we were to spend the night — with a last warning from the drivers to be as quiet as possible.

We slept there — old men and young men and women and children and babies — and early in the morning we heard someone opening the door from outside, and we all turned to see who it was. A very fat woman entered, carrying two pails on a yoke, followed by a boy of about sixteen carrying a sack. She put the pails down, and we could see one was full of milk, the other of tea, and the sack was full of tin cups. The woman said something in Polish which I did not understand, but other people did and said: 'Come on, let's have some tea.' We queued up for the tea, which had already been sweetened, and each time a woman with a child came to her the fat Polish woman give the child a mug of milk and the mother tea. When the buckets were empty the woman and the boy went away, saying they would be back in five minutes, and locking the door behind them. True to her word she returned soon, this time with a large bag of fresh buns which she gave to the children, and then went away again, locking the door, and there all day long we waited, and nobody came to us, but at least we had had a cup of tea each, and most of us had brought some food with us for the journey.

When the sun had set we heard noises in the yard, and the door of the barn was opened; there in the yard were four carts, each pulled by a pair of horses; beautiful horses, they were, fit to be exhibited in shows. In each cart were two Poles; they told us to climb in, and warned us that if anyone should stop and question us we were to say that we were going to a wedding.

The carts moved off, and in the dim evening light I found that we were being driven slowly along a narrow path through a field of corn. The corn on either side grew very high, and I asked what would happen if we met another cart coming the other way. One of the passengers who spoke Polish put the question to our driver, and the driver replied that no carts would be passing that way at this time of evening — it had all been arranged.

But a little later, suddenly there was a cart ahead of us, and voices calling out of the dusk: 'Stop or we shoot!' Our drivers hauled the horses off into the corn, which almost covered us, and round and back on to the path again, urging them into a gallop — it felt as if even a train couldn't go any faster. Behind us the cart that had tried to stop us was backing and trying to turn, but in the narrow pathway that took some doing, and before it had got moving we were out of the field and bumping and jolting into a wood. We pounded on, until the carts pulled under the trees and stopped, and the drivers ordered us all out. We could not scramble out quickly enough for them, so they picked up our cases and threw them out to make us go faster. They told us to go and hide in the wood, to run on as far into the wood as possible. One man asked what we were going to do all night in the woods, but the sweating drivers only said: 'Hurry — don't ask questions but do as we tell you, or we'll all be in trouble.' They pushed us out, and then whipped up their horses and rattled away, leaving us there; old men, young men, women with small babies, young children.

We were lucky it was not yet winter, but it was very cold as the night wore on; few of us could sleep — I didn't sleep at all that night. It was pitiful; some of the children were crying with cold and fear, and we had to hush them and implore them to be silent as we were in danger of being heard. At last, very early in the morning, the same four carts came up, with the same drivers; we crowded into the carts and they whipped up the horses and we were off again. They were quick, those horses, and in half an hour we reached a farm.

Here we were ushered into two barns, the men in one, the women in another, and the carts turned round and set off back the way they had come. The two barns were linked by a door, and after a while some of the women got it open and told us that they had been given tea again, and milk for the children, and that we could buy milk and soft cheese from the farmer. We stayed in our barns all day, with one woman attending to us; she spoke only Polish but there were some of us who could speak Polish so we knew what she had to say. In the loft above the barn there was a window, and through that we could see men and women working in the fields.

When it was getting late the woman told us that we must get ready with our bags and baskets, and the women must get the children dressed, because we now had to walk to the border. She lined us up four abreast, with those who spoke Polish in front next to her so that they could translate her orders and pass them on; then when we were all ready she opened a door at the back of the barn, and there in front of us was a wood, so we stepped out quietly, marching into it and soon hidden among the trees.

We walked for about half an hour, and then the woman stopped us and sent word back down the line to take off our shoes and stockings because we were going to have to cross a river; it was shallow, but about twenty-five yards wide, she said. In our bare feet we moved off again, until we came to the river bank. I was horrified to see, not far down the stream and on our side of it, three Russian soldiers, their rifles on their shoulders. They were moving away from us, but what would happen if they turned round and saw us? But the word came down the line from the Polish woman; we were not to worry; the soldiers had been bribed not to see us, and they would leave us alone. And we stepped off into the shallow water.

When we climbed on to the far bank, the Polish woman disappeared and we found ourselves in a small enclosed area. At one point there was a gate, and standing by it was a man who demanded a ruble from each of us 'to pass on to German soil'. When we had all paid and passed through the gate he told us to walk to a house about twenty or thirty yards beyond the enclosure. We stopped to put on our boots and stockings again, and the women cleaned the mud of the river from their children's feet, and we set off for this house. Only then did I begin to realize that I had left Russia at last, and feel a little easier in my mind.

As we approached the house we saw it was very large and brilliantly lit. A German woman stood outside and invited us in. Already there must have been more than three hundred people in the house, but they found room for us too; I suppose they were people like we were, without passports. There was a corner where people could buy food and drink, and we were all sitting down beginning to relax when two men came in and asked all those who had just arrived to stand up. We stood, and they said that each of us had to pay five rubles, three for a child, to continue the journey. We paid and sat down again, eating and drinking, and some of us sleeping, for it was already night and we were weary.

After about two hours I heard the approach of many horses and carts, and once again we had to move on, going out of the brightly lit house and climbing into the carts. There were two horses to each cart; I'd seen some good horses in Russia, but these excelled them all, and when we moved off they sped along like lightning. We soon arrived at a railway station called Mislovitz. A train was waiting for us there, empty, and we boarded it. At last the illegal part of our journey was over and we were proper travellers again.

All through that night and the next day and on into night again we jolted across Germany; and early in the morning we reached Bremen. Cabs were waiting, respectable-looking cabs, to take us to the emigration centre. When I walked in the size and the noise overwhelmed me. I could not believe my eyes. The main hall was enormous, and people were everywhere, sitting on chairs, sitting on the floor, standing about talking; there were children screaming and crying; noise everywhere. There were shops of all sorts inside the hall; toy shops, ladies hairdressers, barbers, tool shops — I could not take it in, it was so vast. There were dormitories, with about twenty-five beds in each, and though we wanted to discuss the day's happenings the beds were so comfortable and we were so tired from our long journey that we could none of us stay awake.

In the morning there were places where we could wash, and warm water too; and a café where we could get some tea and food. Afterwards I found my way to an inquiry office to find out when the next boat would sail for London; it was in two days' time. There was a long queue at this office, and as I came out a man in the queue shouted to me in Yiddish, 'Are you going to London? Wait for me, I want to talk to you.' I waited for him, and when he had finished in the inquiry office he came over, saying: 'I'm going to London as well. Let's keep together.'

We walked away together, away from the noise of the emigration hall. This man, Isaac, could speak a little German, and he went up to the first policeman we saw and asked if we were allowed to go for a walk away from the hall because we had two days to wait for our ship. The policeman looked at our tickets to make sure we were telling the truth, and then told us we could go wherever we liked, but it would be wiser not to go too far or we might get lost. We thanked him and walked on. When we came to a hat shop, Isaac wanted to buy a bowler hat, and urged me to buy one as well. I did not know how I would make myself wear it, but I let him persuade me. I looked in the mirror and could hardly recognize myself, the hat looked so funny, but Isaac said I'd get used to it in time, and I thought, 'This is the first of many things I will have to get used to before I am settled with my family in England.'

In spite of the first policeman's assurance that we could go wherever we liked, Isaac and I ran into trouble. We discovered that there was an underground railway station in the town, and went down stairs to have a look at the trains standing there under the ground. A railway inspector soon came up to us, questioned us and then told us to wait; and soon two policemen arrived and took us off to a police station, where we were searched and made to empty our pockets. A man speaking perfect Russian questioned us. I was very worried that they might send us back to Russia; I would certainly be punished severely for escaping from the country without having done my military service; but Isaac told me nothing like that could happen, and after questioning us both closely the police let us go, warning us that it would be better if we both waited in the emigration centre so that we wouldn't waste our time or theirs by getting arrested again.

Back we went to the great noisy emigration hall. There was nothing to do, and we passed the time by playing cards, though after a time the noise was so great that I got up and went to wait outside. I was very depressed now, so far from home and everyone I knew, and Isaac saw it and tried to help, though there was nothing anyone could do. At last we could go to bed, and when we got up it was a new day and our ship would be arriving.

We were to leave the emigration centre at twelve, and all morning it seemed to me the hands of the clock would not go fast enough, but at last it was time, and forty-six of us went out, to climb on to three carts for the journey, an hour and a half, to the harbour. An inspector stamped our papers and looked at our tickets, and then we were allowed to go aboard the ship. That was at one-thirty, and there was another four-hour wait before the sailors began untying the ropes and the ship moved out slowly into the river. Isaac asked a sailor how long the journey to London would be: thirty-six hours, the sailor said.

Only there and then did I realize that I had left Russia for ever. But my soul was with my wife and child, who were still there.